WITHDRAWN
From the
Dean B. Ellis Library
Arkansas State University

DEAN B. ELLIS LIBRARY

PROMISES TO KEEP

Promises to Keep

THE MIAMI DOLPHIN STORY

by Bill Braucher

ILLUSTRATED WITH PHOTOGRAPHS

DODD, MEAD & COMPANY

NEW YORK

Copyright © 1972 by Bill Braucher

All rights reserved

No part of this book may be reproduced in any form without permission in writing from the publisher

ISBN: 0-396-06694-1
Library of Congress Catalog Card Number: 72-3921

Printed in the United States of America
by The Cornwall Press, Inc., Cornwall, N. Y.

For Susan and Mike
. . . championship forbearance

Introduction

Once the baseball writer was king. He abdicated amid light towers, a new generation's apathy toward his game, and the limitations of television. The schematic beauty and grace of baseball became lost in the confines of the glowing box, which depicted the players as scattered idlers compared with the infighting gladiators of pro football. The change has elevated the football writer's status. Allotted more space between tire ads, he has become analyst as well as chronicler, filling the gaps television leaves between third and four situations. He travels only on weekends. Except for the inconvenience of an occasional night game, he works on Sunday afternoon in a comfortable press box replete with a squad of statisticians attending to the drudgery of figures. Even the Philadelphia Eagles have been led to a new stadium. No longer is it possible for a visitor complying with a morning deadline to get locked in Franklin Field on Sunday night with a plane to catch.

Poignant evidence of pro football's burst to prominence is

offered in the ghostly outposts that only yesterday accommodated the ragamuffins of the American Football League. Shambles such as Youell Field, Fenway Park (where the baseball writer still toils), Jeppeson and Balboa and Kansas City Municipal stadiums have been abandoned within a decade of incredible prosperity. The way has even been cleared for a new Buffalo arena that will eliminate War Memorial Stadium, the ultimate relic.

But of the 10 AFL stepchildren grudgingly adopted by the National Football League in 1970, the most insolent is the brat in Miami. The Dolphins began in 1966 as the lowest of species, an AFL expansion team. In established NFL citadels, the Dolphins until very recently were regarded with tolerant amusement.

Who are the Miami Dolphins anyway? What were they doing in the 1972 Super Bowl? Having watched the Dolphins leap from the ludicrous to the incredulous, I feel an explanation is in order. There is obviously more than meets the eye to an outfit that achieved the most dramatically successful turnabout in more than 50 years of pro football, and did it apparently overnight under an impatient martinet named Shula.

Miami's time came too quickly, in fact, as the Dallas machine demonstrated in the Super Bowl. At least the 24-3 loss to the Cowboys returned the scene to humbler perspective. No organization so ill-conceived and undedicated as Miami's in the beginning, deserved too much too soon.

During their formative years the Dolphins were a somewhat dubious assignment. But it bared a truth to the dressing-room intruder: He may exult with a winner or, in his sapience, vent ridicule on mediocrity; but without trying he can court a deep affection for a loser. For a bond of agony develops between reporters and chronic losers like the old

St. Louis Browns on the diamond, Sam Snead in the U.S. Open or Harold Stassen in a presidential race. The dressing-room historian cannot simply limit himself to third and four. He must try to understand something of the tough yet sensitive men who play the game, or even the discards who risk their bodies at one training camp. Such an effort is usually rewarding and sometimes unforgettable. Could there be a warmer person or more adamant individualist, for example, than Cookie Gilchrist? Or a man with more compulsive integrity than Howard Twilley?

Since the subject is history, however, first downs and records and intercepted passes must intrude upon occasion. But they are incidentals. In confessing his own flaws as a reporter, Heywood Broun described the perfect reporter as "an associate member of the light brigade, and when cannon roar from the right or left his mission is to keep precisely in the middle of the road in the hope that he will find the truth, which is always said to lie between the two."

Such a perpendicular might be accomplished by a robot, provided he was not operated by a human. Even a Swiss reporter cannot remain neutral if humanity is more important to him than games. So be it. To stray toward the cannon is to discover, in Kipling's phrase, "more than seven watchmen sitting in a tower."

Some of these discoveries are set forth here.

BILL BRAUCHER

Miami, July 1972

Contents

Photographs following page 82

1.	The Divine Right of Kings	1
2.	Cutting Down the Old Pine Tree	10
3.	Who Needs the AFL in Miami?	22
4.	A Very Nice Party	34
5.	Les Bingaman's Busloads	44
6.	Let's Win One for the Flipper	55
7.	Clifford, Dammit and Joe Auer	65
8.	Old Men Come and Go	74
9.	Unhappy Warrior	85
10.	My Son, the Quarterback	96
11.	A Drive, a Nine-Iron, a Mingo	104
12.	The Playing Fields of St. Andrew's	115
13.	Paper Cups and Motorcycles	122
14.	How to Succeed in Business	134
15.	Controlling the Press	142
16.	The Worst Is Yet to Come	151

17.	The Dolphins Lose a Father	160
18.	Don Shula's Ordeal	169
19.	Summer of 1970: A Conversion	175
20.	No Miracle Man	187
21.	An Indestructible Heavyweight	199
22.	High Road to Muddy Oakland	202
23.	Butch and Sundance	208
24.	Tiptoe Through the Poly-Turf	220
25.	Blackouts 1971	228
26.	Christmas in Kansas City	239
27.	The Ultimate Confrontation	248
28.	Gree-Gree Gertie's Revenge	258
	Index	267

PROMISES TO KEEP

> ... Ah, love, let us be true
> To one another! for the world, which seems
> To lie before us like a land of dreams,
> So various, so beautiful, so new,
> Hath really neither joy, nor love, nor light,
> Nor certitude, nor peace, nor help for pain;
> And we are here as on a darkling plain
> Swept with confused alarms of struggle and flight,
> Where ignorant armies clash by night.
> —MATTHEW ARNOLD

1. *The Divine Right of Kings*

Joe Robbie was discouraged yet determined, an attitude perfectly plausible in the binary scope of the Mediterranean mind. This combination often gripped him in his first four years of running a turbulent football operation called the Miami Dolphins.

The 1970 draft completed that day had gone uncommonly well from the start. Paul Warfield, perhaps the game's most brilliant receiver, had been acquired from Cleveland in trade for Miami's No. 1 choice. That in itself was an accomplishment making the entire two-day process successful. But Robbie was restless. His thoughts were not of the draft as he fidgeted behind the big desk in his paneled office 11 floors above Biscayne Boulevard. He had a spectacular view of John F. Kennedy's Torch of Freedom and the washday rows of charter sailboats swaying in their Biscayne Bay docks.

On Jan. 28, 1970, most men would have considered themselves lucky to be in such a milieu. Though politicians, land racketeers and automobiles had long since despoiled the

"Magic City" euphemism advertised by the Chamber of Commerce, Miami was still more comfortable than smog, chapped lips and snow shovels.

Robbie by nature is rarely content, however. He has thrived on controversy. In Minneapolis, before he assumed a $7.5 million debt for openers to join the American Football League, he was a practicing lawyer with a wife and 11 children, prosperous if not affluent. He was certainly in no financial position to buy a football team. Before becoming an instant owner, he had never worked a day in professional football.

He paid for the inexperience. In four Miami seasons of walking a financial tightrope, Robbie's trademark was agitation. He staved off creditors, critics and buyers while maneuvering to sustain a football team that succeeded only in arousing apathy. For his efforts Robbie was cast as the town villain. A scathing *Sports Illustrated* article labeled him a "prairie pirate" among other appellations, few of them flattering.

He possessed the tenacity of an octopus. And concealed inside the Lebanese profile, Irish eyes and acerbic approach was the soul of a romantic. Once, pondering his problems and his battered image, he offered a typically disarming change of pace: "And we are here as on a darkling plain," he said, "swept with confused alarms of struggle and flight, where ignorant armies clash by night." With atypical shyness he added, "That's my favorite, *Dover Beach,* by Matthew Arnold. I forget the whole thing, but I like the last eight or nine lines in particular."

A few moments later he was raging over some petty injustice he had been dealt. Robbie's side of any argument was always prominent, often to the exclusion of any other side. He entertained few distractions in his passion to build a football team that would be acceptable in South Florida. In that sense he embodied an observation of his political idol Harry Truman: "We'll give 'em a fair trial and then hang 'em."

In January 1970 all Robbie's energies were aimed at drastically revising the football team regarded by most South Floridians with more amusement than interest. The Dolphins were shunned to the extent that only 17,478 season tickets had been sold for the 75,312-seat Orange Bowl in 1969. That figure represented a record. The first year, 1966, season tickets totaled 12,503. Average attendance was 26,062.

Attendance was creeping up, but debts were descending on Robbie at a much faster pace. As president, managing general partner, exchequer, comptroller and virtually everything else connected with the operation, Robbie was discouraged not only by the reception his club was getting but by its performance as well.

In their first four hapless years, the Dolphins had won 15 games, lost 39 and tied 2. Robbie was determined to replace George Wilson, the 56-year-old coach whose club had only won three games in 1969.

"Injuries killed us," Wilson protested. "More than anything else, injuries were the story of our season." And Wilson was right, as far as he went. Even Bob Griese, the promising young quarterback, had gone down with a sprained knee on a muddy November afternoon in Boston. Griese was lost for the last five games of the 1969 season. A dozen other players, including both regular wide receivers, had succumbed for all or part of the disastrous episode.

Reporters and others around the scene felt that Wilson had been a victim of circumstances and deserved another year toward a goal he defined on Jan. 29, 1966, when he was initially hired to coach the new AFL entry. "We'll be competitive our first year," Wilson said. "It takes time to be a contender, but we should be ready to challenge for a championship within four or five years."

Robbie felt that, after four years, the Dolphins were not close to challenging. Moreover, he was weary of excuses. Wilson had already gained an extra year when his original three-year contract was extended for the 1969 season.

Wilson was a genial and charming man, with a reputation for toughness from his days as an end on George Halas's Chicago Bears—a trait seldom exercised in Miami. He was accustomed to long luncheons with cronies and occasionally members of his staff at Johnny Raffa's lounge on Biscayne Boulevard. These sessions particularly irked Robbie, who felt that no man could prepare a football team while entertaining such daily distractions.

After the 1969 travesty Robbie made up his mind to find the best coach available. At the Senior Bowl in Mobile, Ala., Robbie sought out Paul (Bear) Bryant, who particularly in the South is regarded with awe bordering on veneration. He offered Bryant what amounted to a lifetime coaching job complete with stock options that, in effect, gave the coach part-ownership.

Bryant turned it down. Why abdicate as ruler of Alabama for a job offering more uncertainty than security, more headaches than promises?

Robbie was stymied as he pondered where to find a coach so late in the offseason. The Miami press was pushing to give the popular Wilson another year. And Wilson, a shrewd politician, was telling friends the difficulties of doing business without a contract. "But I still think I'll be the next coach," he said. "Nobody could have done the job with all those guys hurt."

Robbie was once again the target for criticism from those who believed the Dolphins were worth criticizing. Robbie reckoned that if he had signed Bryant, the critics would have been silenced, or at least soft-pedaled. More important, the Dolphins would be pointed toward success. Though independently wealthy through various investment and business sidelines, Bryant had been tempted by Robbie's offer. In the end, University of Alabama administrators had helped make up his mind. They asked him to deliver a successor on the spot, a request Bryant could not fulfill.

So Robbie was casting about for another choice. He was discussing the situation with Ed Pope, sports editor for *The Miami Herald,* when Pope suggested somewhat jokingly, "How about Don Shula?"

Robbie reacted vigorously. He shot forward in his chair and slammed a fist on the desk. "That's the man!" he snapped.

Robbie's mind works like a ferret. Scarcely had he responded so exuberantly than he paused, searching other considerations. "There's a problem," he told Pope. "How would I go about contacting Shula? The man is under contract to the Baltimore Colts. You just don't go around dickering with pro coaches without permission from their owners."

In the tight circle of 26 National Football League owners, protocol dictates that these shoguns are at all times aware of their coaches' intentions. The logic reverts to the divine right of kings, but that's how it is in the NFL.

At this point Braucher came in. I had been covering the Dolphins for the *Herald* all four years and knew Robbie was determined to dismiss Wilson. If every other avenue was shut off, Robbie felt certain that Bill Peterson, then coaching Florida State University, would jump at the Miami job. (Peterson jumped soon enough following Wilson's firing. After turning down at least two pro offers prior to 1970, he took the job at Rice the following year, then switched to the Houston Oilers in 1972.)

I also knew Shula. We had been classmates at John Carroll University in suburban Cleveland. And while we were only casual acquaintances, I knew enough about Shula to feel sure he would succeed in Miami.

I told Robbie so. "I'll give Shula a ring tonight or tomorrow and see what he says. If he's interested, he can ask Baltimore's permission to talk with you."

Robbie agreed, his eyes dancing with excitement over the prospect of landing the coach who in seven pro seasons had built a better won-lost record than the legendary Vince Lombardi at Green Bay.

Robbie has a sixth sense. He already suspected that Shula and Carroll Rosenbloom, Baltimore's owner, were not getting along. Their problems began in January 1969 when Joe Namath and the New York Jets shocked everybody but Namath by upsetting the Colts in the Super Bowl, 16–7, vindicating the AFL.

Shula was a bit incredulous the first time I phoned. He had been occupied with his own draft and with internal shake-ups following an 8-5-1 Baltimore season, his worst since taking over in 1963. Don Klosterman had recently been hired from Houston as general manager and special assistant to Rosenbloom. Others in the Colts' family, including Shula and Upton Bell, the personnel director, resented Rosenbloom's shift of authority. Klosterman had earned a sound reputation with the Oilers but was regarded as an intruder in Baltimore.

I phoned Shula again the next day to assure him I was serious. "I know Robbie offered the job to Bear Bryant and included an ownership deal," I said. "It seems he could hardly do less for you."

Shula expressed concern over George Wilson. In 1960 Wilson had introduced Don to the pros as an assistant at Detroit. And Shula worked three years under Wilson in Detroit before replacing Weeb Ewbank at Baltimore. Don hesitated to usurp the man who first hired him.

Just as Robbie had assured me Wilson's time was up, I assured Shula. Then he began to express interest. He said he would get permission from the Colts and discuss the job with Robbie. But there were problems, the foremost being that Carroll Rosenbloom was vacationing in Japan. So Shula went to Carroll's son Steve, whose permission as a member of the official family would serve protocol.

"I can't stand in your way," Steve told the coach, "if you're convinced the Miami job would represent a big advancement for you."

Robbie, right in character, entertained no such distractions as the Rosenblooms. Joe cranked up the conversations with Shula as soon as I told him the coach was available and, I suspected, more than willing to change jobs under ownership conditions.

Because Robbie ignored the rules of the NFL fiefdom and hired his man directly, he was later charged by Carroll Rosenbloom with tampering. Commissioner Pete Rozelle decided Rosenbloom was right. As compensation, Rozelle awarded the No. 1 Miami draft choice in 1971 to Baltimore.

Robbie complained publicly, but privately could not have cared less as things turned out. Shula was worth a dozen draft choices.

Robbie and Shula talked by phone several times in the next few days. Once Robbie reached the coach just as he was bundling up his family for an evening of ice-skating. Both men laughed at the notion of ice-skating while discussing a job in Miami.

On Tuesday afternoon, February 3, Robbie flew to Washington and checked into the Marriott Hotel. Shula met him and they talked for nearly three hours. By this time they were getting down to dollars and cents. Robbie set forth the terms he had in mind, including a percentage of the franchise—which was losing money, but still worth an estimated $15 million in an era dominated by pro football—and then decided to sound out his man. He does not believe in wasting time on maybes, and in this he and Shula are alike.

"Don," Robbie popped at him, "are you any less interested right this minute than you were when you walked into this room?"

Shula grinned and introduced a Socratic play of his own, countering the question with a question. "What would you do if I said I was less interested?"

"I'd walk out of here," Robbie said, "and I wouldn't bother you any more."

Shula grinned again. This is the kind of honest approach he appreciates, and is among the qualities he continues to admire in his employer. "I'm interested," he said.

Between conversations with Robbie, Shula spoke with me. Painstakingly thorough, Don pumped me with the cunning of an experienced reporter, wanting to know every imaginable detail about the franchise, its reception in Miami, the players, the office personnel, the coaching staff. Shula was drawing close to accepting the contract that Robbie had left for the coach's lawyers to ponder.

On Thursday, February 12, Shula flew to Miami and went directly to The Jockey Club, a posh private establishment at 11111 Biscayne Boulevard. Robbie's wife, Elizabeth, had planned to attend the races at Hialeah the afternoon Shula checked into The Jockey Club. Instead, Robbie asked her to pick up Shula. So far the secret was intact, and he didn't yet wish to be seen with the Baltimore coach in so public a place.

Mrs. Robbie drove Shula to the family home in Miami Shores. And that day the conversation was productive enough to give both principals the notion that the situation was all but settled.

Now it was the *Herald*'s turn to sweat. We were sitting on a monster of a story that could elude us with one slip. Elinor Kaine, the lady NFL-watcher who can add two and two, had seen Shula at The Jockey Club. Fortunately, sports and entertainment personalities were not uncommon visitors there. But that was just one potential leak.

Once, panicked by the possibilities, I phoned Shula. "Don, I've got to run the story. I can't sit still on it any longer."

"No," Shula said. "We're all committed to silence, so stop worrying. Besides, how can you be certain I'll take the job when I'm not yet sure myself?"

I discussed the situation with Ed Pope as well as Ed Storin, the *Herald*'s executive sports editor. We decided to sit tight.

Finally, on Wednesday, February 18, Robbie called a press conference at The Jockey Club. We got our stories into the first edition, which had reached the street by 7:30 P.M. when Shula strode briskly and a little self-consciously onto the patio where the reporters were assembled under a full moon.

Incredibly, the secret had been preserved for 22 days, from the first phone call until the press conference. But George Wilson never recognized the commitment to silence of all concerned. He was bitterly wounded.

The Wilsons and Shulas belong to the same Catholic parish, Our Lady of the Lakes, in northwest Miami. They meet rarely, and only by accident. Since 1969, Wilson has never seen the Dolphins play.

> When I was a kid growing up in Chicago, I had to make pickups and deliveries in a lot of rough spots. I'd walk down some streets in the South Side with rocks in my pockets. Just because I'm not the type to go around hollering all over the place, like some coaches I could name, is no sign that I won't get tough if I'm pushed.
>
> —GEORGE WILSON

2. Cutting Down the Old Pine Tree

George Wilson had his suspicions but refused to believe the worst until an hour before the 7:30 press conference the evening of Feb. 18, 1970. Summoned to The Jockey Club by Joe Robbie, Wilson drove hurriedly through rush-hour traffic to meet the Dolphins' president.

When Wilson was hired in January 1966, Robbie hailed him as "a lifetime winner." More pertinent was another observation by another coach: "I wouldn't want to be the first coach of the Miami team. I'd rather be the second." He knew the frustrations to be expected from an expansion team, hastily stocked with hand-me-down veterans and rookies of unknown talent.

Wilson had the patience for the task. He suffered and cajoled and occasionally exulted in the rare victories that came his way over four unpredictable years. Yet South Florida had little use for losers.

Finally, with a nucleus of established football players and improvement if not prosperity in sight, Wilson found himself smiling for photographers at The Jockey Club while shaking hands with his replacement.

During his last three days as Miami's head coach, Wilson was in a courtroom testifying for the Dolphins against Earl Faison. The 275-pound plaintiff had been an all-AFL defensive end at San Diego before Coach Sid Gillman dismissed him in 1966. The Dolphins grabbed Faison for the $100 waiver price, a bargain except for one catch: They also acquired the two years he had remaining on a contract worth about $30,000 a year.

Faison proved useless. He had lost his "pop," he said, because of a back ailment incurred at the Dolphin training camp. He was another in a series of unlucky gambles taken to find a quality performer during Robbie's uphill struggle to establish a major league franchise in Miami.

When doctors could find nothing wrong with Faison's back, the Dolphins turned him loose. He sued but lost, with Wilson's testimony among the deciding factors.

"Just think," Wilson said bitterly a few days after he was fired, "I knock myself out in court to help Robbie, and that's the thanks I get."

But at The Jockey Club, when Robbie broke the news at suppertime, all concerned played out the *noblesse oblige* charade. Wilson shook Shula's hand. Both smiled for the cameras. Robbie said the 56-year-old coach took the blow "like a man."

"By his attitude when I told him, which by the way wasn't the easiest thing in the world for me to do, I admired and respected George Wilson even more than when our association started four years ago."

Robbie added that Wilson "will always have a place with

the Dolphins as long as I'm connected with the club." The Dolphin president, who in grabbing Shula from under the nose of the Baltimore owner had achieved the most significant coup since Washington's Edward Bennett Williams hired Vince Lombardi from Green Bay, added that he would sit down "within the next few days" to discuss Wilson's future with him.

But "the next few days" never came. After the act for photographers, George left The Jockey Club in a hurry. He didn't attend the press conference, and he shut himself off from reporters the rest of the night.

Wilson had desperately wanted another year, even though critics wondered what he would do with it. For all his grandiose plans, George had never been disposed to work long hours at his job and to pore over game films.

"George is a good guy," one of his old Detroit assistants once said. "But down deep, I don't think he even wants to coach. I think he'd be far better off in the front office. He knows football politics and football people, and I think he'd make somebody a good general manager."

Wilson was never renowned for the dedication of a Paul Brown or Don Shula. He preferred the personal touch, including a pregame fight speech in the style of his old Chicago coach, George Halas.

Once in his later years, before finally yielding his coaching job (if not his guiding hand) to younger men, Halas delivered an impassioned speech to the Bears on the supreme effort needed that day to overcome Lombardi's Green Bay Packers. Halas resurrected Lord Baltimore, a courageous leader who inspired a battered army and by sheer desire and determination defeated a foe far superior in manpower. Most of the Bears were apparently getting the message, banging fists against open hands and shoulders and helmets into dressing-room walls. But as the mercenaries filed from the dressing room into the tunnel leading to the arena, 6-8 defensive end George Atkins cupped hand to mouth and shouted, "Calling Lord Baltimore!"

Atkins' reaction reflects today's cerebral, cash-oriented athlete. Ranting and raving have yielded to meticulous, individual planning and concentration. Modern coaches disdain such orations as those that once persuaded Wilson into ferocity as a $100-a-game end for the Monsters of the Midway. No NFL coach will ever win a Super Bowl with a Lord Baltimore.

Yet Wilson, like many warriors of earlier and less complicated days, could never be convinced that his ways needed revision in a computer era. He resented both Robbie and Shula for "conspiring behind my back without ever telling me a word about it until the last minute."

Until January 14, George had been optimistic that he would be rehired. On that day one of his three daughters was married, and not one of the Miami owners he invited to attend the wedding or reception chose to come.

"Look around, Bingo," Wilson advised his old friend and defensive line coach, Les Bingaman. "Do you notice something funny?"

Les had noticed. Beneath a hulking frame and Tennessee mountain approach, the old Detroit middle guard possessed a shrewdness and sensitivity no casual acquaintance would suspect. But Bingo's active days were gone by January 1970. Les had been stricken with a heart attack on the Orange Bowl sideline a month before. He merely shrugged when Wilson reminded him that the owners were conspicuously absent from the wedding party.

Still the wedding went well. As usual, Wilson was persuaded to the microphone at the Kings Bay Yacht and Country Club. A willing singer whose enthusiasm was infectious, he rendered his medley of favorites. The climax inevitably came "When They Cut Down That Old Pine Tree."

In four years with the Dolphins and seven as head coach of the Lions, Wilson had sung that pine tree down "and hauled it away to the mill" hundreds of times, "to make a coffin of pine for that sweetheart of mine."

But this time his heart wasn't in it. Though still overtly confident, he was beginning to fear that Robbie was out in some forest sawing on a tree of his own, and that it was he, Wilson, who was bound for the mill.

During a lull in the ceremonies George told a few friends: "I'm not going to hold it against any man for taking my place. I'm not built that way. Besides, I'll do all right whatever happens. But I'm concerned for my assistants and their families, who've been sweating out their jobs the last two months. I don't think it's right they should be left hanging.

"This club is on the verge of becoming a big winner," Wilson added. "I started with it and I've seen it mature. I'd hate like hell to leave just when the team was ready to make its move."

George then went off on a favorite tangent. "You know," he said, "it's a funny thing. Scooter McLean, my old Detroit roomie, began building Green Bay the year before Lombardi took over. It was McLean who made a halfback of Paul Hornung, built the offensive line and made many of the moves Lombardi got credit for. Not to knock Vince. I know he's a fine coach. But he got all the praise for building the Packers while McLean got nothing."

Wilson often drew a similar parallel in Detroit, where overnight he had succeeded Buddy Parker in 1957. Parker walked out at a "Meet the Lions" banquet shortly before the season was to start. His speech that night consisted of, "I can no longer handle this team." And he left.

Wilson has ascribed Parker's success in the 1950s to his predecessor, Bo McMillin, who "laid the groundwork." And he has even conceded that his own success—a 1957 NFL championship in his first year as head coach—might have been linked by the same reasoning to Parker's groundwork. "I was in the right place at the right time," Wilson noted.

In any case, the suspense for all concerned was ended February 18 when Shula's appointment was announced. Wilson's disappointment was aggravated when he read the reported terms of the 40-year-old Shula's contract: Five years at $70,000, with a vice-presidency and part-ownership through stock options that could make him a millionaire if the club were successful.

Equally galling to Wilson was Robbie's definition of Shula's power. "He will have complete control of the football end of the operation," Robbie said, "and he will be consulted in every policy decision of the club."

Wilson had never exercised such control, and was particularly cautious the last two years when he became concerned over retaining his job. George's timidity to make changes was most evident in his reluctance to give up on such high-priced bonus failures as quarterback Rick Norton and middle linebacker Frank Emanuel. And he shrank in pitiful contrast to the self-sustaining man who had abruptly and dramatically quit the Lions in 1964 when management refused to rehire his assistants.

Wilson began losing his authority in 1967, his second year with the Dolphins, when his son was traded to Denver despite his objections. Although George Jr. had a slight frame and limited ability, his success was his father's fondest dream. In truth, young Wilson had once rescued the Dolphins in 1966, when three other quarterbacks fell out with injuries.

But Robbie considered the father-son arrangement an "impossible situation" the next year, after Bob Griese was plucked from Purdue as the club's No. 1 draft choice. Joe Thomas, the Dolphins' personnel director, was of the same mind. So was Denver coach Lou Saban, as it turned out; he acquired young Wilson and then cut him in two days, lending weight to Coach Wilson's theory that the trade was a "put-up job."

Young Wilson's case was closed when Robbie and Thomas remained adamant against giving him another chance. From then on the coach lost authority steadily. He was reluctant to make a move that might displease his employer, even though Norton in particular was to prove a disappointment from start to finish. Shula cut him after the new coach's first camp.

Norton was with Wilson to the end. "What can I do?" Wilson would say, shrugging when the subject arose. Robbie, however, maintains that Wilson had the authority to dismiss Norton or any other player whenever he chose. Lending weight to Robbie's contention was the fact that the Dolphin president rarely intervened in pure football matters.

Wilson wasn't around to hear it, but Shula gave his predecessor due credit at the press conference. "One of my biggest regrets at taking this position," Shula said, "is that the man I'm relieving is a personal friend and my former head coach.

"I'm thankful for the three years I worked as his assistant in Detroit. I think he's done a fine job with an expansion football team, and any success I may have in the future can be partly attributed to the groundwork laid by George and his assistants."

Honesty is among Shula's strong points. But whether he meant what he said is moot in view of his subsequent tactics.

By September Shula had dismissed or traded half of the 40-man squad that finished the 1969 season with its tenth defeat, a 27–9 pounding by the New York Jets.

In eight tries Wilson's Dolphins never beat the Jets, while Shula's Dolphins were to whip them three times in four games over the next two seasons. Admittedly, though, the Jets were playing without quarterback Joe Namath in two of these games.

"I learned a great deal under Wilson," Shula said, "particularly in the art of handling men. There is no better psychologist in the game."

The psychologist in Wilson emerged the day after he was fired. On Biscayne Boulevard, below his eleventh-floor office, he looked almost relieved. "Well, I'm a businessman now," he said, grinning and tapping cigar ashes on the sidewalk. Smartly clad in yellow check jacket, green tie, brown slacks and yellow shoes, George seemed to have lost the drawn, apprehensive expression that so ill became him the previous year.

A golfer who shoots in the 80s, George was arranging a date with Tom Kelleher, the 12-year pro back judge and a long-time friend. Kelleher represents Wilson Sporting Goods in the Miami area. And Wilson, as a member of the advisory board (though no relation to the founder), a lagniappe proffered to many coaches and athletes, had recently been presented with a new set of clubs.

"My boss said you can keep the clubs," Kelleher told Wilson. "We're not ready to fire you—yet."

"Thanks a lot," George replied, laughing.

Upstairs in his office, Wilson regarded the plaque sitting on the desk he would have to clean out before March 1, when his contract officially expired. "George Wilson," the inscription read. "Never Give Up. Go-Go-Go."

Wilson grinned, sadly. "I bear no animosity toward anybody. I'm not built that way," said Wilson the psychologist. "But I'm out of it now. They've got a new coach, a darned good one, and I have nothing more to do with it. So I've made up my mind that I won't say anything to anybody or about anybody, even though I could say a thing or two if I wanted to. But what for? I'm no longer the coach, and that's it.

"But I'll say this: I can walk into this office any time and talk to anybody with my head up. Pro football has given me 33 good years. And Joe Robbie gave me four good years in Miami. I'd wanted to be down here for a long time, and now I have the opportunity to go into business here. I can't complain about that."

Wilson and his partner, Raleigh Tozer of Miami, had invested successfully in an apartment on Bayshore Drive in downtown Miami. They were also planning a condominium, since completed, at the Country Club of Miami. Their five children married or at college, George and Claire Wilson have now moved from their large Coral Gables home to an apartment in the condominium.

Tozer had also purchased rights for the Dolphin Radio Network from Robbie, but that was the end of their association.

Tozer and Robbie, both volatile and outspoken, had many a loud argument. Once, in the bar at the Colonial Inn where the Dolphins were first quartered in St. Petersburg Beach, Tozer loudly advised Robbie that "this club will succeed in spite of you." Robbie never forgave him, and the Wilson-Tozer relationship irked the Dolphins' president to such an extent that it became a factor in Wilson's dismissal.

Wilson knew it, but he liked Tozer's camaraderie, his impudent Don Rickles' approach and his loyalty. Over the years, as Wilson came in for increased criticism because he wasn't winning, Tozer consistently defended his partner and pal. But Wilson was wise enough to know that a coach is hired only to be fired, and prudent enough to prepare for that day.

"I'm gonna stay right here in Miami and enjoy it," Wilson said, his eyes turning to a portrait of himself on the sidelines during a game. Beside him is No. 2, worn briefly but with a regal flourish by the inimitable Carlton Chester Gilchrist.

A legendary fullback in Canada and in the early AFL years, "Cookie" Gilchrist had grown bulky and stepped over the hill when he came to Miami in the fall of 1966 after a typical Gilchrist impasse with Denver's management. A foe of all front offices throughout his illustrious career, Cookie brought to Miami the same independent air that characterized his past adventures. Eloquent and distinguished, Cookie swept into Miami like The Man Who Broke the Bank at Monte Carlo. The first item he demanded of Robbie was a Cadillac, which his Denver contract called for.

Eventually, he got it. But Gilchrist was among numerous crosses afflicting Wilson in the Dolphins' formative years. In New York, Cookie refused to honor the 11 P.M. curfew, explaining that such sophomoric regulations were below his stature as a sophisticated man of the world, particularly in sophisticated Manhattan.

"We had our share of characters around here," Wilson said, studying the portrait, "and our disappointments. But I know this: It'll be 20 years before another football team gets as many injuries as we did last year.

"But that's the way life goes. A big part of this game is being in the right place at the right time. Don Shula will make a great coach for anybody, and I think he's made a fine move for himself. Hell, I wish him all the luck in the world."

George studied his cigar, thinking. "But I wish my assistants had been given some warning about this. It's pretty late to catch on somewhere now. I wish someone would have let somebody know in the 22 days it took to sign Don.

"Oh well," he added, "you take the bitter with the sweet and that's it. When I'm out teeing the ball up next summer, I'll think of training camp and maybe hit the thing a little harder."

Wilson was bitter. Egocentric as most head coaches and given to brooding, he could not sustain his magnanimous attitude when Shula became a spectacular success overnight. The psychologist yielded to the coach scorned, particularly when his bitterness was encouraged by well-meaning friends.

George has never used four season tickets Robbie sent him "for life." Nor has he ever attended a Dolphin practice. Once he attended a team banquet, sitting inconspicuously in the rear of the hotel dining room with friends. Wilson was unnoticed and went unintroduced—"purely by oversight," as emcee and Dolphin radio commentator Larry King explained. Wilson walked out in silent rage.

After smoldering nearly two years, the rancor erupted during, of all times, the week the Dolphins were in New Orleans for the Super Bowl—a long-shot achievement beyond imagination when Shula took over.

Yet Wilson, interviewed by Charlie Nobles of *The Miami News,* decided at last to speak out. "I've been silent too long," Wilson told Nobles, while predicting the Dolphins would beat Dallas in the Super Bowl. "As far as I'm concerned, Don Shula took over a ready-made team. Joe Doakes could have coached that team.

"I don't think the true story is out on this thing. You go over the first three years and you'll see we equaled or bettered the record of any expansion club in the history of pro football. In the fourth season we were taken out by injuries. You go over the roster and you'll see most of the guys who are doing the playing were committed to the Dolphins before Shula ever got here," Wilson said.

Wilson's reference to Joe Doakes, the hapless character in the old Hearst comics, animated Super Bowl week for the national press in New Orleans.

The game was billed as a confrontation between Joe Doakes and Plastic Man, the tag hung on Tom Landry, the Dallas coaching stoic, by running back Duane Thomas. Hubert Mizell, irreverently comic Associated Press reporter, once ended a Shula interview with, "Say hello to Dorothy and all the little Doakeses."

Shula took the kidding in stride. In New Orleans he repeated his original Miami observation that "Wilson deserves credit for his accomplishments in the early years." Shula added, "He's entitled to his opinion, and I'm certainly not going to lose any sleep over it. But I am disappointed to hear these things coming from George."

Wilson's timing could not have been more unfortunate, as Ed Pope wrote in *The Miami Herald*. Wilson was attacking the man who had created The Little Miracle of Biscayne College (the Dolphins' training base), just as they called Bobby Thomson's Giant home run of 1951 The Little Miracle of Coogan's Bluff.

Said a Dolphin assistant coach over the Joe Doakes' accusation: "It was like the Pharisees denouncing Christ on Easter Sunday instead of Good Friday."

Wilson realized this later on. Although he can be goaded into anger and displays of temper, George is not vindictive. "The newspapers," he said, "twisted my words around."

> I want our team to be comparable to the New York Mets. When a Met hits a foul ball, he gets a standing ovation. When we make a first down, I want a standing ovation.
>
> —DANNY THOMAS, *August 1966*

3. *Who Needs the AFL in Miami?*

Danny Thomas looked trim, black-haired and younger than his 53 years. His enameled smile and euphoric cuteness were contagious as usual. The entertainer pumped hands, exchanged pleasantries and joined in the fuss over the Miami Dolphins he had helped into existence.

To hear Thomas, in fact, an innocent bystander might suspect he'd personally brought the Dolphins to Super Bowl VI on the end of a leash. Danny's "God-given" exuberance flowed.

This was Friday night before Super Sunday, at the Roosevelt Hotel in New Orleans. All the king's men and their women had turned out as usual for the annual NFL party, a sybaritic excess of rich food and bonded spirits and Ella Fitzgerald singing George Gershwin tunes. The affair extravagantly illustrated how far professional football had advanced in the 52 years since A. E. Staley of Decatur, Ill., permitted George Halas and the rest of his football-minded employees to practice two hours a day on company time.

Thomas seemed to be enjoying himself. His audience was properly obsequious. He laughed and laughed at the recollection of racing down an Orange Bowl sideline after a running back named Joe Auer on the Miami Dolphins' first play of their first season. On that muggy September night in 1966, when Auer returned Oakland's kickoff 95 yards for a touchdown, Thomas had dashed into the end zone to bear-hug the hero.

That was about the last people in Miami saw of Thomas, who quietly backed out of the financially flattened organization the following year "to fulfill television contracts in Hollywood."

His reappearance five years later in New Orleans startled those who knew he'd left Joe Robbie, his original co-owner, to scrounge for a new partner and fresh capital lest his football team sink in red ink scarcely after its launching.

Robbie found a new partner and repaid his friend a profit on an investment pegged at $600,000, no questions asked and no hard feelings. Now Robbie had invited Thomas to New Orleans "to share in the fruits of the Dolphins' success."

So Danny shared. "My daughter and I made about $320,000 in commercials, all donated to St. Jude's," Thomas said, referring to his more recent occupation as a coffee salesman on television. Thomas and Robbie had become acquainted through a mutual interest in St. Jude's Children's Research Hospital in Memphis, Tenn., where both have contributed money and time to the cause of handicapped youngsters.

As he moved among the Super Bowl guests, Thomas recognized an occasional face and insisted he still retained "a little bit" in the Dolphins. (When later apprised of the remark, Robbie grinned in good humor and said, "If he does, I haven't heard about it.") It was a harmless remark in any case. Besides, Thomas had such high praise for Robbie, Coach Don Shula and the Dolphins that everybody knew Danny was on the side of the angels, as always.

His elation matched his mood of an evening some seven years before, one spent at Miami's Palm Bay Club, a breezy haven dedicated to the jet set and others seeking respite from life's cares. Thomas was in top form the moment he landed at Miami International Airport that Aug. 16, 1965. "What are you guys doing here?" he demanded of the police escort on the runway. "You ought to be in Los Angeles." A murderous riot was destroying the black Los Angeles ghetto of Watts at the time.

No sooner did the comedian's black alligator shoes hit the marble floor of the Palm Bay Club than he was sprawled flat on his back for the cameras. His triangular nose pointed toward the ceiling to serve as a kicking tee for Joe Foss, the American Football League commissioner, who had formally announced the birth of the Miami franchise just that afternoon.

"With this nose," Thomas announced, "how can we miss the point after touchdown?" And though for a moment Foss seemed tempted to try, he never got the chance. The irrepressible Thomas leaped to his feet and turned on the enameled smile for the television cameras. His brown eyes glowed as he painted a bright pro football future for the new team. "You can't show me any Lebanese boy raised in Toledo, Ohio, who doesn't want to own a Miami ball club," he said. "Seriously, although we know we're not walking into the biggest financial bonanza of all time, we must expect to at least break even. An old arithmetic teacher taught me that nobody can take losses forever. But I have confidence in this town. It's a big city. It's no longer just a citrus grove where people come to escape the winter."

For all his hopes, the most significant symbol Thomas displayed that evening was a lapel medal honoring St. Jude, the patron of lost causes. "Absolutely no connection with the football team," he said.

Historically, St. Jude represented the perfect patron for Miami's pro football team until the indomitable Robbie kidnaped Shula out from under his contract with the Baltimore Colts in 1970.

The pros had made passes at Miami since 1946, when a round-faced, good-natured Atlantan named Harvey Hester introduced the Seahawks of the All-America Conference. The Seahawks were an immediate disaster—artistically, financially and barometrically. For an opening opponent, Hester's team drew Paul Brown's Cleveland Browns, a dynasty from the beginning. Through four years and 49 games in the doomed AAC, the Browns of Otto Graham, Marion Motley, Dante Lavelli & Co. would lose only four times. They wiped up the Seahawks 44–0 at Cleveland's Municipal Stadium.

At home in the Orange Bowl things got worse for the Seahawks. Unwanted by the University of Miami and the locally powerful Orange Bowl Committee, an esoteric group dedicated to the success of its college game every January 1, the Seahawks were compelled to play on Monday nights.

Their home opener was delayed one night because of a hurricane. The next night they were beaten in the rain by the San Francisco 49ers, 34–7. Another game was postponed by a hurricane, and others were drenched in rain. On one balmy night the Seahawks drew 242 customers. At the end of the season the Seahawks disappeared.

Still, Hester's sense of humor remained intact. A reporter once opened an interview by asking him, "Didn't you have the old Miami Seahawks?"

"Yes," Hester replied. "And vice versa."

More than 20 years later, Hester attended a Dolphin game. "Why isn't it raining?" he asked.

When the AFL was being conceived in 1959, Ralph Wilson of Detroit was anxious to put a team in Miami. Again, the Orange Bowl Committee and the University of Miami combined to repel him. The Orange Bowl people termed the AFL "the Garbage League." Discouraged, Wilson set up his franchise in Buffalo.

In 1965 Thomas and Robbie at last found a friend in Miami. Their champion was Mayor Robert King High, a feisty battler who before his death in 1967 was used to going up against entrenched interests. High fought the notorious clip joints in downtown Miami and managed to close most of them. He even bucked the utilities to the extent of winning a rate decrease from Florida Power & Light.

High had a confidence few others shared, namely that pro football would become a source of economic assistance to an area that was growing too rapidly to depend exclusively on tourists. One who shared his confidence was Robbie, although the brash Minneapolis lawyer went practically unnoticed.

The eloquent Robbie was one of only 19 Democrats elected to the South Dakota Legislature in 1946, the year hurricanes were blowing Hester's Seahawks off the face of the earth. The Legislature included 111 Republicans, among them a World War II Medal of Honor winner named Joe Foss, with whom Robbie had been friends at the University of South Dakota. Four years later Robbie won the Democratic nomination for governor but lost in the general election. Foss was defeated for the GOP nomination the same year.

In the winter of 1964 Robbie came to Miami Beach to relax and meet a law client. Their business finished, the client asked if Robbie knew Foss, who by then was commissioner of the AFL. Could Robbie speak to Foss about an AFL franchise for Philadelphia?

At a meeting in Washington, Foss told his old classmate that Philadelphia was out. However, he considered Miami an excellent possibility if someone could sell the idea to the other league owners and to the city officials themselves. No one had to tell Robbie or his client of Miami's hostile indifference in the past.

Robbie's client balked, but Robbie retained the notion even though money has a habit of eluding a man with 11 children.

Still, lack of money has never stopped Robbie. He sought out Thomas, his friend and co-worker in Lebanese-American charities. And with the endorsement as well as enthusiasm of Thomas, but not yet the money, Robbie decided to pursue a Miami franchise on his own.

Obstacles were everywhere. Ralph Wilson, still miffed over being snubbed by Miami in 1959, said the town would support only college football. Lamar Hunt, the Kansas City owner and Texas millionaire most responsible for the AFL, warned that the tourist city hadn't enough civic unity to support a pro team.

Thus advised, Robbie characteristically paid no attention and pushed on. High's support further encouraged him, except for one seemingly insurmountable barrier—Orange Bowl bonds reputedly required rental to be 17.5 percent of gross receipts, a self-defeating figure as far as both the AFL and NFL were concerned. High's source of information regarding this last matter was Melvin Reese, Miami's city manager; so Robbie went to Reese and asked if he might look over the stadium bonds. Thus began a beautiful enmity that Robbie and Reese still hold for each other.

Robbie discovered that the bonds said nothing at all about

any rental percentage. This was the turning point. Robbie was now prepared to pitch Miami at the AFL expansion committee meeting in July 1965, at New Jersey's Monmouth Racetrack, owned in part by Sonny Werblin of the New York Jets.

While the owners were not prepared for either Robbie or Miami, they were prepared to sell their first expansion franchise for $3.8 million to Atlanta. At the meeting to accept the award was J. Leonard Rensch, former Democratic Party treasurer, head of Cox Broadcasting, Inc., and a member of the Peachtree Street elite. Rensch's credentials were impressive. They were certainly better than Robbie's, whose equipment consisted of lance, shield and unmitigated gall.

Robbie had angles, though. He was riding in the colors of his pals, Foss and Thomas, and had the unqualified support of High. The mayor had also found out about the expansion meeting, supposedly a clandestine affair, and was on hand to extoll the virtues of his Magic City.

Furthermore, Robbie refused to discourage. When the owners' committee suggested $7.5 million for starters, other interested groups were frightened off. Robbie didn't budge.

The owners were just playing, however; they had already ordained that the ninth AFL franchise would go to Atlanta in the care of Rensch. Then came help for Robbie from an unexpected source. His biggest benefactor that day proved to be NFL Commissioner Pete Rozelle.

While the AFL committee was losing money on the horses at Monmouth, Rozelle had read its offense and beaten it to Atlanta. On the same day, Rozelle was awarding the NFL's fifteenth franchise for $6.5 million to a personal friend, Rankin Smith, with the blessing of Atlanta Mayor Ivan Allen and his huge new stadium.

Now with Atlanta securely locked into the NFL establishment, owners of the wildcat league began calling the swarthy Minneapolis lawyer "Mr. Robbie." In turn, Mr. Robbie said he was amenable to the $7.5 million, except for a few details.

Among the details, Robbie's forensic proclivities succeeded in extracting $500,000 a year in television revenue for his team. The committee had not planned on cutting in an expansion team for any of this treasure trove. When the Cincinnati franchise was awarded two years later, the Bengals didn't get a dime.

With the groundwork completed and the franchise practically in hand, Robbie and Hunt flew to see Thomas at Lake Tahoe, where the entertainer proved as ebullient as he was the following month at the Palm Bay Club.

Robbie's work was only beginning. Still faceless as far as this suspicious Florida community was concerned, he now had to field a football team.

Sports had been Robbie's consuming passion as a boy in Sisseton, S.D., and he had been writing a sports column for several years in the weekly newspaper, but at 120 pounds Robbie was no athlete. Until he found himself with his own pro team, the closest he had come to the mercenaries were the $5 seats at home games of the Minnesota Vikings. So Robbie went right to the Vikings for assistance. There, his sixth sense told him, a man was available for the right inducement.

Norm Van Brocklin, Minnesota's plainspoken coach, was having his problems both on and off the field. Seeking a scapegoat, Van Brocklin was venting much of his wrath on Joe Thomas, the Vikings' personnel director and a man of unquestioned ability and experience in the game.

After a series of nerve-jolting defeats, Van Brocklin called the athletes Thomas supplied him "a bunch of stiffs." Robbie had a notion such appellations were not being smoothly digested by Thomas. And it took Robbie less than a month to get Thomas to sign with Miami in October 1965 as director of player personnel.

Thomas, a man of responsibility and self-discipline, proved perfect for the lonely task of finding football players. He was the first employee Robbie hired. His ability was reflected in the fact that the jilted Vikings locked up his personnel files on his departure. Among the Thomas recruits and draftees therein were names such as Tommy Mason, Fran Tarkenton, Lonnie Warwick, Roy Winston, Paul Flatley, Carl Eller, Dave Osborne, Jack Snow and Lance Rentzel. Thomas had also been the first employee hired by the Vikings as an NFL expansion team in 1960. He knew his job.

Specifically, Thomas was to draft 32 experienced AFL hands from among a group of expendables placed on the expansion list by the other eight teams to stock the Miamians. He could select up to four from each team. The procedure was liberal, even if the quality of material in 1966 was decidedly below NFL standards. The AFL draft allowed existing clubs to protect only 23 players, and no freeze was permitted on taxi-squad personnel or reserves inactive the previous season because of injuries or for other reasons.

Of the 32 names Thomas selected, only offensive right tackle Norm Evans (from Houston) remained on the active roster when the Dolphins reached the Super Bowl six years later. But the others helped create a memorable saga.

A more difficult task for Thomas was signing up his college draftees in what turned out to be the last year of the all-out bonus war between the NFL and the upstart AFL. (The leagues signed an agreement in June 1966 calling first for a common draft and then total realignment into a single organization by 1970.) But the common draft was only a hope when Thomas started chasing his first draft choices around the country, competing with the far more organized and heavier in the wallet "baby-sitters" of the NFL.

At the same time, Robbie was busy lining up office personnel and financial support. A lifelong subway alumnus of Notre Dame, Robbie reached under the Golden Dome for Charlie Callahan, a 50-year-old native of Lexington, Mass., who had been preserving the legend of the Fighting Irish for 20 years.

In the stormy, incredible years that followed, Callahan was to remain a loyal constant. And he is now the only employee left from the original cast Robbie recruited. During the first few years, while Robbie was a favorite target of opprobrium even in his own office, Callahan would answer all complaints with a stock phrase: "No Joe Robbie, no Miami Dolphins."

Robbie and Danny Thomas made two significant financial moves before the end of 1965. In October, John H. O'Neil of Miami bought a 10 percent share of the club, representing an investment of $750,000. O'Neil was the only Miamian in Robbie's original partnership group, a step both men were subsequently to regret. In December, a substantial share was purchased by George A. Hamid, who owned the Atlantic City Steel Pier and the Hamid-Morton Circus and had been a close friend of Danny Thomas for more than 25 years. A colorful personality, Hamid had been brought to America from Beirut, Lebanon, by Buffalo Bill to perform as a boy acrobat in Cody's Wild West show.

Hamid was taught to read English by Annie Oakley. And at 69 he could still hold seven men on his shoulders, according to his son, George Jr., who joined him in the Dolphin family. Though both men vowed to take an active interest in the club, this turned out to be short-lived.

Robbie consulted Joe Thomas in the search for a head coach. Above all, Robbie wanted a man who was well known, as he wished to assure skeptical South Florida that the Miami team was in town to stay.

George Wilson was an excellent choice in many respects. He had brought his Detroit teams to three consecutive play-off bowls in Miami and had won them all. Over eight seasons in Detroit, his record was 58-45-6. And the roughhouse, rowdy character of the Lions in those years pointed to Wilson as the ideal man to guide an eclectic Miami squad gathered for the first time from all Gaul.

Alex Karras, a defensive tackle as loquacious as he was tough, had called Wilson "the best damn coach I ever played for." And the quote was a familiar one in Miami, where Karras was a frequent winter visitor at the home of Archie Stone.

Stone, a 73-year-old chucklebag weighing 155 pounds, had been an unofficial mascot of the burly Lions in the eight years Wilson presided as head coach. Dedicated to pro football and underprivileged children, Stone adopted the Miami team from the start. He was—and remains—a frequent host to athletes and celebrities. The walls of his southwest Miami home are covered with inscribed photographs of his idols, from Jimmy Durante to Bob Griese. And "Little Archie" remains the quiet, introverted Griese's closest friend in Miami.

Archie's atavistic generation, abundant in South Florida, could identify with Wilson as a two-way end for the Chicago Bears in their glory years under George Halas.

After 10 years as a player, Wilson joined Halas as an assistant coach for two years before moving to the Lions as an aide first to Bo McMillin and then to the neurotic genius Buddy Parker. In 1957, when Parker abruptly quit in anger and frustration over "back-door politics and disloyal players," Wilson took over. He promptly won the NFL championship with Parker's unruly but talented squad, driven by indomitable Bobby Layne. Wilson built a reputation among the mercenaries as a "player's coach." But critics of Detroit's cavalier style and absence of discipline said that Wilson was letting the inmates run the asylum. Neither the superintendent nor the inmates won another championship.

On Jan. 29, 1966, Wilson signed a three-year contract as head coach of the Miami Dolphins.

The nickname, submitted by Mrs. Robert W. Swanson of Miami and 822 others, won the 33-year-old housewife two lifetime passes. "I really don't know why I picked Dolphins, except that the dolphin is supposed to be an intelligent animal and the name just came," said Mrs. Swanson, who eliminated rival dolphin fanciers by correctly guessing that the 1965 Miami-Notre Dame game would end in a tie.

"My daughter, Holly Ann, has this eight ball that makes predictions," Mrs. Swanson explained. "When we asked it about a tie, the answer came up, 'Definitely.'"

> The thing that impressed me is that everybody on the team came out clawing and hitting on every play. Even little Twilley was knocking linemen down. We just got beat by a better team.
>
> —DICK BUTKUS, *after Chicago's 34–3 defeat at the Orange Bowl in November 1971*

4. *A Very Nice Party*

Howard Twilley's contorted, sweating face reflected the pain in his right knee as he bobbed around the St. Petersburg Beach practice field in breezeless, 90-degree heat.

"I can tell the time by Twilley," said Joe Thomas, commiserating on the sideline. "He comes gimping past every five minutes."

Thomas had made Twilley his twelfth pick at the American Football League college draft held the previous November 1965. A consensus All-American despite his 180 pounds stretched over a 5-10 frame, Twilley had set 10 NCAA records on a pass-minded Tulsa team.

Thomas had offered him a $20,000 bonus with a no-cut contract before the Minnesota Vikings got into the bidding. The Vikings had picked Twilley in the National Football League draft and offered him more money. But despite the urging of his father to take the more lucrative offer, Twilley declined with the explanation that he had given Thomas and the Dolphins his word. He would keep it, and with part of his bonus money would set up a scholarship fund at Tulsa.

An honor student who had majored in electrical engineering, the 22-year-old Twilley represented the kind of employee Thomas was seeking: *mens sana in corpore sano*—sound mind, sound body. A native of Houston, Twilley's wide-angle features and protruding ears give him the appearance of a hayseed. An object of amicable ridicule, he returns most of it with a good-natured grin. Meanwhile, he has doggedly stayed with the Dolphins while becoming a consummate pro.

He wasn't grinning on the practice field that July, however. He knew he needed every ounce of effort in his compact body to gain a job and to keep it. And this was impossible, since he had twisted the knee in a spring game while playing for Tulsa's alumni.

With his leg tightly wrapped from ankle to thigh, Twilley dragged his burden ceaselessly around the field's perimeter while 84 rookies took turns scrimmaging in the middle. Coach George Wilson had his newcomers hitting from the first day, July 5, which only added to Twilley's discomfort.

"I'm no use to the club at all," he said between deep breaths during a break in his running program. "Sometimes I wonder what I'm doing here."

But the determination Twilley displayed during his reconditioning ordeal impressed Wilson and his staff, just as it would Don Shula five years later. Written off at the outset as through for the year, Twilley would come back to get his jaw fractured that same season at Kansas City by a shattering forearm blow delivered by cornerback Freddie "The Hammer" Williamson.

In retrospect, Twilley was among the rare assets the Dolphins possessed in a training camp where almost everything else went wrong from start to finish.

The Happy Dolphin Inn, a bright new hostelry overlooking both Boca Ciega Bay and the practice field, was promised to the Dolphins in an arrangement promoted by a group called Suncoast Sports. They had agreed to underwrite camp expenses for five years at $50,000 a year in order to bring the new team to the Tampa-St. Petersburg Bay area as a promotional fillip. The arrangement was completed with Chuck Burr representing the Dolphins.

A pleasant man, if somewhat officious, Burr had been among the AFL pioneers as publicity director for the Buffalo Bills in 1960. But his front-office experience was limited, and he was a neophyte in the fast-buck operations of Florida. So when a salesman named Charlie Proper put Suncoast's $50,000 proposition to him, Burr leaped at the chance. "This is the greatest training-camp bargain a pro football team ever had," he exulted.

Indeed the deal looked perfect, particularly for a new team with limited capital. The Dolphins would be quartered at the Happy Dolphin and train just across Gulf Boulevard on a field freshly sodded for their convenience.

The promises came in March. By the middle of June, Suncoast informed the Dolphins that the inn would not be available. It was too expensive at $15 a room. Reports from the Tampa-St. Petersburg area that the promoters were scratching for cash had contributed to a pervasive uneasiness. And though Mayor Bill Colletti of St. Petersburg and other civic leaders were talking of staging a night of entertainment to raise money, such measures were unspecified in the original "bargain."

But Suncoast had a solution. Arrangements were made for the Dolphins to stay at the Colonial Motor Inn, just down the road, where the $11.50 room charge was feasible. Wilson and

Burr inspected both the partly sodded practice field and the Colonial in June, and found the facilities "excellent."

Nobody was really responsible for the sight that greeted the Dolphins on the sandy finger of land known as St. Petersburg Beach. Bikini-clad girls were abundant by day. At night the neon lights of the strip catering to vacationers twinkled until all hours. Saxophones in the motel lounges and guitars on the beach made the place a better training camp for swinging singles than football players. "I don't believe this," was the opening comment of Wahoo McDaniel. Wahoo, a stumpy Choctaw Indian whose flamboyant style made him a favorite in Manhattan before Joe Namath came along in 1965, was among the expansion draftees obtained from the New York Jets.

"Remember one thing, Wahoo," cautioned Al Dotson, a 270-pound defensive tackle. "Remember the words of Austin O'Malley."

"Austin O'Malley?"

"Yes," replied Dotson. "O'Malley said, 'The harder you throw down a football and a good character, the higher they will rebound; but a reputation once thrown is like an egg.'"

Wahoo walked off, shaking his head. If he remembered O'Malley's advice, he disguised it adroitly in four seasons as a courageous and inscrutable middle linebacker for the Dolphins.

Wilson himself encountered problems even before he reached camp. One of the six assistants he had hired, Ralph Hawkins, quit in June. Disenchanted with the Miami setup, the 30-year-old Hawkins decided to join Tom Cahill's staff at West Point. As a last-minute replacement to coach the receivers, Wilson hired Bobby Walston from Philadelphia.

An old-school advocate, Wilson surrounded himself with aides who had played or coached professionally. The exception was 38-year-old John Idzik, whom Wilson had known when Idzik was coaching at the University of Detroit and upon whom Wilson came to rely heavily as the architect of his game plans.

The offensive line coach was Ernie Hefferle, a 52-year-old veteran from college and professional ranks who the year before had been with the Pittsburgh Steelers. The others hired were defensive line coach Les Bingaman, Wilson's great middle guard at Detroit; linebacker coach Bob Pellegrini, fresh out of uniform with the Eagles; and defensive backfield coach Tom Keane, a 1953 all-pro at Baltimore who had coached the previous season in Pittsburgh.

None of them was ready for the St. Petersburg Beach fiasco. The Dolphins were greeted with more suspicion than warmth by Jack Krug, manager of the Colonial Inn. Krug, who had not yet seen his first check from Suncoast Sports, was worried and remained worried while gradually and understandably reducing both the quantity and quality of the training-table fare.

By the second week chow mein and other such starchy items began to appear, until McDaniel was moved to note, "If I face any more of this goddam Chinese food, they'll have to carry me to practice in a rickshaw."

Rick Casares, the former Chicago backfield great acquired a month before from Washington on waivers, said that he looked in a mirror one night and found his eyes were slanting. "I may be the guy pulling you," Casares told McDaniel.

Krug was desperate, despite the efforts of Wilson and Burr to conciliate him. Robbie, grounded at home in Minneapolis by a nationwide airline strike, knew nothing of the club's plight. Wilson and Burr, hoping that Suncoast would come through, continued to deliver encouraging reports to Robbie in their regular phone conversations, for they did not want to steam up the team's volatile president.

Then Krug began cutting down on the fruit punch, a succulent red beverage the dried-out athletes consumed by the vat. The murmuring increased.

"Jack, I know your problems," Wilson said. "But you've got to keep that punch flowing. These guys' bodies are drained after practice. They've got to have liquids, and plenty of them."

The punch kept flowing. Krug understood. But as manager of the motel he was on the edge of panic. "I don't like to do this. I'd like to serve steak every night," Krug said. "But I have to get paid." (The Colonial served the Dolphins steak every Wednesday night, for an additional charge of $1.50.)

Then the air-conditioning shorted out in the players' wing. This rapidly became a twofold curse, for in the absence of locker-room facilities, the players used their motel rooms to change and store their equipment. After a day without air-conditioning, the entire Colonial complex reeked of sweat. To ease this problem, some of the players hung their equipment outside. As a result, pads, shirts, shoes and helmets were stolen.

The only visible hope for relief was a gentleman named John Burroughs, a local businessman and the only self-acknowledged member of the Suncoast Sports group ever seen on St. Petersburg Beach that July. Burroughs would appear at the Colonial, to be eagerly collared by Wilson, Burr and Krug. He would tell them he would do his best to instigate some action from a group that did not seem to exist. Burroughs protested to Wilson that he was "not a wealthy man" but would do what he could. He did his best. At times he would take a huge roller, apparently abandoned on the field when the sodding was more or less completed, and strain valiantly against it in an attempt to roll the field. He was saved, however, when the city shut off the water supply to the field for lack of payment. Out of respect for his Herculean efforts, and still hoping Suncoast would come forth, Wilson kept Burroughs' son around as a rookie linebacking candidate, though it was evident that Billy Burroughs would never cut it as a pro.

The field itself was positively dangerous. The sod had been plopped haphazardly over sandshells. And when receivers or backs made sharp cuts, ankles and knees were vulnerable. After a week of practice, the strewn sod looked as though a dozen duffers had been practicing 9-iron shots.

Even Wilson's astounding patience and good nature began to yield. Except for a few quality performers, he was not only dealing with flotsam and jetsam of pro football but was also compelled to train them on a beach.

Onto this depressing scene came two flamboyant spirits so determined to lift the depression that the result was a brouhaha big enough to move Vietnam off the local front page. John O'Neil, the Miamian who had bought 10 percent of the club, decided to throw a dinner party marking the birthday of Julian Cole, an effervescent public relations man on temporary duty as a promotion and advertising consultant for the Dolphins. Cole had done publicity for stock cars, Sally Rand, politicians and racetracks. As publicist for Miami's Tropical Park, Cole's reputation for getting things done was as consistent as his unpredictable methods.

O'Neil invited coaches, press, officials and visiting wives to Cole's birthday dinner. The affair was held at a smart, sedate restaurant called The Careless Navigator. Drinks and supper progressed smoothly. Too smoothly.

O'Neil had alerted some of the guests that this was to be no ordinary birthday celebration. As the time came for dessert, an ominous air of anticipation was evident. The *pièce de résistance* turned out to be a huge, splendid cake that O'Neil ceremoniously presented to Cole by flattening it over Julian's head. Knowing the prankish Cole, guests began to slide their chairs away from the hysterically laughing O'Neil.

Methodically Cole began gathering pastry from his face, his clothes and the tablecloth. He then returned the fire. Of course, by now the entire Careless Navigator clientele was paying attention, as O'Neil and Cole dripped and threw and ducked. Stalactites of frosting began appearing on The Careless Navigator's paneled walls.

A few days later, despite O'Neil's checkbook which seemed to soothe the proprietors and succeeded in averting a Dunkirk-style exit, the St. Petersburg *Independent* bannered the story on page one. The article suggested a prandial riot involving a mob of Miami Dolphin ruffians who besmirched both the reputation and decor of the town's prestige restaurant. A remark by Charlie Callahan appeared ridiculous in the context: "It was a very nice party," the old Notre Dame man was quoted as saying.

This was among the nuggets that greeted Robbie when he arrived in Miami after the airline strike had delayed him more than two weeks.

Taking a dim view of O'Neil and Cole from that point on, Robbie set out to do something about the Colonial Inn and the miserable field on which his football team was preparing for its first season. Characteristically, Robbie moved in like Toro. "We don't intend to let these people stick guns in our backs," he announced. "Nor can we be expected to tolerate these conditions any longer." Absent from Robbie's meeting with Krug, as usual, was Suncoast Sports, the supposed angel of the entire camp enterprise.

The Dolphins moved immediately to a new practice field

across the causeway at Boca Ciega High School. Robbie dispatched Joe Thomas on a statewide search for a new training camp.

With the opening exhibition game August 6 at San Diego just 10 days off and Suncoast Sports now established as a myth, Robbie weighed some $75,000 in totally unexpected bills. At the same time, he learned from Miami that the free offices promised him in the Dupont Plaza Hotel had fallen through.

Word had spread that the club was in trouble and, predictably, front-running Miamians were leaping off the ship. Robbie, operating on a shoestring after contracting for enormous bonuses to rookies he had not yet seen in action, sifted sheafs of bills and began a holding operation.

Burr joined O'Neil and Cole in the doghouse. Although Robbie acknowledged the responsibility was his own, Burr was not forgiven for permitting himself to be gulled into the Suncoast disaster.

Robbie might have been portrayed in the Bill Veeck mold if his often and abrasively expressed anger did not so aggravate both his business associates and employees. His candid if one-sided approach is simply out of kilter with the necessary Janus-faced art of politics. He makes enemies of his acquaintances simply by walking past them without speaking or nodding or otherwise acknowledging their existence.

At the 1972 Super Bowl, Mayor Steve Clark of Dade County wondered aloud, "What's the matter with that man? We bumped into each other a little while ago and he didn't even say hello."

Though no charmer, Robbie is a responsible man and as brutally honest with himself as he is with others. From the beginning he brooded over bills and the cold reception accompanying his efforts. He found nothing remotely humorous in the mad month of St. Petersburg Beach. Perhaps Robbie suspected a conspiracy of Brutuses intent on his destruction, and even now he cannot erase the notion from his mind.

On August 7 the Dolphins returned from their exhibition at San Diego to Boca Raton, a tranquil community some 40 miles north of Miami. They resumed training at St. Andrew's, an Episcopalian prep school for boys hidden in the Everglades, about a 10-minute drive from the nearest Boca Raton bar. Serene, rustic St. Andrew's was indeed the antithesis of the beach. Clean if plain dormitories, a spacious cafeteria, two well-kept football fields, showers and locker facilities made the place a welcome haven.

> Better limp all the way to heaven than not get there at all.
>
> —BILLY SUNDAY

5. *Les Bingaman's Busloads*

Les Bingaman punched M6 on Charlie Wren's jukebox and sat back on the barstool. Les enveloped the barstool. It just disappeared under his 320-pound bulk. He looked like he was sitting there on a pole.

M6 was a country tune called *Please Release Me*. Les could sing the lyric with the proper Tennessee inflection—"Plaeez reeylees meee, layit meee goooo"—when in the mood. He was not in the mood. He had spent the whole hot day busing 84 rookies from the Tampa Airport across town to St. Petersburg Beach. "Bingo," as George Wilson called his old friend, was tired from the grinding bus. He could still hear the gears in his ears. And he didn't particularly take to rookies anyway, especially the diaper cases.

He ordered another draft beer from Charlie Wren, the high-aproned, 63-year-old proprietor of Dad's Rendezvous on Gulf Boulevard. Charlie had already taken to the gruff-voiced "big guy" who could quaff draft beer "till the cows come home."

Veteran that he was, Bingo had only needed five minutes to find Wren's beer-and-wine bar near the Colonial Inn. By July 5, the reporting date for the rookies and the second day on the beach for Wilson's coaching staff, Bingo had already figured the lay of the land. The food at the Colonial was not to his taste, the motel bar was too expensive and the whole place too "vacationish." So Les established headquarters at Dad's Rendezvous, where Charlie Wren had Polish sausage, pickled pigs' feet, hot peppers and an assortment of nuts that went just fine with the beer. For diversion, Charlie had a bowling machine and the jukebox with its M6.

Sitting there in his shroud of a T-shirt, thigh-length coaching shorts and a scowl, Bingaman was an imposing figure, still a lion of a man at 40. It had been 19 years since Bingaman, Buddy Young and their Illinois teammates made a shambles of the first Rose Bowl game involving the Big Ten and the Pacific Coast Conference. The Illini walloped UCLA 45–14. Bingaman handled the Bruins' backs as though they were Shakespeare's "slight, unmeritable men meet to be sent on errands."

Bingo was as clever, sensitive and humble as he was huge. One Sunday in Denver, after another gut-wrenching Miami defeat and another disappointment from his defensive line, Bingaman could not be found in the dressing room. He was in the rear of the team bus, crying. A three-time all-pro with Detroit and six years there with Wilson as an assistant coach, Bingaman idolized Wilson and was unswerving in his loyalty, even in the trying seasons to come when the allegiance of the staff was split.

He was worried now, as he punched M6 for the ninth time and ordered another round. "The old man's got a big job, we all do, but him especially," Bingo growled. "I hope these rookies are a little scared, because being a little scared helps." Bingo sighed, drained his glass and equivocated. "Still," he said, grinning, "you can't be sure till you get them on the field. Hell, with a little luck a good pro can earn $14,000 or $15,000 a year right off and start a good career. I hope they keep that in mind."

Most of them apparently did not. Of the rookies who Bingaman shuttled into the Colonial Inn that day, including 11 of the 20 Miami draft choices Joe Thomas had signed in competition with the NFL, only 15 were still around when the season opened in September. Of these, seven were draft choices, most with no-cut contracts offered as inducements in the last year of the signing struggle between the leagues.

Two came enormously high, even for those days when collegians grew rich overnight. Rick Norton, the quarterback from Kentucky and Miami's No. 1 choice, signed for $350,000 in salaries and bonuses. Frank Emanuel, a middle linebacker from Tennessee, commanded even more money in Miami's battle with the Philadelphia Eagles for his services. Emanuel was considered one of the three linebackers that year who couldn't miss. The others were Tommy Nobis of Texas and Carl McAdams of Oklahoma. Nobis, reputedly given more than $600,000 in salary and material considerations, remains a fixture for the Atlanta Falcons. McAdams went to the New York Jets' camp with an ankle injury and never fulfilled his promise. Emanuel stayed four seasons with the Dolphins, most of them disappointing. But when Don Shula came on the scene, Emanuel was dismissed before Shula's first training camp ended.

Emanuel's price came to nearly $400,000. In a relentless campaign to get him, Joe Thomas tried practically everything. Emanuel was given vacation trips to Hawaii and Mexico, with credit-card privileges enabling him to live in almost any way he chose. But still the 6-3, 225-pound linebacker came to camp after the All-Star game as tight as a spring. Fully aware of the money invested in him, Emanuel wanted badly to produce.

The athletes of consequence whom Joe Thomas lost to the NFL included fullback Jim Grabowski of Illinois, Miami's bonus choice (as a new team), who signed with Green Bay for $400,000 despite a higher offer from the Dolphins, and offensive tackle Larry Gagner of Florida, who signed with the Chicago Bears. Gagner and George Allen, then pursuing prospects for the Bears, gave Thomas fits in New Orleans when all three were on hand and maneuvering before Florida and Missouri collided January 1 in the 1966 Sugar Bowl. And when Gagner went over to Allen and the Bears that weekend, his defection completed a maddening New Orleans visit for the Miami personnel man. A ruthless competitor who had played football under Paul Brown at Great Lakes and coached in the pros before moving to the front office, Thomas took such defeats as personal insults. He stayed angry and sullen for days.

The defection of Jerry Oliver at St. Petersburg Beach incensed him. A 6-6, 285-pound tackle, Oliver had been drafted fifteenth and had been given a substantial bonus to sign. He was the largest rookie reporting to Wilson. Oliver simply left after the second day of practice and went back home to Freeport, Texas.

"He felt real woozy," reported Lindy Lyles, Oliver's friend and roommate at the Colonial Inn. "So he just took off for home. Ol' Jerry gets these down-and-out feelings sometimes, and ain't nothin' you can say to him. It's just like talkin' to an ol' yeller houn' dawg." Lyles said Oliver had a job waiting in Texas. He was going to be a prison guard.

The other looming rookie in camp was 6-7, 275-pound Ron Berger from Wayne State. Berger was even greener than

Oliver. The first day he kept sliding off a 400-pound tackling dummy, tumbling awkwardly to the sodded sandshells.

"Easy, son. You can't kill it," said Bingaman, draping an arm around the huffing shoulder of Berger. "Now go around and try again. Just come straight at the thing. Remember, it won't scare. Ain't no use tryin' to take it by surprise."

Berger never did master the dummy. But he had more determination than Oliver. He lasted a month before being cut. Berger then spent four seasons bounding around the minors, mostly with Los Angeles satellite teams, before attaching himself to the Boston Patriots and gaining a first-string defensive end job. Berger was to contribute three of seven sacks quarterback Bob Griese suffered in a 27–14 Boston victory that ruined Shula's Miami debut in September 1970.

The candidates that first summer included the inevitable Walter Mittys who'd always known they could play pro football if only given a chance. Jesse Holt, a 5-7 sprinter with college experience, sold a pint of blood for bus fare from Miami to St. Petersburg. The Dolphins paid his bus fare back after a one-day trial. "I guess my wind and strength were not as good as I thought," said the tiny Holt.

Bob Brown, a 6-2, 271-pound Miamian, waited all day in the Colonial Inn lobby for Wilson, who finally could no longer avoid a confrontation. "I'll play anyplace where it's rough, Coach," said Brown. But after one drill he disappeared.

Between the exits and cuts, only 34 rookies were left when the experienced AFL personnel reported at the beginning of the second week. Joe Thomas had picked 32 players in the expansion draft, four from each AFL team. These players, acquired team by team, presented a curious, disunited front.

Boston—quarterback Eddie Wilson, guard Billy Neighbors, linebacker Jack Rudolph, safety Ross O'Hanley.

Buffalo—fullback Billy Joe, flanker Bo Roberson, offensive tackle Jim Davidson, defensive tackle Howard Simpson.

Denver—safety John McGeever, linebacker Tom Erlandson, defensive end Ed Cooke, defensive tackle Tom Nomina.

Houston—offensive tackles Norm Evans and Maxie Williams, center Tom Goode, fullback Jack Spikes.

Kansas City—flanker Frank Jackson, defensive tackle Al Dotson, defensive end Mel Branch, linebacker Ron Caveness.

New York—middle linebacker Ed (Wahoo) McDaniel, safety Willie West, defensive end LaVerne Torczon, center Mike Hudock.

Oakland—quarterback Dick Wood, defensive tackle Rich Zecher, guard Ken Rice, placekicker Gene Mingo.

San Diego—tight end Dave Kocourek, tackle Ernie Park, cornerbacks Jim Warren and Dick Westmoreland.

Six of these athletes, vital to any success the new team might have, failed to report at first. Joe Thomas, a hard man to refuse because of his sheer persistence, went out and collared three: Jackson, Branch and Rice. All were entertaining thoughts of retirement rather than suffer with an expansion outfit.

Simpson, Spikes and Caveness never did report. Thomas had yielded Caveness for the draft rights to Bill Anderson, Twilley's former batterymate at Tulsa, whom he lost to the NFL anyway. Simpson retired. But the Dolphins got a draft choice when Spikes decided he would return to football, though not to Miami.

Davidson left camp the first week with a knee that required surgery. O'Hanley incurred a severe thigh injury and was lost for the season. Eddie Wilson was knocked out in an August exhibition with a bum knee. Of the expansion draftees, however, 26 survived to open the season with the Dolphins.

Another experienced hand was found in the spindly-legged, 35-year-old torso of Rick Casares, released by the Washington Redskins after breaking two ribs in the 1965 opener and sitting out the rest of the year. Wilson signed him in June, desperately hoping to extract a few more yards from the old warrior. Casares had once been an all-pro back with the Chicago Bears, where he had racked up 5,657 yards in 10 seasons to surpass the record of Bronko Nagurski, Wilson's old teammate. Furthermore, Casares was a University of Florida product, so his presence might help the gate. And judging by early returns, the gate needed all the help it could get.

Wilson, a great believer in building a player's ego through newspapers and television, received Casares like the prodigal son. "When I coached at Detroit I tried to trade for him twice," the coach said. "When I coached the West one year in the Pro Bowl, he did a very fine job for me. I think with his ability and experience he can be a tremendous help to our offense."

Casares, who almost retired before the Miami deal, proved just as gracious. "The whole situation was too tempting," he said. "And George Wilson being the coach—well, I just can't find words to tell you how much respect I have for Wilson."

Wilson acquired three more experienced hands in the discouraging training weeks that followed. One of these additions, a running back from the Los Angeles Rams named Joe Auer, was to be a saviour that season, as well as a source of constant attention from Wilson or the press.

Despite Wilson's optimistic nature, he soon realized that he had problems in every category on the squad. Of more than 60 free agents gathered from the collegiate highways and byways, only seven remained by September, and most of these were on the taxi squad. One, however, was George Wilson Jr., the slender 21-year-old son of the coach. The presence of the younger Wilson represented the fulfillment of his father's fondest hopes, a coach-quarterback combination without precedent in NFL history.

At Detroit, George had drafted his son as a "future" or "redshirt" choice, a collegian eligible to graduate with his class but held out of athletic competition for a season. The Buffalo Bills also drafted young Wilson, but by the time he graduated they were not particularly interested. So the Bills sent him to Miami for a twelfth-round draft choice.

At Xavier of Cincinnati, young George seldom played. He never surpassed second-string status, although he did the punting for the Musketeers, at which he was better than average. But Junior had confidence in his ability. "At Xavier," he explained, "the emphasis was on a quarterback who could run and block. We ran power stuff, practically everything to the strong side."

From the time he was seven, the boy had accompanied his father to Detroit's training camps. As he matured and learned to throw a football, he patterned his style after the dropback, spot-passing pattern of the pros. Both father and son believed that despite his 6-1, 180 pounds and poor eyesight, the young man had the mental toughness and intelligence to succeed, for young George had been brought up with such stalwarts as Bobby Layne, Tobin Rote, Doak Walker, Joe Schmidt, Alex Karras and the freewheeling Lions of the 1950s.

In Miami a few days before camp was to open, the Wilsons held a cookout at their Coral Gables home. After steaks, father and son began discussing football. What else? The game had always been an integral part of their lives.

"George," his father asked, "what's the first thing you'll do when you get to camp?"

The young man grinned, mischief in his eyes. "Oh, I dunno," he said. "I guess I'll have a few beers."

The coach exploded. "I'll tell you this, Mister," he shouted, nose to nose with his son. "You'll have a few beers over my dead body. I'll run you out of camp so fast it'll make your head swim."

Proud as he was of his son, Wilson was also determined that the boy should make it on his own. The coach went out of his way the first month to avoid his son. There were five others in the quarterback contest, and nobody looked fit to win.

The coach later described that first month: "My son never even came to my room unless I asked him to. On the field, he would walk away from me to avoid getting into conversation. In turn, I treated him like any other player. Once you begin to play favorites in this league, you'd better get out while the getting's good."

By the time the coach ventured this opinion, his son had survived four sizable cuts, including rookie quarterbacks Mike Vincent and John Stofa. Nobody thought much of Stofa's credentials at that time, even though the University of Buffalo alumnus had spent two creditable seasons in the minor leagues. Stofa was to return before that first season was over, however, and furnish it with an Horatio Alger capstone.

Going into the exhibition opener at San Diego, the three other quarterbacks were Dick Wood, Eddie Wilson and Rick Norton. All were suspect, but Coach Wilson leaned toward Wood because of his intelligence and experience.

A quiet, gentlemanly Georgian, Wood hadn't even been

a regular at Auburn, though this was in part because he was always having knee surgery. By the time he reached the Dolphins in the expansion draft, at 28, he had undergone six operations. He was virtually immobile because of the surgery and the braces on both knees. And although he could still whip the football, at 6-5 and barely 200 pounds he presented an incredible picture of rail-thin delicacy. "An advance man for a famine," the Dolphins called him.

Dick had been on the Baltimore taxi squad for two years under Weeb Ewbank before drifting to San Diego, where he sat behind John Hadl until Ewbank grabbed him again as a free agent in 1963. Weeb then built his New York offense around Wood for two years, as the Jets struggled through identical 5-8-1 seasons.

When Joe Namath came along, Wood wound up in Oakland behind Tom Flores before the Raiders made him expendable in the expansion draft. Wood could throw a mile and, perhaps because he preferred the long pass, was vulnerable to interceptions. In his two New York seasons, Dick hurled 35 touchdown passes and 42 interceptions.

Eddie Wilson had sat for three years behind Len Dawson at Kansas City, and another year behind Babe Parilli before Boston let him go. His college coach, Jim LaRue, called him "the greatest player in Arizona's history." Eddie conducted himself with poise and called signals with authority. He looked good. But he was not quite six feet tall, he had thrown less than 200 times in four inactive seasons, and he looked erratic in camp. The personable New Englander eliminated himself by rupturing a knee ligament in an August exhibition against Denver.

Norton reported to camp as the most coveted of the 1965 college quarterbacks. His three-year record at Kentucky included 302 completions of 573 passes for 52.7 percent and

24 touchdowns. But 1965 was a poor year for quarterbacks, and Norton was simply the best of the lot.

The 22-year-old Louisville native also reported with a six-inch scar along the left side of his right knee, the result of surgery necessary when Norton was engulfed beneath a pile of Houston University rushers the previous December in the Astrodome. Even though the ligament tear had healed satisfactorily, Norton was obviously failing to anchor his right leg as he threw. The results included wobbly passes—"wounded ducks" in the parlance of his teammates—and an attendant lack of confidence. A severe attack of hemorrhoids further handicapped him.

So the quarterback situation was literally tender when the Dolphins at last boarded the plane for San Diego. The month at St. Petersburg Beach had seemed in some ways like a year. Still, it wasn't time enough for Wilson and his staff to sort out the most capable performers, much less install offensive or defensive refinements. So the Dolphins went into San Diego with a basic four-three defense and a minimum of plays.

For a time it appeared they might not get to San Diego at all, as the effects of the airline strike were still limiting traffic. The club was forced to charter a private DC-7 operated by an independent firm out of Detroit, Zantop Airlines.

Bob Pellegrini, the linebacker coach who had qualms about flying anyway, crossed himself when he saw the DC-7 on the runway. Pellie was a rough, earthy character given to thersitical language. But he spent most of the eight-hour grind to San Diego in subdued prayer.

The DC-7 rattled and bobbed at a low altitude across the nation, over the Mojave Desert in stifling heat, and finally into San Diego on Friday afternoon, August 5, for the Saturday night game.

> I've been misunderstood all my life.
> —GENE MINGO

6. *Let's Win One for the Flipper*

People coming off planes, unlike those getting on, are usually in good spirits. The Dolphins who deplaned at San Diego were feeling salubrious if leggy after their eight-hour ordeal in the DC-7. Most were anxious to meet Danny Thomas, who was supposed to speak to the squad.

Thomas had been in California during the St. Petersburg Beach fiasco. He was still considered the titular head of the club, although by this time Joe Robbie had all the headaches and was up to his neck juggling bills—from those of the Colonial Inn to the laundryman. Of course, Thomas was also a celebrity, and the players wondered what the star of "Make Room for Daddy" was like.

They never found out. Thomas was too busy to address the squad. Most of his talking on the subject of football was delivered at high pitch from the press box of Balboa Stadium and was directed at San Diego Coach Sid Gillman on the field below. "Attaboy Sid," Thomas yelled as things for the Dolphins went from bad to terrible, "run up the score." And

Thomas continued to berate Gillman until the closing gun for the unsportsmanlike attitude of his Chargers to so dominate the game.

Curious as this sentiment was in an enterprise conducted by professionals, it was echoed by many of the Dolphins, including George Wilson. However, from his long association with professional football, Wilson must surely have known that no quarter is to be expected in the arena. Indeed, anything less than all-out performance would be more insulting than considerate.

Ernie Park, the guard acquired from San Diego in the expansion draft, issued fair warning before the game. "Sid never calls off his dogs," he told his new colleagues. "Even though he'll be experimenting, we'll probably see a lot of John Hadl."

In 1965 the talented Hadl had experienced one of his big years. He passed for 2,798 yards and 20 touchdowns while running an offense that averaged 364 yards a game, as the team won the AFL's Western Conference title. His associates included Paul Lowe, AFL Player of the Year and leading ground gainer in 1965; Lance Alworth, the incomparable receiver who snagged 69 passes (14 for touchdowns); and seven-year receiver Don Norton, San Diego's all-time leader in receptions. No rival was able to shackle this combination until the championship game, when the Buffalo Bills shut out the Chargers.

Wilson started Wood before 25,712 who were curious to see the new AFL outfit. With Wood in that first-game backfield were Billy Joe and, of all people, Gene Mingo. The 28-year-old Mingo represented the first of numerous reclamation projects attempted by Wilson the psychologist, who sometimes viewed controversial athletes on potential rather than performance.

A 6-1, 215-pounder with a mighty kicking leg, Mingo had run sparingly but occasionally well in six pro years prior to joining the Dolphins. His excellent practice-field form prompted Wilson to note one day that Mingo "has a smooth, easy running motion, like Jim Brown." On a Friday night at Boston in 1960, it was Mingo who had returned a punt 76 yards to win for the Denver Broncos in the first AFL game. He certainly looked like money in the bank that first season despite his lack of college experience. Fresh from the Norfolk (Va.) Naval Base, Mingo led the league in scoring with 125 points including 6 touchdowns, 18 of 28 field goal opportunities and 35 touchdown conversions. And he set a league distance record with a 53-yard field goal in 1962, when his 137 points established an AFL scoring record.

Between successful seasons, however, Mingo was mysteriously ineffective. In 1961 he made only 3 of 34 field goal attempts before he was replaced by King Hill. In 1964 he was finally dismissed after another ineffective spell, and was picked up by Oakland. "Al Davis just ignored me," he said of the Oakland majordomo.

Like nearly all the mercenaries who toiled for Wilson, Mingo had respect and affection for the coach. "I've been accused and abused in my career," said Mingo, "but right now I'm doing very well and I think I'm going to like it here."

Another Wilson hopeful in the lineup at San Diego was a thin, swift, cocky Texan named John Roderick. At six feet and 180 pounds, Roderick had been clocked at 9.3 in a 100-yard dash and was easily the fastest athlete in camp. Tapped by Joe Thomas as his first choice in the 1965 redshirt draft, Roderick left Southern Methodist early for a shot at the pros. Unencumbered by false modesty, he never doubted he would be a star. His early progress, however, was retarded by the flu as well as his continuous vocal sparring with reporters who considered the brash newcomer to possess more mouth than ability. Still, he opened at split end. There were several reasons for this: Bo Roberson had been balky over signing a contract he considered beneath his reputation. Howard Twilley had started working out with the receivers but remained handicapped by the knee injury. And free agent Karl Noonan of Iowa had been unimpressive.

Indeed, Noonan would have been dismissed the first month but for an unusual clause in his contract containing a no-cut provision during training camp. Aware he was a slow starter, Noonan had insisted on this clause when signing. This was a fortunate decision for both Karl and the Dolphins, because Noonan developed into a productive and reliable receiver, particularly in clutch situations. He was the only 1966 free agent who remained on the 40-man active squad Don Shula took to New Orleans six years later.

Also in the offensive lineup were Maxie Williams and Norm Evans at tackles, Ernie Park and Billy Neighbors at guards, and Tom Goode at center. Williams, Evans, Neighbors and Goode proved mainstays up front the first four seasons.

On defense the Dolphins lined up with Ed Cooke and LaVerne Torczon at ends, Tom Nomina and Al Dotson at tackles. The linebackers were Tom Erlandson and Jack Rudolph flanking Wahoo McDaniel in the middle. Jim Warren and Dick Westmoreland were the cornerbacks, John McGeever and rookie Bob Petrella the safeties.

Wilson hoped the Dolphins would get the ball first. For openers, he had planned a bomb from Wood to the sprinting Roderick, a fly pattern utilizing Roderick's speed and Wood's ability to unload. The Dolphins won the toss and got their wish.

Rookie Wes Matthews, the littlest Dolphin at 5-9, returned the kickoff to his 33-yard line. Wood then backpedaled in his inimitable Whooping Crane fashion and looked for Roderick. But the rookie had been held up at the line of scrimmage by cornerback Kenny Graham, and defenders were already pouring in on the jelly-kneed quarterback. Wood got rid of the football, in the general direction Roderick was supposed to take. Graham was back there instead. To avoid an interception, Roderick gave Graham a shove. Result: a 15-yard transgression that marched the Dolphins back to their own 18.

On third down, Wood hurled the first of many interceptions. Once again it was Graham who cut in front of Roderick to seize the ball and run 39 yards for a touchdown.

The fun was only beginning for the Chargers as Hadl completed five of his first six passes. Before the Dolphins could come near a first down, running back Keith Lincoln joined Hadl in the passing act by firing 47 yards to Alworth for a second score. All this with less than six minutes gone in the game.

The 38–10 final was not indicative of San Diego's domination. In the dressing room George Wilson was smoldering. All he needed was a little encouragement to blow a fuse. And this came when somebody told him that Danny Thomas had been accusing Gillman of pouring it on.

"I don't care what he does," Wilson said of Gillman. "If he wants to play a championship game in August, it's his right. Now some of our guys know what they're up against in this league."

The conversation turned to Wilson's Lions, who had beaten Gillman's Rams in 6 of 10 engagements during the 1950s. "And all of 'em were regular season games," Wilson snapped.

That night the bus driver took a wrong turn en route from Balboa Stadium to the airport, and the second bus followed him. The prospect of the DC-7 journey back home was aggravated when the buses wound up on a muddy path next to the airport, but apparently leading nowhere. Everybody piled out and groped through pitch-black fields to the runway.

Robbie remained behind in San Diego. Tim, his 10-year-old son, had been stricken with acute appendicitis Friday night and was recovering in a San Diego hospital.

The radio network became another of Robbie's problems. He squirmed through the trial-and-error period of announcers beginning with Johnny Bell, a disc jockey unfamiliar with the game, Mel Allen and Red Barber before finding a competent football man in Bob Gallagher. Allen and Barber were baseball announcers, neither of whom would devote the time necessary to master Miami's personnel or the pro game.

Gallagher, the voice of the Boston Patriots in the early AFL years, capably took over in 1967. And if Gallagher was prone to overdramatize ("Well, it's third down and a cab ride for the Dolphins, folks"), the Dolphins then needed a little Aristophanes with their defeats.

Drama was the principal Orange Bowl ingredient the following weekend against the Kansas City Chiefs. (A more worthy opponent could hardly have been selected by the Marquis de Sade.) The first dramatic dash was supplied by George Wilson, who announced on the trip back from San Diego that his son would start at quarterback.

"He deserves it," the coach said. "After all, his scrimmage record was the best of our four quarterbacks. And at San

Diego he was the only one who scored for us. Besides that, he didn't throw an interception."

Young George had started the second half and scored the touchdown by surprising a stacked defense with a four-yard sweep. But Junior also suffered a sticky baptism in the third quarter when "one of those big damned hods stuck a finger in my eye."

Wilson's right eye was swollen shut on the trip home. Complicating the condition were contact lenses. The poke jammed a lens into the quarterback's eyelid, forcing him to leave the game after a 12-minute stint that proved convincing enough to his coach. Although Rick Norton relieved Wilson and produced the best figures of the night—five of seven completions for 101 yards—two interceptions spoiled this $350,000 rookie's debut.

The San Diego weekend was not over when the Dolphins deplaned in the wee hours at Tampa. From there, car pools and buses were arranged to move the squad some 225 miles southeast to the new training headquarters at St. Andrew's in Boca Raton. After St. Pete Beach, the players didn't know what to expect.

Boca Raton, however, turned out to be a quiet, clean town typical of the retiree-based communities along the Florida east coast. Certainly more pleasant than its Spanish name, "mouth of the rat," would lead tourists to believe.

St. Andrews, built back in the brush between the town and the Sunshine State Parkway, was a neat complex of white concrete dormitories and utility structures facing two large, flat, green fields. Ideal for football. "Hey, all right, all right," were the comments of the Dolphin contingent on arriving at their new Everglades outpost.

Jim Davis, the school's athletic director, was out to greet them when the bulk of the pro athletes arrived. "Welcome to St. Andrew's," Davis would say, extending his hand to each one.

"He must have thought we were the Green Bay Packers, for crissake," Bob Pellegrini said.

Except for squadrons of bugs that zoomed in from the Everglades and eventually drove the Dolphins out of St. Andrew's, the place afforded three more summers of practically ideal conditions.

After the first grateful impression had passed and the training grind resumed, a favorite guessing game among the Dolphins concerned their reception in Miami. Season tickets had been crawling at a disappointing pace. Only 12,503 were eventually sold that year. The game against Kansas City, a fearsomely physical outfit that was supposed to win it all every year, figured to draw a crowd. But the Chiefs were likely to make the Dolphins look as though they belonged in the Continental League.

Intrigue and show business were added to the home exhibition opener that week by Julian Cole, the promotional stunt man, who managed to set up the most notorious tank job since marvelous Willie Pep suffered himself to get hit with three overhand rights by Lulu Perez in a studio farce during the televised boxing glut.

Cole's tank, a cylinder 8 feet high and 20 feet across, was delivered by crane into the Orange Bowl the week of the Kansas City game. The tank held 16,500 gallons of water, to which $3\frac{1}{2}$ tons of salt were added. The water was pumped in from a fire hydrant. This whole arrangement was designed to provide the oceanic comforts of home for a 7-8, 300-pound dolphin called Flipper. At the time, Flipper was a pelagic star of films and television.

The curvaceous cetacean was installed in the tank behind the east end zone to retrieve field goals and extra points landing in his area, and to leap joyously after every Miami score. Flipper responded, much to the SPCA's concern, to an electronic buzzer jabbed by his keeper. Animal lovers were placated when it was explained that the dolphin would not be shocked into action but would merely respond to sound waves set in motion by the buzzer.

The evening of the Kansas City game, Flipper was loaded on a stretcher and vanned from the Seaquarium to the Orange Bowl. Six attendants bathed and sponged him constantly—dolphins breathe air, but their skins peel out of water.

Flipper made national headlines. This marked the second coup for Cole, who had also managed to get rookie Frank Emanuel's torso on the cover of *Sports Illustrated*. Emanuel looked impressively tough, but his critics in the seasons to come swore that the Time, Inc., jinx claimed the $400,000 middle linebacker early.

The Kansas City game quickly demonstrated that Flipper was not the only dolphin to operate as though hauled in on a stretcher. The Chiefs overpowered the Miamians 33–0.

Subjected to a befuddled performance and a fourth-quarter downpour, the crowd of 34,277 expressed disenchantment. The athletes, anxious to do well, were jittery and gave the game away with four interceptions as well as two fumbles.

The four quarterbacks, beginning with young Wilson, threw 41 passes, completing 16. Wilson had brought the offense 74 yards in the first series, exciting the fans until the drive petered out inside the 10, and a high snap from center ruined Mingo's field-goal attempt. Wood hurled two interceptions and Eddie Wilson one, the last resulting in a 20-yard touchdown run. By then, however, Len Dawson and Chris Buford had collaborated on a 15-yard scoring pass, and Bert Coan had crossed over twice on runs of five and three yards.

The final Dolphin embarrassment occurred after the game.

Hurrying off to escape the crowd in the privacy of their dressing room, the players found themselves locked out. Wet and miserable, they milled about outside the door for nearly 15 minutes until somebody found a custodian.

With the explanation that "we can't experiment any longer," Wilson reduced his squad to 46 while preparing for the next game, against the New York Jets in Jacksonville. The cuts included a receiver named Doug Moreau out of Louisiana State University, the nineteenth draft choice.

But Moreau wouldn't go. He didn't have to, he explained, because he had a no-cut contract. So Moreau was retained and, in fact, managed to cling four years as a tight end. "On such details does greatness hinge," said Moreau.

> He was to be in all the wars that followed, of his own volition, always a strain on discipline but a delight to all good men at arms.
> —BEN HECHT *on Charles MacArthur*

7. *Clifford, Dammit and Joe Auer*

Whether Joe Auer arrived on a white charger in August of 1966 is not known. "I would have come on the lion, only I had to get rid of it," he said. The lion was Clifford, purchased while Joe Auer was applying himself on the football field and in the classroom at Georgia Tech.

"When I got the lion, he was just like a kitten, about 15 or 20 pounds," Auer explained. "Actually, he wasn't dangerous. He didn't really know he was a lion. It takes them about three and a half years before they know that.

"I had to teach him to growl. I'd get down on my knees and go, 'Gr-r-r-r, g-r-r-r,' and finally he got it. They don't come by it naturally, you know."

Artist and dreamer, Auer was also a mechanical engineering graduate and good enough outside the classroom to be drafted as a future by the Dallas Texans, who had become the Kansas City Chiefs by the time Auer arrived.

In Kansas City Auer found a wife but lost his job. After four exhibitions he was first waived and then traded to Buffalo, where he functioned nobly while gaining 191 yards in 63 carries as the Bills won the 1964 AFL championship.

"I was sure I had it made," Auer said. "Actually, I'd beat out Wray Carlton and was first-string running back until I had to leave the club. I didn't play the last two games or the championship game, but I got a full share and thought things were perfect." Auer had received permission to leave the Bills when his wife, Donna, became ill in Kansas City. And there were also financial problems.

The impetuous Auer had realized a lifelong dream and bought a farm—"25 acres of golden carpet"—in Buffalo. "I thought everything was fine until I got back to camp the following summer. Lou Saban suddenly had me listed as third-string. It seems he didn't think I should have gone to my wife when she was sick. Anyhow, I never got my job back.

"After they cut me, I talked to Elroy Hirsch in Los Angeles. I had to have money, as there was a mortgage and Donna was pregnant.

"Well, I hung on in LA until the season was over, thanks to Elroy. He believed in me, even though I didn't get to carry the ball."

Between the farm and the family, Joe was strapped when he reported to the Dolphins on the Thursday before the Jacksonville game against the Jets. Joe's problems were further complicated by his love for animals. He had horses on the farm, plus an alligator, goat, possum and raccoon. The alligator's name was Dammit. "I named him when I stuck my hand in his box one time and he bit me. I left Dammit in the house one day and turned down the heat to save on bills. Dammit died of exposure. And then I tried weaning the goat on a special formula I invented. He died, too. I was a rookie farmer."

Auer was familiar in Miami. He had been a star at Coral

Gables High School in the late 1950s and his name had appeared frequently in the sports pages. Therefore when Hirsch and George Wilson got together over Auer's future, the result was a natural. Wilson needed running backs desperately, and here was a home-grown product whose credentials were at least as good as anybody's in camp. Rick Casares, Billy Joe and rookies Sam Price, George Chesser and Rabbit Brown had established a common denominator of inconsistency.

So Auer came as a free agent to Miami, where he had spent the previous winter scraping to pay off his debts. "I worked as a civil engineer days, then I'd run over to Coconut Grove Playhouse and park cars at night," he said. "In between I did some painting. They tell me my stuff has good perspective. I guess you'd call it objective op art, a series of lines creating an optical illusion."

Auer was made to order for George Wilson, who more often than not was able to motivate other people's problem athletes. After practice one day at St. Andrew's, Wilson triumphantly announced that Auer had all the potential of a great runner and would play Saturday night against the Jets.

For a change the game was not a complete disaster, despite Miami's third straight exhibition defeat, 31–14, and an all-day rain that limited the Gator Bowl crowd to a generously estimated 11,500. Adding to the woes of promoter Abe Fletcher, Weeb Ewbank announced during the week that Joe Namath's surgical knees had not mended to the point where the $427,000 quarterback was worth risking in August.

Mike Taliaferro played quarterback for the Jets and fared worse than Norton or Wood, who divided the job for the Dolphins while young Wilson did the punting. Taliaferro was 6 for 22, but his efforts included a 46-yard touchdown pass to flanker Sammy Weir in the third quarter and a flare pass that fullback Matt Snell turned into a final touchdown in the fourth quarter. Snell had put the Jets in front to stay with an 18-yard first-quarter touchdown run up the middle after Price's fumble on the game's first series. The rookie from Illinois was playing in his first game after being idled with an ankle injury incurred on the sandshells of St. Petersburg Beach.

So the Jets were never in danger, although the Dolphins gave it their best effort of the summer while outgaining the New Yorkers in total yardage, 407 to 216. Playing the second half in relief of Norton, Wood amassed 219 passing yards in a 12-for-28 performance that included touchdown tosses of 27 yards to Jackson, 43 to Roberson.

The performance was significant in that, for the first time, the Dolphins actually had a chance in the fourth quarter. With the score 27–14 after Roberson's touchdown, rookie Hal Wantland recovered Jim Gray's kickoff fumble on the Jets' eight. On third down, however, cornerback Johnny Sample intercepted Wood's pass in the end zone.

Wood fired two other interceptions, a tendency that was beginning to aggravate Wilson. But the coach decided to forget them in the game's aftermath. He was anxious to bring together his collection of strangers, and decided on the positive approach.

"We played much better tonight than we did in our first two games," he told the squad. "There were times I was downright proud of you guys out there.

"We could have won this game, but we got hit with three interceptions, a fumble and a bad pass from center on a punt attempt. Though it's probably the first bad snap Tom Goode has ever made," Wilson said, apparently misplacing the high snap that ruined a Mingo field-goal try two weeks earlier at San Diego.

Wilson was happy to see at least a trace of a running attack. Casares gained 44 yards in six carries as the ground offense surpassed 100 yards for the first time. "I thought Joe Auer did a very fine job for his first game, particularly after one day of practice," Wilson said, even though Auer had been restricted to 18 yards in eight traffic-laden trips.

Wilson, the master diplomat, talked Fletcher into picking up the tab for a squad party after the game at Charlie Thoma's Oyster House in Jacksonville. And for the first time, Miami's rookies and expansion draftees joined Wilson in cutting down that old pine tree and hauling it away to the mill—"to make a coffin of pine for that sweetheart of mine"—and were vowing by the beer in their mugs that, by God, they'd have a winning season.

The mercenaries were impressed. Wahoo McDaniel, who on his arrival in New York a few years earlier had said, "This town is not big enough for both of us"—meaning Wahoo and super-publicized middle linebacker Sam Huff of the rival Giants—lingered over coffee after most of the party had left. "I'll say it again," Wahoo volunteered. "It takes more than figures in a playbook to make a ball club, and our bunch is getting the idea. It won't be long now before we put it all together, and then somebody is going to get hurt." Wahoo could be dramatic.

The Dolphins had hardly settled back at St. Andrew's when it was time to leave for Memphis and their final exhibition against the Denver Broncos on Wednesday night. The game was an artistic and financial disaster. The midweek date, a $6 price scale and two terrible AFL teams all contributed to limit attendance to 18,106 at a time when Robbie was desperate for operating capital.

It was a bad night for anybody named Wilson. Eddie

started the game at quarterback and was carted off in the first quarter with a torn knee ligament that was to end his pro career.

Young George, whose punting had averaged 48 yards in an excellent Jacksonville performance, shanked a 27-yarder that led to Denver's first score. And a few minutes later he was swarmed under by a fourth-down blitz, giving the Broncos possession at the Miami 13 and shortly thereafter a 14–0 lead. The Broncos held on to win 28–16.

With the Orange Bowl opener against Oakland coming up in 10 days, Wilson still had seen nothing to give him a great deal of hope. In fact, the Dolphins suffered their most damaging injury of the summer as Frank Jackson, who after reporting late to camp had demonstrated that he was easily the most skillful of the receivers, was carried off in the second quarter with a back injury that would cause him to miss almost half the team's games.

In five seasons with the Dallas Texans and Kansas City Chiefs, Jackson had caught 154 passes, including 62 for 943 yards and nine touchdowns in a banner 1964 year. While accomplishing these figures, Jackson was also embarking on a somewhat varied academic career.

At Southern Methodist he had studied for the ministry. Later he attended East Texas State University and grew interested in osteopathy, a science he pursued in Kansas City and intended to continue without reporting to the expansion team. But the persistence of Joe Thomas and a long-term contract that made allowance for his postgraduate studies (Robbie is a fanatic on education) induced the 6-1, 180-pound flanker to appear.

So it was at Methodist Hospital in Memphis that Jackson, a student of osteopathy, knew exactly how he wound up in traction after getting whacked in the second quarter.

"The transverse processes are broken in three lower back vertebrae," Jackson reported. "I don't mind saying the pain is excruciating at times."

Jackson's misfortune brought Karl Noonan to the foreground. Saved from unemployment a month earlier by the no-cut-through-training-camp contract he'd demanded, this quiet, diligent Iowan had indeed been improving. And as Jackson's replacement in the game against the Broncos, Noonan seized an 11-yard touchdown pass from Wood to at least put the Dolphins on the board. His catch reflected many more to come.

By default, the fragile but arena-wise Wood was named to open the season at quarterback against Oakland. In the Denver game Wood had completed 11 of 19 passes for 211 yards, including a second touchdown pass to Noonan. Wood had also gone without an interception—for a change—before retiring in the fourth quarter with a damaged nerve in his right elbow. But the diagnosis was that the much-battered Georgian would recover before the Oakland encounter.

After the team's fourth straight exhibition loss, Wilson was despondent if not yet discouraged. It was a silent and chastened group that returned to St. Andrew's to prepare for the season opener.

The Dolphins had been beaten by a cumulative 130–40 points. The ground game was negligible. At Memphis, Wilson rested Casares and Auer most of the night to test Billy Joe and Sam Price. They amassed a total of 13 yards.

Joe had been AFL Rookie of the Year at Denver in 1963. Injuries handicapped the 6-2, 230-pound fullback the following year; he was traded to Buffalo for the celebrated Cookie Gilchrist. In Miami, the gentlemanly Philadelphian could simply not get started. An assistant coach observed that Billy Joe was the best north-to-south runner in the league.

Price, a compact 217 on a 5-11 frame, blocked three years for Jim Grabowski at Illinois and ran enough himself to merit fond expectations as Miami's eleventh draft choice. But the sensitive, intense Toledoan was beset with anxieties throughout his three struggling seasons with the Dolphins. Among his well-hidden convictions was the inescapable notion that a black athlete would need an abundance of luck to succeed in the pros. And rare is the football coach on any level who qualifies either psychologically or sociologically in the complex dimensions of race relations. Wilson had occasional racial problems. One such eruption in the summer of 1969 over a black linebacker he had cut almost resulted in the enraged coach literally tearing a reporter's head off.

But this same man who insisted, after a popular lyric, "Don't Call Me Coach, Call Me George," was a master at manipulating emotional faucets. And after the Memphis debacle he began what turned out to be an astoundingly effective job of motivating his uncertain squad for the opener.

That Friday, an oppressively muggy afternoon with thousands of tiny sandflies visiting from the adjacent Everglades, the Dolphins had finished pre-practice calisthenics when Wilson ordered everybody to take his shoes off. Mystified, the players removed their cleats.

"All right," Wilson yelled, "everybody, right-face. Now, forward march!"

With co-captains Dave Kocourek and Tom Erlandson leading the way, Wilson marched the Dolphins off the field, up a flight of concrete steps next to the dressing room and into the St. Andrew's pool.

After the happy dunk came freedom and lifting of the 11 P.M. bedcheck for this last night at St. Andrew's. The athletes could now disperse to apartments or, in a few cases, to homes they had managed to rent, for beginning the next week they would practice at Miami Stadium downtown. The bartenders of Boca Raton circled that Friday night on their calendars.

Many players who survived the final cut—particularly blacks—were less than fortunate in finding living accommodations. South Floridians were indifferent to the newcomers, and many were hostile to the blacks. Sam Price, born in Margret, Ala., and raised in Toledo, Ohio, knew what the brothers would be in for. Although Sam shunned controversy over racial matters, he once blurted out a basic and saddening truth: "How can a white man possibly understand what a black man goes through?" Sam asked. "As long as I can remember as a kid and growing up, our family was never even allowed in a decent restaurant." And Toledo is a long way from Miami. For the Prices with their three-year-old son Kevin, for safetyman Willie West and others, Dade and adjacent Broward counties were difficult testing grounds.

Even white players had their troubles. "It was a long period of answering ads and knocking on doors before my wife and I could even get an apartment landlord to give us the time of day," offensive tackle Norm Evans said. "They just laughed at us or shut the door in our faces." Between the year's lease demanded by tourist-oriented landlords (but unacceptable to athletes in town four or five months a year) and racial inhumanity, most Dolphin families segregated themselves the first few years. In 1970, winning changed all that. The Dolphins were accepted as celebrities. But by then the bulk of the originals were gone.

> Wahoo intrigues me. Look at his eyes. He has the eyes of Chief Irontail. Firm, clear and ruthless. I'm glad we've got him.
>
> —GEORGE HAMID

8. *Old Men Come and Go*

The opening kickoff of the Dolphins' first season dropped into the hands of Joe Auer. "I knew I would do something unusual as the ball was hanging up there," said the incomparable halfback. "I felt strong and confident."

Auer was right. He did do something unusual. Before a scattered audience of 26,776 in the vast Orange Bowl saucer, Auer returned Oakland's kickoff 95 yards into the east end zone, where Flipper soared from his tank and Danny Thomas pounced in jubilation on the runner's back.

Auer almost jammed an elbow into the entertainer's mouth. "He came from behind," Joe explained. "I thought it was one of their guys giving me a cheap shot."

Auer's feat enabled the Dolphins to hold the lead for 22 minutes in a remarkably close game; and his heroics that Friday night, September 3, started the blue-eyed blond from Coral Gables off on a season of redemption.

With Joe Auer, however, there was always a hitch. That same month, beset by creditors, he filed for bankruptcy and lost his 25 acres of golden carpet. "Upstate New York is God's country, gorgeous country," he said. "We had the farm all fixed up. We even had 3,000 Christmas trees on the land. We could have sold them for a buck apiece easy. But that's life."

The contest evolved into a combination of offensive mistakes and defensive stubbornness on both sides. Dick Wood suffered a terrible debut, hurling four first-half interceptions before Rick Norton took over with but slight improvement. Norton hit Rick Casares for short yardage and a second touchdown with seven minutes left, narrowing Oakland's lead to 17–14. But the Raiders, obviously superior despite two lost fumbles and four interceptions, came back to clinch the game on a 16-yard pass from Tom Flores to rookie tight end Tom Mitchell.

George Wilson, pleased over the defensive performance, thought he should have had the game. The five interceptions (one lofted by Norton) were compounded by Gene Mingo's ineptness at field-goal kicking. Mingo, already written off as a runner, blew potshots of 19 and 17 yards, and a third opportunity from 43 yards out. This, despite his ability to boom 50-yard field goals in practice.

The opening defense remained intact most of the season. Wahoo McDaniel seemed to have regained his youth. "He has the eyes of Chief Irontail," observed George Hamid Sr., harking back to his younger days as a tumbler in Buffalo Bill Cody's Wild West show.

Flanking McDaniel that night were Tom Erlandson and Jack Rudolph. Frank Emanuel came on later to be a linebacking regular, replacing Rudolph and sometimes Wahoo.

The front four had Ed Cooke and Mel Branch at ends, Rich Zecher and Tom Nomina at tackles. LaVerne Torczon and Al Dotson supplied relief. Dick Westmoreland and Jim

Warren were at the corners, Willie West and Pete Jaquess at safeties with occasional help from John McGeever and rookie Bob Neff, also the punt returner.

On offense, Billy Joe and Casares shared fullback assignments. Auer was set at halfback. Bo Roberson and rookie John Roderick opened at flanker and split end, respectively, with Karl Noonan and the still-limping Howard Twilley behind them.

Dave Kocourek was the tight end, Norm Evans and Maxie Williams the offensive tackles, Billy Neighbors and Ernie Park the guards, Tom Goode the center. Ken Rice, an expansion-draft guard who delayed reporting until August 25, worked his way in as a replacement on either side.

The quarterback situation was being handled by nobody. "Everyone who saw the Oakland game knows we have quarterback problems," Wilson said. "But on the bright side, I think our running game and our blocking will continue to improve, along with our defense."

The immediate problem was the New York Jets and sophomore Joe Namath, the AFL's premier quarterback. Namath was reasonably healthy on his scalpeled knees, but Mike Taliaferro of the Jets started against Norton. Taliaferro had been the quarterback in four straight exhibition victories, and Ewbank was letting him play out the string.

In the first 20 minutes Norton completed two of seven and was dumped three times by defenders, including once in his own end zone for a safety. Taliaferro managed to complete only 4 of 17 in the first half before Namath replaced him. One of Taliaferro's tosses, however, was a 20-yarder to George Sauer for a first-quarter touchdown.

When Namath took charge, the Jets padded the lead with a four-yard scoring burst by Bill Mathis and a 45-yard field goal by Jim Turner.

Down 19–0 after three quarters, the Dolphins began to cut into the lead. Dick Wood had relieved Norton with terrible results—one for eight in the second quarter—before Wilson sent Norton back in. And Rick got lucky. From the Jets' 43, he fired to Roberson cutting across the middle. The ball bounded high off Roberson's pads. But Kocourek, trailing the play, seized the ball in stride and hustled the rest of the way.

A few minutes later, backed up to his 14-yard line, Namath took a chance on a third-down pass. Jaquess intercepted and dashed 27 yards to make it close. But the game ended at 19–14.

On the face of the Dolphins' two close losses, Wilson was encouraged, particularly with his defense. Yet the quarterback situation continued to haunt him. He benched the personable but unfortunate Wood, whose interceptions in two games matched his completions—six and six. Still reluctant to start his son, Wilson announced that Norton would get his second starting opportunity the following Sunday at Buffalo in the first of three road games.

Norton was a nerve-ridden rookie, sensitive and responsible, who remained keenly conscious of both the scar on his surgical knee and the $350,000 bonanza that made him an object of instant interest in South Florida.

"I've always been a slow starter," said the quarterback. "I found at Kentucky I had to throw a lot in the summer to get my arm in shape. Because of the operation, I didn't get a chance to throw before I came to camp.

"And I was never real sure of myself. That was worst of all. The money and the knee were on my mind, and what the other guys thought about me, particularly the veterans. I can't shrug things off with a wisecrack. I just want to be one of the guys doing his job."

But from the day Norton signed on Dec. 12, 1965, he was

a *cause célèbre*. He received a $25,000 signing bonus immediately, $30,000 in March 1966 and a similar sum that September. He also got bonuses of $15,000 each December for the following three years; $140,000 in all. His salary over the four-year term totaled $115,000—$25,000 annually until 1969, when he received $40,000. And Norton still has $105,-000 coming from the Dolphins, in $15,000 annual payments from 1975 through 1981, wherever he may be.

Norton would be up against the two-time defending AFL champions, in Buffalo. But his coach expressed optimism if Norton could click. The Bills had lost their first two games. There were reports quarterback Jack Kemp was having elbow problems and that his understudy, Daryle Lamonica, might start.

"Our defense handed us the Oakland and New York games on a platter," Wilson observed. "But the offense didn't take it. I'm as disappointed in our offense as I am pleased with the defense. I doubt that any team in this league will run away from us now. Our defense won't let it happen."

The Bills won 58–24. Scoring every way imaginable, they came within a point of the AFL record owned by Kansas City. They ran up a 41–3 lead in the first 20 minutes, intercepting three passes on the beleaguered Norton. Butch Byrd brought one back 60 yards for a touchdown, and fled 72 yards with a punt return for another score.

"It just goes to show," said linebacker Mike Stratton, who intercepted two Norton passes deep in Miami territory, "that there are other imperfect people in the world besides us." Stratton and his colleagues had been taking a verbal lacing from Coach Joel Collier for their apparent complacency.

One positive aspect emerged from the rout. George Jr. entered at quarterback with five minutes gone in the second quarter and the Dolphins down by 18. Although completing only 10 of 30 passes (to Norton's 3 of 10 and 3 interceptions), he totaled 185 yards by air and threw touchdown passes to Roderick for 4 yards, Roberson for 54 and Kocourek for 13.

The shot to Roberson followed an imbroglio that finally had settled a howling crowd of 37,546 in Buffalo's perfectly named War Memorial Stadium. Buffalo crowds, mollified by defeat, are more orderly now. But in 1966, television cameras on the field were protected by wire cages. Steel-helmeted police were armed with clubs, and the beer cans that flew were not always empty. Booth Lusteg, the peregrinating kicker, was once soundly beaten up by a gang outside the stadium for blowing a field goal and the ball game.

The fuss started when little Wes Matthews, who had hung on despite his chunky, 5-9 frame, was hit while fair-catching a punt at the Miami 16. The shot cost the Bills 15 yards and vocalized the crowd. Showing poise for a rookie in his first start, Wilson simply threw up his hands and recalled the offense. Twice he did this, as the people kept roaring.

Finally, a 15-yard penalty was assessed against the customers, moving the ball up to the Miami 46. Definite progress was being made, and by now even the Bills were motioning their disciples to simmer down.

The din let up just enough for the fleet Roberson to hear his signal called. He darted straight down field, took a perfect lead floater from Wilson and went into the end zone standing up. The noise abated. The fans settled for a rout rather than a pogrom.

After the game George's father announced, "My son is now the No. 1 quarterback." Why not? Futility would be euphemistic in describing the problems of Wood and Norton.

Asked what he thought was the turning point of the Buffalo game, Wilson replied: "If Emanuel had intercepted that pass in their first touchdown drive, maybe we could have turned it around a little." He was referring to a Kemp toss that bounded off the rookie linebacker's hands. (Emanuel was playing the middle at this time and Wahoo the outside, much to the veteran's dislike. The coaching staff never did resolve this dilemma, which caused constant jealousy between the two.)

"Too anxious," was Emanuel's comment on the muff.

In a scrimmage Wilson called after the Buffalo debacle, Roberson broke his ring finger, leaving the Dolphins four rookie wide receivers—Roderick, Noonan, Matthews and Twilley, now gradually working into action as his right knee mended. Fortunately the squad had a week off before West Coast dates at San Diego and Oakland.

The running game was suffering, as usual. A foot injury kept Casares out against Buffalo. Auer, though bothered by a twisted left knee, was playing. Jackson returned from the hospital, his mending back in a corset, to make the San Diego trip. Casares made it seven hours late, which cost him $200 plus air fare.

The Chargers, who had won three straight, captured their fourth, 44–10, from the Dolphins. Although the spread was wider than Miami's exhibition loss, the Chargers trailed for nearly three quarters and only pulled away with a 28-point fourth quarter, which included three touchdown passes by Steve Tensi in relief of John Hadl.

Young Wilson's debut was brief. The reedy quarterback sprained his right ankle and suffered a partial ligament tear when his cleats caught in the Balboa Stadium turf on a first-quarter rollout pass pattern.

Mingo's 27-yard field goal had produced a 3–0 lead at the time. Wood came in and pegged a 20-yard touchdown pass to the fast-improving Noonan, and Mingo's point after gave the Dolphins their biggest lead in the AFL, 10–0.

When linebacker Rick Redman scooped up an Auer fumble and sprinted 58 yards for a touchdown, the game started "turning around" in Wilson's opinion. The Dolphin bench protested so violently that end Steve DeLong had jumped offside on the play that they drew two 15-yard penalties. One was against Danny Thomas for being on the sideline and the second was against Wilson and his volatile linebacker coach Pellegrini for language unbecoming gentlemen.

Still, the Dolphins clung to a 10–9 lead with 2:14 left in the third quarter. Then Tensi fired 25 yards over the middle to wide-open fullback Gene Foster for the score that put the Chargers ahead to stay.

Dick (Night Train) Lane tried to cheer up Wilson after the game. But his old Detroit defensive star only made George feel worse.

"What would you do with this club?" Wilson asked, without really seeking an answer.

Lane grinned. "Punt," he suggested.

The coach had to laugh. His son's ankle injury had pressed McDaniel into service as the punter, and Wahoo had experienced a rough afternoon. "Hell," Wilson said, "we can't even punt."

The quarterback confusion was already an old familiar story by the time the Dolphins reached Oakland to play the Raiders, who had not won since their opener at Miami. The Dolphins cured that, 21–10.

In dropping their fifth straight (and ninth including exhibitions), the rudderless Miamians did find a quarterback, however. Young Wilson, playing despite the ankle injury, completed 11 of 19 passes for 142 yards, including a 43-yarder to Jackson that set up Auer's three-yard touchdown effort. And Miami had battled until the fourth quarter, when quarterback Tom Flores opened up with three touchdown passes.

The Dolphins returned home to a faithful audience of 23,393 against the Denver Broncos, a team South Floridians barely knew existed, as most continued to follow the NFL's adventures on television.

The Broncos had not come very far since their own inception in 1960, when General Manager Dean Griffing would vault into the stands to fight fans for footballs after field goals and extra points.

Before the small Orange Bowl reception the Dolphins produced a 24–7 maiden-breaking victory. Auer scored twice on short plunges, after Billy Joe took a screen pass from Wilson and hustled 67 yards for a first-quarter touchdown that put Miami in front to stay.

Wilson's mother witnessed her son's best performance, 9 for 18 and 176 yards, plus a 19-yard bootleg escape just before Mingo's 35-yard field goal.

Early in the course of Denver's troubles, John McCormick was relieved at quarterback by 38-year-old Tobin Rote, who had recently been coaxed from retirement. Rote was dumped four times for 40 yards by a pass rush that had been heretofore absent.

"What a shame," Mrs. Wilson said while the ponderous Rote was being attacked. "George was just a baby when Tobin was a star in Detroit."

After the final gun, Joe Robbie said, "I won't believe it for five more minutes."

The patrons and players exulted as though they had won the Super Bowl. Evans, all but weeping, leaped into the arms of Kocourek as fans poured onto the field. Eventually a crowd gathered at the dressing-room door and chanted, "We want George! We want George!" They meant "Junior," who at

Joe Robbie, an activist on the sidelines.

George Wilson is presented with a cake by Dolphin security guard Manny Castro after Miami's victory over Houston in the 1966 finale. Behind Archie Stone, the team's #1 fan, is Tom Goode (left), Dave Kocourek, George Wilson, Jr., and assistant coach Les Bingaman.

Both Photos: John Pineda

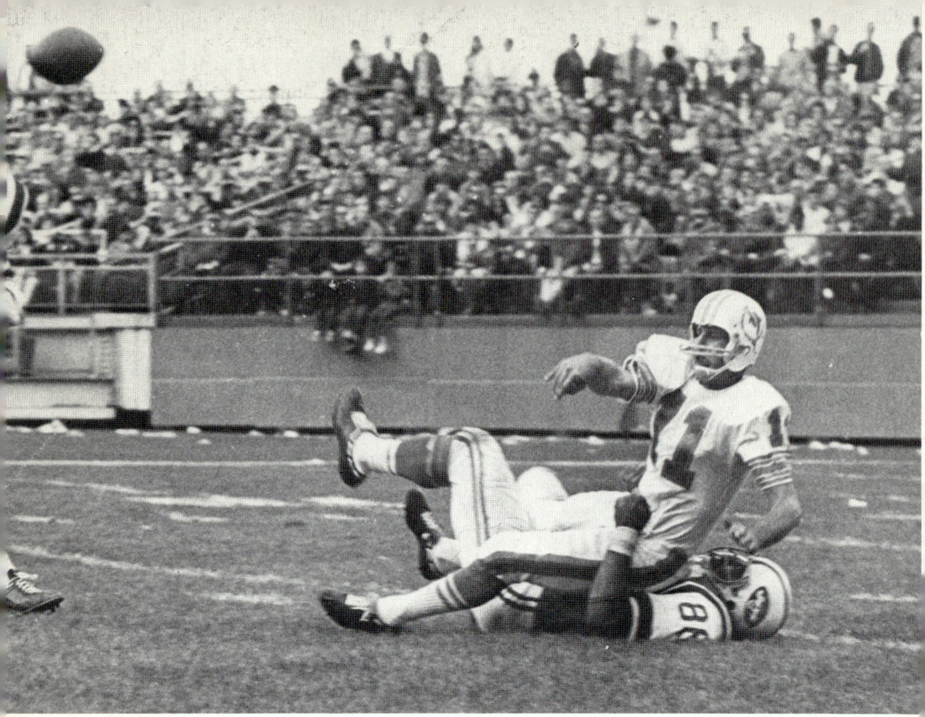

UPI

Rick Norton is pulled down by Mel Branch during Miami's 29-7 loss to the Jets in October, 1967.

Sam Price scores Miami's lone touchdown in the same encounter.

UPI

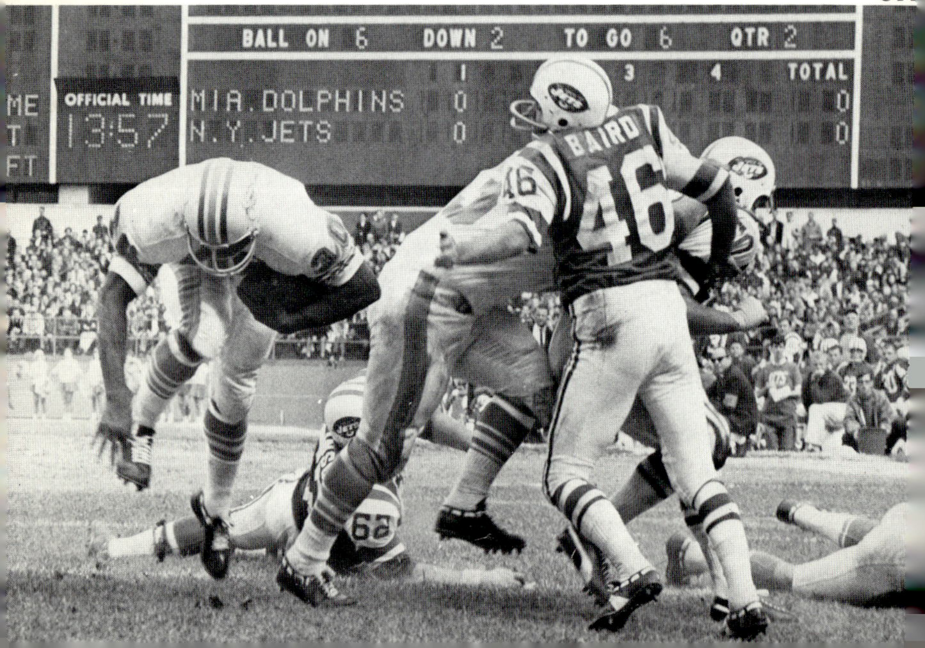

Both Photos: John Pineda

John Stofa runs for his life against the Chargers.

Karl Noonan seized eleven touchdown passes in 1968.

John Pineda

John Pineda

Left: Les Bingaman and his first love. *Right:* Larry Csonka inspects his water-cushioned helmet.

John Pineda

After a great rookie year, Jack Clancy was beset by injuries.

Howard Twilley.

Vernon Biever

Mack Lamb takes an enforced respite.

John Pineda

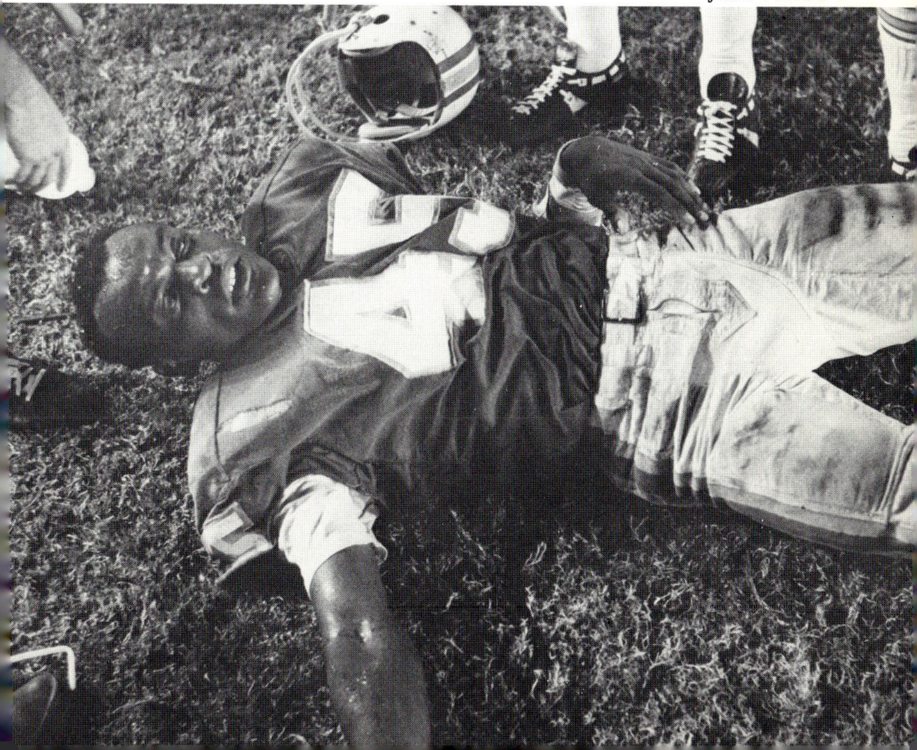

John Pineda

Larry Little.

John Pineda

Bob Griese in the huddle.

Griese drops back to throw with Jim Kiick out front.

Griese runs one across.

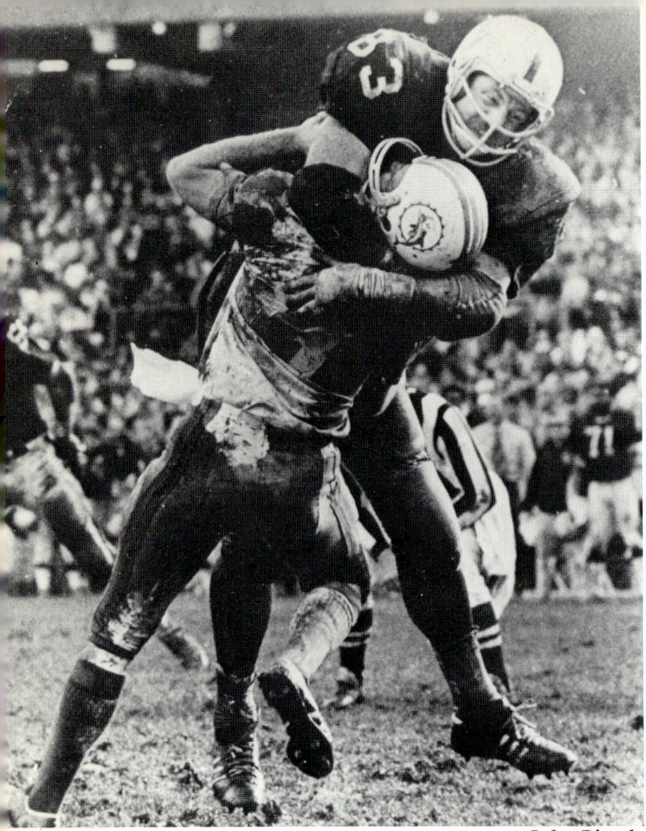

John Pineda

Ben Davidson sacks Bob Griese in the Oakland playoff game.

UPI

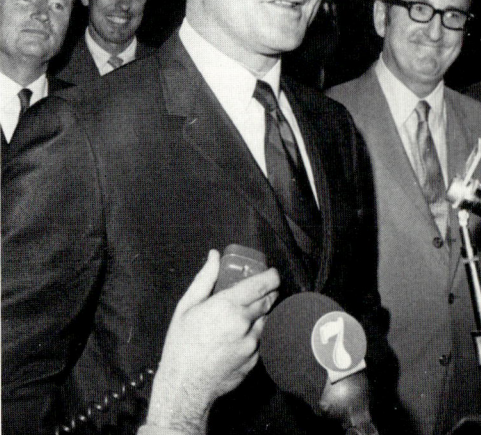

Don Shula accepts a new job, as Robbie lights the way.

John Biever

Jim Kiick.

Vernon Biever

Larry Csonka on the move.

John Pineda

Csonka as the Sundance Kid and Kiick as Butch Cassidy.

Garo displays his ties.

John Pineda

Yepremian puts his foot to one.

Vernon Biever

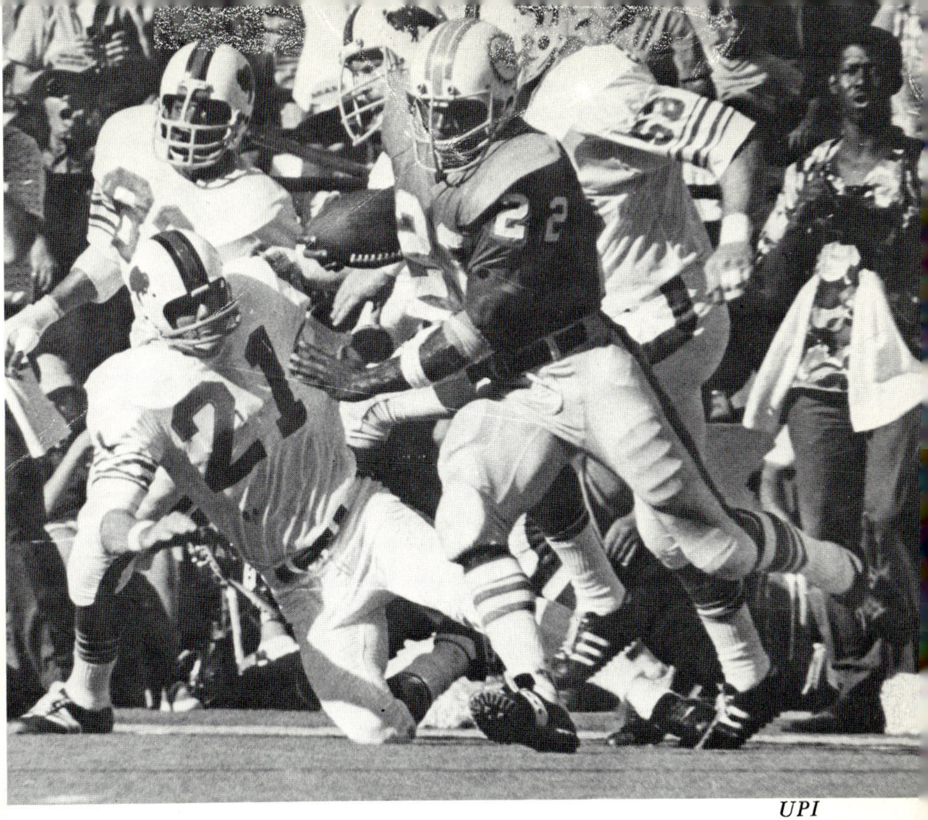

UPI

Mercury Morris cuts past a host of Bills enroute to a 45-yard TD run. The Dolphins defeated Buffalo 34-0 in this November, 1971, game.

Joe Thomas welcomes Paul Warfield.

John Pineda

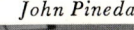

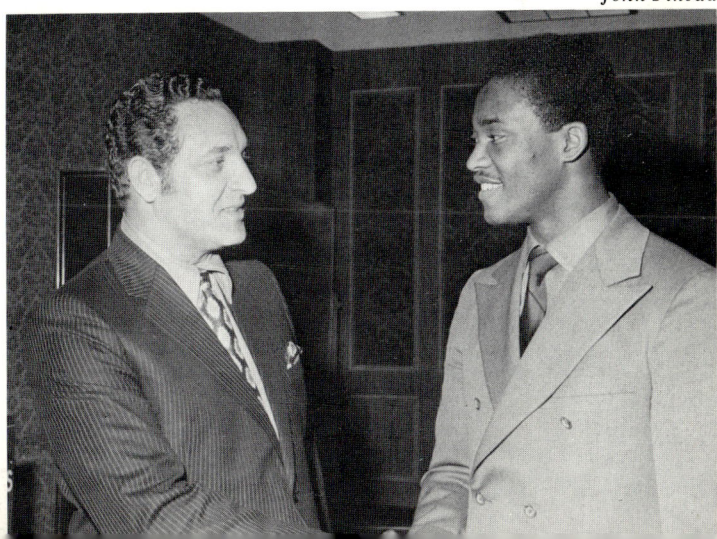

Vernon Biever

The blockers set against Green Bay.

Some gang tackling in the Packer game.

Vernon Biever

UPI

Kiick dives into the end zone for a score against Green Bay. The Dolphins defeated the Packers 27-6 to win the Eastern Division title after Baltimore was upset by New England.

Larry Csonka scores against Kansas in the Christmas classic.

UPI

Warfield takes a pass from Griese over the head of Baltimore defender Rex Kern and starts a long run to the end zone for Miami's first touchdown in the AFC Championship game.

UPI

Bob East

Bubba Smith pursues Bob Griese.

UPI

ob Lilly (74) and Larry Cole (63) were unremitting in the Super Bowl.

im Kiick and Herb Adderly jostle for the ball.

John Biever

John Biever

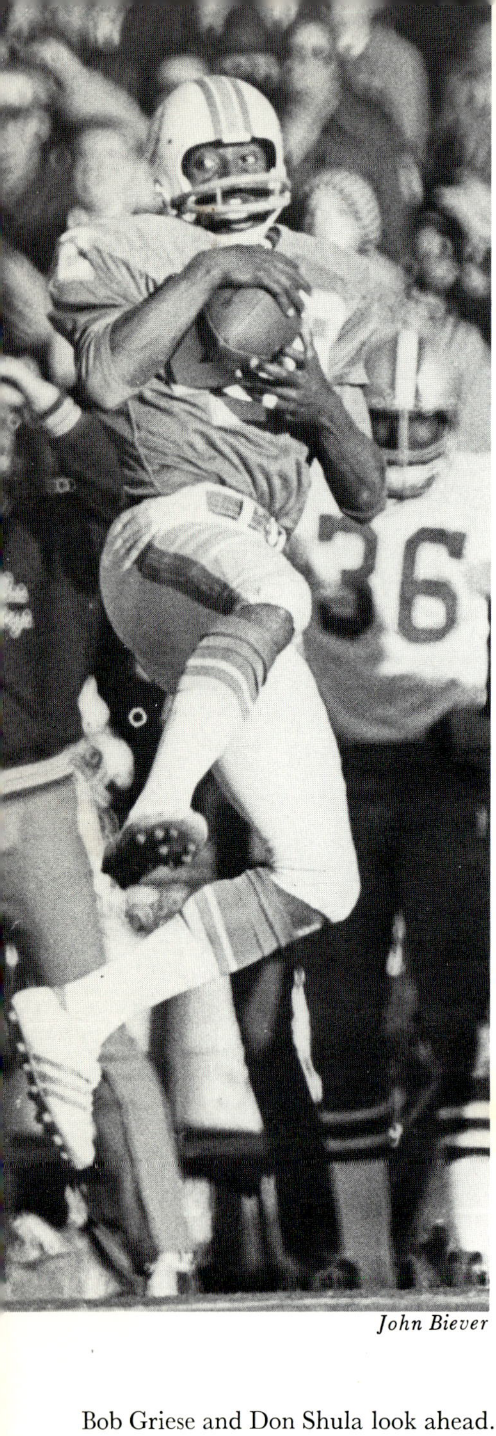

Warfield pulls one in against Dallas.

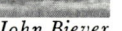

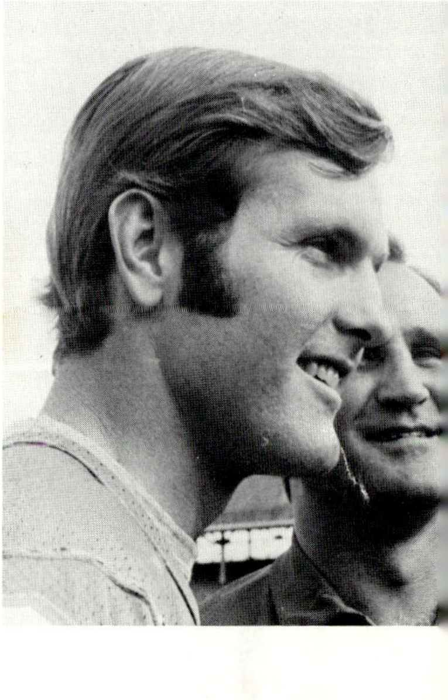

Bob Griese and Don Shula look ahead.

least for the day had fulfilled a dream long cherished in the Wilson family and well-known to the fans.

The elder Wilson, his face drawn from weeks of frustration, was almost too exhausted to enjoy it. "Boy," he said slowly, "what a feeling to get over the hump."

"Dad's not a poor man," young Wilson said. "That makes it difficult for me to buy him a gift. And that's why I want so much to make good as a quarterback."

Casares had spent most of the Denver evening (Sunday games then started at 4:30 in deference to the early afternoon heat) on the bench. He had missed Saturday's practice and drawn his second $100 fine in three weeks. The following Wednesday, his picture still on a few Miami billboards for having once been named Player of the Week by a local milk company, Casares was released.

"The hardest thing I ever had to do," Wilson said.

"I'm still shocked," Casares said, knowing his dismissal meant the end of a 12-year career. "But this thing is just as hard on Wilson as it is on me. I appreciated the chance to play for him."

Casares knew his best was behind him. He had gained 135 yards in 43 carries and caught one touchdown pass for the Dolphins. He accepted his fate with grace and later opened a bar in Tampa.

Roderick also caught his last pass in the Denver game, although he returned briefly the following season after a long surgical bout with a congenital condition in his lower back which football had aggravated.

To replace Casares and Roderick, the Dolphins completed negotiations the same week for two more athletes who quickly enhanced the club's blossoming reputation as a haven for unusual characters. One was Earl Faison, the 6-5, 265-pound former all-AFL defensive end waived by San Diego. Coach

Sid Gillman, angered by Faison's "cavalier" attitude after gaining a three-year contract estimated at $90,000, dismissed him with the comment that he would be "better off anywhere else."

The other newcomer was Carlton Chester Gilchrist, tagged "Cookie" by his uncle because of the boy's fondness for sweets. In a 13-year career extending from Canada to Miami, Cookie had become a legend.

"The Dolphins' should be complimented," Cookie was quoted as saying, "for bringing in quality at any cost."

> What kind of a player is Cookie Gilchrist? Well, he's just like any other fullback who has a gold Cadillac with a gold telephone in it. When I got rid of him I thought my Christmas present came early.
>
> —MAC SPEEDIE

9. *Unhappy Warrior*

When Cookie Gilchrist reported to the Dolphins Wednesday before the Houston game, he had been inactive since leaving the Denver camp in July. "I didn't even bother to take out equipment," he said. "The Broncos attempted to renegotiate my contract, which was already signed, and I felt they were unduly antagonizing me."

The Dolphins, on the other hand, relinquished their third and fifth draft choices for 1967 as payment to the Broncos, while assuming Gilchrist's $45,000 contract, which included a Cadillac among other fringe benefits.

Tapped out of high school by Cleveland's Paul Brown who sent him to Canada, Gilchrist prospered so well in football and investments that he remained nine seasons. He said he possessed mineral rights under lake beds in Canada, a zinc mine in Brittany, tungsten in Wales and copper in France. Lured to Buffalo in 1962, he at once became an all-AFL back. But after three seasons, Cookie was suspended and eventually traded by the Bills because of his constant misunderstandings with the club and Coach Lou Saban. The swap was to Denver in 1965 for Billy Joe, who the following year became his rival for the Dolphin fullback job.

Gilchrist said he weighed 259, "nine over my playing weight," when reporting to the Miami Stadium practice field. Wilson took Cookie aside and the two talked for about 10 minutes, Wilson sitting on the outfield grass and Gilchrist reposing in a lawn chair. The scene prompted McDaniel to note that "Cookie has already learned how to handle the coach."

The delicacy management felt over Gilchrist's arrival was demonstrated by the brass accompanying the fullback to the stadium. Robbie and Joe Thomas were both smiling at his side as Cookie announced, "I feel that coming to Miami is a step in the right direction for both myself and the ball club."

Indeed, his credentials seemed to confirm it. While chiding AFL hierarchy in his four seasons, Gilchrist had also established league records for rushing attempts (928), years leading the league in rushing (two), and touchdowns rushing (13) for Buffalo in 1962. On Dec. 8, 1963, Cookie set game records with 36 carries, 243 yards and 5 touchdowns.

After his talk with Wilson, Gilchrist was enthusiastic and expressed confidence that he would work himself into condition in a very short time. "Wilson understands individuals. And he know what I'm talking about."

Wilson, who campaigned strenuously to get Gilchrist, reciprocated the understanding. "I don't care what has happened in the past," the coach said. "He'll play Sunday, if we need him in crucial situations. He's a helluva player and we're very happy to have him."

Wahoo, never one to miss an opportunity, removed his helmet to display a cauliflowered left ear. It had been generally assumed that Wahoo had the ear massaged in his moonlight occupation of wrestling. Not so, said the redoubtable Choctaw. "Cookie did this to me. He's not only a runner, but he's the best blocker in football. He hit me so hard he cracked my helmet and impaired my hearing."

Thus fortified, the Dolphins went into Houston's Astrodome and emerged with a 20–13 victory, their second straight.

Young Wilson began the game auspiciously. At his 20, on a play sent in by his father via Bo Roberson, the quarterback popped the 9.4 receiver in full stride just beyond the line of scrimmage. Roberson dashed all the way for the score. A few minutes later, however, the delicate Wilson took off on a scramble and gained a first down, but injured his right shoulder in the process.

Norton replaced him. He tossed a 13-yard touchdown pass to Gilchrist, then in the third quarter was leveled by a shot from linebacker Johnny Baker. Norton's lower jaw was broken on both sides and he retired for the season. Mingo came through with field goals of 43 and 42 yards to pad the lead as Wood finished up without distinction—but without interception either. The Dolphins had caught 38-year-old George Blanda on an off day.

Baker, who put Norton in the hospital, was among the enigmatic performers in a sometimes puzzling business. This Elmer Gantry was a Baptist lay minister. When signing with the Oilers, Baker tithed his bonus to his parish church in Meridian, Miss. On the field he is an employee bent on punishment. At Kansas City in 1965 he broke Len Dawson's jaw. However, the 6-4, 238-pound linebacker had nothing but remorse and regrets for Norton's mishap. "Look, I don't go out to hurt anybody," he said. "Miami teaches Norton and Wilson to sprint out of the pocket if they see the outside linebacker pinching in. It's my responsibility to contain that play, to prevent the quarterback from getting outside.

"Wilson got outside of me once earlier in the game, and I didn't want it to happen again. I sure hope the kid will be all right."

"The kid" was an appellation often used to describe both Norton and Wilson, to their aggravation. Each had dropped below 180 pounds by midseason, each had a boyish face and neither looked mature enough to direct hired men. But both were competitors, a quality that particularly sustained Norton in the eyes of his colleagues through a discouraging career.

With Norton out, Wilson hurt and Wood barely ambulatory with his braced-up knees, the Dolphins were desperate for help at quarterback. So Robbie immediately began negotiations for John Stofa, the 6-4 Pennsylvanian who had been chopped from the roster at St. Petersburg Beach.

Stofa had gone from the Miami camp to Pittsburgh, was again dismissed, and wound up with the Florida Brahmans of the North American Football League while also teaching school. In two seasons prior to his Dolphin tryout, Stofa had thrown 73 touchdown passes for the Daytona Beach Thunderbirds in the Florida Football League, an organization as short-lived as the North American was destined to be. Stofa now led the NAFL with 27 touchdown passes.

Wilson planned to put Stofa on the taxi squad. In any case, the Orange Bowl rematch with Buffalo was a week off, and by then young Wilson's right shoulder was expected to be functional.

"All together, things look good," said Wilson, ever the optimist. "These guys have stuck with it and built a pride that gives them a chance against anybody."

For a 2-5 outfit that had been outclassed by the Bills in

Buffalo, all the Dolphins expressed optimism. The Bills were only 4-3-1, the Jets leading the league at 4-2-1.

Billy Neighbors, the philosopher-guard, saw it in perspective: "I was on a Boston club that tied for the Eastern division title with a 7-6-1 record in '63 and lost it with a 10-3 record the next year. Believe me, anything can happen."

"We've got something to settle with Buffalo," said Tom Goode. "They beat us bad up there, but I guarantee you it will be a ball game Sunday."

The Bills romped 29–0. A record Orange Bowl turnout, 37,177, turned the jeers on young Wilson while the visitors were turning the quarterback's fumble and one of three interceptions into two touchdowns. "Junior," who completed just 3 of 13 passes, was relieved by Wood in the third quarter.

The Buffalo setback marked the end of the rainbow-making phase for everybody. The next two Sundays would be spent in Kansas City and New York. Apprehensiveness over these engagements became realities when the Chiefs coasted 34–16 and the Jets won with even less difficulty, 30–13.

Robbie was slightly consoled by his 40 percent cut of the 58,664 attendance in New York, the only bona fide big-league franchise then operating in the AFL. But even this was blunted by the first Gilchrist broadside, delivered three days after the Buffalo defeat.

Cookie began with a threat to leave town. The focal point, it seems, was a Cadillac ordered by Gilchrist that morning in full accord with his version of the contract terms that the Dolphins had assumed from Denver. Robbie pointed out that Cookie already had a Cadillac in Denver and that a Chrysler Crown Imperial with only 10,000 miles on it was available to him now. Hence, Robbie saw no moral or contractual obligation on the part of the Dolphins to furnish Gilchrist a second Cadillac.

"Penny wise and pound foolish," Gilchrist countered. "I spelled out my terms for coming to Miami, and the club agreed. If they don't intend to live up to their agreement, I cannot in good conscience remain here. It's as simple as that."

Cookie's Denver contract called for a $37,500 salary, plus fringe benefits of (1) $5,000 if Cookie rushed for 1,000 yards, (2) $5,600 or $200 weekly for the 28 weeks of the offseason if Cookie were unemployed, (3) a $5,000 Cadillac or its equivalent.

How much was a 10,000-mile Chrysler Crown Imperial worth?

"That's not the point," Gilchrist said. "See these pants?" he demanded, fingering a smartly tailored yellow pair of obvious quality. "They're thirty-five-dollar pants. But I consider them worth every penny because they fit to a tee. I am not a bargain-basement player. I don't come cheap. The Dolphins knew what I required when I came here. But they are hedging. This is how it started wherever I had differences with management. And I don't intend to let it continue. I am not a man with whom you cut corners."

Gilchrist claimed the Denver Caddy cost the Broncos $8,500 and had been driven 28,000 miles. The Broncos were willing to sell it for $5,500.

"Too much money for a used car," Cookie contended. "Besides, I'm entitled to a new one. I'm only asking what's in my contract. I've been in this game 13 years. I've played in Canada for eight dollars a game. Another season I got fifteen hundred for the whole year. But I didn't mind. That's all the man could pay. He told me so, and I respected him. At the end of the year my phone bill was fifteen hundred. I told him to pay the bill and forget it. I don't want any more than is coming to me. But I won't settle for anything less."

Cookie got his Cadillac a few weeks later.

Adding to everybody's discomfort, Gilchrist was woefully out of shape. Try as he did, Cookie's long layoff and advancing years combined to make the old warrior more colorful than effective.

Problems were accumulating. Neighbors suffered a concussion in the Buffalo game. McDaniel tore an arch in the same game, and yielded his middle linebacking post to the green and overanxious Emanuel.

In Kansas City, Twilley was retired for the season when his cheekbone was fractured by cornerback Freddie (The Hammer) Williamson. Howard had just grabbed a sideline pass at the Kansas City 17 and was tumbling out of bounds when Williamson swung his extended arm and struck the rookie flush in the face. The Dolphins were furious.

Later in the dressing room Williamson just shrugged. The play was legal. There had been no penalty. Besides, he had been warning receivers for years not to trifle with his celebrated "Hammer."

"I don't just stick my arm out, baby," Freddie said. "I move it. I put it where it hurts. Sometimes I move it laterally, sometimes perpendicular. But the idea, baby, is to hammer them."

Two months later in the first Super Bowl against Green Bay, Williamson's fortune boomeranged. He was knocked cold while tackling Donnie Anderson and was carried from the field. "There goes the Hammer," fullback Jim Taylor observed.

On the field at Kansas City, Wilson had thrown four of the six interceptions that helped relegate the Dolphins to their proper humble place. Wood threw the other two. Robbie scored the only success during this depressing period. He succeeded in getting Stofa out of Lakeland and on the Miami taxi squad, and just in time.

In New York young Wilson made his last appearance as a pro quarterback. Obviously struggling with the same right shoulder bruised in Houston, "Junior" completed just three passes of nine attempts before a weak toss resulted in Jim Hudson's third-quarter interception to help the Jets put the game away.

"I saw Jackson open but didn't have the strength to get the ball to him," Wilson admitted.

George's father sat alone outside the dressing room as the November cold swept through the steel and cement corridors stretching like catacombs beneath Shea Stadium. "I guess I should have taken the kid out sooner," he said softly, jaw hardening. "One thing for sure. I'm not putting him on the spot any longer. Not until his injuries are completely healed."

Adding to Wilson's woes was Gilchrist. In Manhattan, Cookie had seen no reason why a cosmopolite of his distinction should observe the 11 P.M. bedcheck. It cost him $300 and a fatherly lecture from Wilson, who had been something of a mischief-maker in his own day.

Faison's contributions were minimal since the bulky end arrived from San Diego. And Earl was even defiant about it. During home games in December, everyone was surprised to see Faison resting cross-legged in a sideline chair at midfield simply viewing the action.

Wilson called a full-scale scrimmage the week the club returned to Miami. Evidently the roughhousing did some good, for the Dolphins came up with one of their better games in losing to the Patriots 20–14.

Wood, who hurled 52 passes, hit touchdown throws of 32 yards to Jackson and 38 to Auer before finding Jackson open at the Boston 35 with two minutes left. But Jackson coughed up the ball when cracked by safety Ron Hall, and that was it.

The game at Denver the following week was only memorable for Gilchrist historians. Cookie's Cadillac, the one he got before departing from Denver, would be raffled off at halftime, and the great man himself would preside at the drawing. A record crowd of 32,592 packed Denver's converted baseball park to see the show in which the Dolphins furnished the fun and lost to Denver 17–7. Gilchrist was held to 11 yards in five gang-tackling carries. Mingo fouled off a field-goal try from the Denver 33. Another Mingo effort from the nine-yard line boomeranged off the goal posts. Warren, in full stride with an interception inside the Denver 10, was hit from behind and fumbled away the ball. Auer, behind a seven-man line, failed to score from inside the three on three successive downs.

Stofa, activated for the first time, relieved Wood in the fourth quarter and threw seven straight incomplete passes before connecting with Moreau, also activated for the first time as Wilson desperately shuffled his troops.

Just before the game McDaniel turned to Gilchrist and said, "As long as you're gonna draw the winning number for the Caddy, why don't you just palm a number off one of the game programs in the dressing room and we can drive back to Miami in style."

Gilchrist gave McDaniel a long, pitying look. "Wahoo, that just shows how many brains you have. Can you really see me winning that car? And then can you see us driving through places like Mississippi and Alabama with those state police?

"I can hear the all-points alarm now," Cookie continued, cupping a hand to his ear. "Attention all cars, attention all cars—be on the lookout for a nigger and an Indian coming through in a big Cadillac!"

Despite Gilchrist's foreboding, the pair would have traveled more comfortably in the car. Scratching on all sides to keep the club going, Robbie had saved $13,000 by chartering an old DC-6 to Denver. The 16-hour round trip had the squad in a sour, irritable frame.

Wahoo was on crutches after pulling a hamstring muscle in the second quarter. And with two games left of a 2-10 season, the 28-year-old Choctaw was excused for the year by Wilson. So McDaniel left for Tampa, where within two weeks he was on a wrestling card, hamstring pull and all.

Establishing a pattern of inscrutable behavior that would remain through the Wilson era, the Dolphins rebounded from adversity to come within one point of embarrassing Kansas City the following Sunday. Just two minutes remained when a 25-yard touchdown pass from Len Dawson to Chris Buford pulled out a 19–18 victory for the Chiefs, who had already clinched their Western Division championship.

Wood's best performance as a Dolphin was his last as a pro. The gentleman from Georgia, who shocked everyone with a stiff-legged, seven-yard touchdown bootleg, suffered bruised ribs and became the fourth quarterback casualty of the season.

Stofa got his first starting chance in the season finale at home, and the 24-year-old wanderer made the most of it. The turnout of 20,045 was at least better than the week before, when the finest team in the AFL, Kansas City, could draw no more than 17,884, the lowest attendance ebb the Dolphins would reach in a milieu of indifference.

Only the hard-core faithful saw Stofa and Auer excel in a 29–28 Miami victory to close the 1966 season on a hopeful note. Stofa's fourth touchdown pass to Auer with 38 seconds to play tied the score. And Mingo's conversion produced the third Dolphin victory in 14 games.

Stofa completed 22 of 38 passes for 269 yards in the best performance of a Miami quarterback all year.

For the redoubtable Auer, the year ended as it started—in the end zone. In between there had been disconcerting moments for the Coral Gables blond, who readily admitted to mental lapses on the field. "Funny what flashes through your head while you're in a game. Somebody once proved that only about 5 of the 60 minutes are spent in actual competition. So what do you do the rest of the time?"

Auer had been recently thinking about how a TV set would add to the apartment he and Donna were renting, pending final settlement of the bankruptcy issue. The $100 gift certificate a local department store awarded each Dolphin scoring a touchdown would make an ideal down payment.

"When we beat Denver," Auer said, "we were going for a score. I took it in, hit Arch Matsos about the three-yard line, then got past Goose Gonsoulin on the one and fell into the end zone. Know what I was thinking out there? I was thinking, My God, we've got the TV."

> Let's face it. I could be as good as Johnny Unitas and some people would still talk. There was just too much pressure on Dad and me.
>
> —GEORGE WILSON JR.

10. *My Son, the Quarterback*

Erratic and makeshift, the football squad was still the smoothest factor in Miami's first-year operation. To watch Joe Robbie juggle to meet payrolls and other obligations was to wonder why he persisted. But Robbie was shrewd as well as stubborn; and besides, he was a fan.

In the press box he squirmed, he paced, and occasionally he exulted with the fortunes of the odd collection of mercenaries who by his own reckoning cost him about $237,500 apiece—the $7.5 million franchise divided by the 32 expansion draftees that came with it. "But I'm here to stay, goddammit, and the sooner everybody around here realizes that, the better."

His need for operating capital was immediate, and his bid somewhat desperate. With a $1 million payment due the AFL by January 1, he set a December 15 deadline for the original season buyers of 12,503 tickets to renew for 1967. The season did not end until December 18, and the customers howled. Robbie then extended the deadline.

"All of us associated with the Dolphins are deeply grateful

to the enthusiastic fans of Miami and South Florida," he said in stretching the date to February 1. "Our fans were major league in every respect."

With Danny Thomas fading from the scene, Robbie was now running the entire office operation. At the Super Bowl in Los Angeles that January, he decided to let Chuck Burr go. Despite a three-year contract, the Suncoast Sports travesty leading to St. Petersburg Beach had marked the beginning of the end. Burr was crushed, though he soon moved back to Buffalo and eventually prospered as an executive in a concessions firm.

As though Robbie's problems were not distracting enough at the time, up popped Cookie Gilchrist to announce from his home in Toronto that he was preparing to sue the club for "breach of contract." Cookie said he had not received "one dime" on his fringe benefit calling for $200 weekly in the offseason. "And Robbie doesn't even speak to me."

The complaint "Robbie doesn't even speak to me," voiced by many of his foes, appears petty to Robbie. "They ought to consider themselves fortunate," he says, grinning. "When I do speak to them, matters usually turn out worse."

Robbie erupted over Gilchrist's interpretation of the offseason income arrangement. "The Miami Dolphins are not going to permit Cookie to take what amounts to unemployment compensation while sitting on his rusty-dusty until July. He is entitled to either the entire $5,200 if he has no employment, makes no personal appearances or endorsements or anything of that nature; or he is entitled to the difference between $5,200 and whatever he has made before training camp opens. That is how his contract reads."

Robbie was correct, and Cookie never sued. Robbie decided that Gilchrist's days as a Dolphin were numbered.

Robbie functions best with his back to the wall. Early in

February he completed a deal bringing two new partners and fresh cash into the organization. Willard H. (Bud) Keland was interested enough to invest in even such a floundering club as the Dolphins. The risk was somewhat lessened since the merger of the AFL with the NFL now seemed assured. At least the common draft effected in 1966 had erased the bidding competition between the leagues for coveted athletes.

The 48-year-old Keland, a Racine, Wis., developer, was a former vice-president of Johnson Wax and the son-in-law of the firm's president and board chairman. He brought along a friend, George Gillett, who left a Chicago consulting firm to join the Dolphins, ostensibly as Burr's replacement.

Keland's presence encouraged Robbie early in March to state unequivocally that the club was not for sale. "There are no negotiations in process for the Miami Dolphins. And I can conceive of no set of circumstances in which an offer would be entertained or discussed. The Miami Dolphins are not for sale."

While Robbie settled his partners, Joe Thomas grappled with a problem of his own. He wanted a quarterback in the draft, specifically Bob Griese of Purdue. The other blue-ribbon passer in 1965 was Steve Spurrier, not only from the University of Florida but also winner of the Heisman Trophy.

Spurrier's local popularity and Miami's high drafting position (only three teams were ahead of the 3-11 Dolphins) stirred excitement among Dolphin followers.

"I want the kid from Purdue. I like everything about him," Thomas said. "But I'm afraid to pass up Spurrier. I'm afraid we'll get lynched or something." However, San Francisco coveted Spurrier. And so the 49ers arranged with Atlanta, drafting just ahead of Miami, to choose Spurrier and trade him off. Thomas then snatched Griese.

As his second choice Thomas selected a badly needed defensive lineman, Jim Riley of Oklahoma. Two other 1967 selections, Larry Seiple (No. 7) and John Richardson (No. 9), remained with the club through the 1972 Super Bowl.

The draft was a success, if only for Griese and end Jack Clancy, a Michigan athlete selected as a redshirt the year before. Clancy, whose maturity delighted Wilson from the start of training camp, was to catch a record 67 passes in his rookie season.

Few other rookies delighted Wilson at Boca Raton that July. The coach and Joe Thomas had never seen eye-to-eye. And so when George Wilson Jr. went to Denver on June 27 in the most significant of a flurry of trades, once again the fur was up. "It's ridiculous to have a situation like that on any ball club," Thomas had said privately. And Robbie agreed. Two more thorns, Gilchrist and Faison, were sent along with Wilson and guard Ernie Park. In return the Dolphins received running back Abner Haynes, linebacker Jerry Hopkins, defensive end Dan LaRose and a sixth draft choice in 1968.

Publicly, the coach whose paternal dream was shattered looked at the practical side. "This will take the pressure off the kid," he said. In private, however, Wilson criticized the judgment of Thomas and Robbie, who "didn't seem to realize that my son was by far the best quarterback we had last year."

Young Wilson seemed to take the news in stride. "The trade could be a big break for me. Let's face it. I could be as good as Johnny Unitas and some people would still talk. There was just too much pressure on Dad and me."

Lou Saban, starting a 10-year contract with the Broncos, cut young Wilson after two practice days.

Both Wilsons were embarrassed. "I can't understand it," the coach said. "I don't know what Saban's thinking. He couldn't have taken a good look at the kid in two days."

Wilson said he would like to have his son back. But Robbie closed the issue quickly. "We do not intend to sign George Wilson Jr.," he said. "Period."

Disappointed as much for his father's sake as his own, "Junior" sat out the 1967 season. When the Cincinnati franchise was organized in 1968, young Wilson asked Paul Brown for a tryout. The coach refused with the explanation that he didn't want to be placed in the middle of a family situation involving an old friend.

Still determined to prove to himself and his father that he was capable, George got a tryout with the Toronto Argonauts. He was cut after three games. "I figured that was it for me," he said. "I was on my way back to Miami when Philadelphia called me and wanted me for their Pottstown farm team. They said if I did well there, I might move up to the Eagles.

"Pottstown had a player salary budget of $3,600 a game in the Atlantic Coast League. My official salary was $175 and I was getting an extra $300 personally from the Eagles through Pottstown's owner. But it came out in the papers, and they said the arrangement couldn't be continued."

The Pottstown Firebirds were the last stop for young Wilson. "The whole bit was hell on my family," he said. "There won't be any more."

Quarterback John Stofa's spectacular finish in the 1966 finale against Houston made him the man to beat in the passing derby. Griese and Jon Brittenum furnished the rookie competition in a camp where personnel was shuffled constantly. Making good a view to "get rid of some of these contented veterans," and stung by his son's departure, Wilson went housecleaning. In one August cut he dismissed five expansion draftees—fullback Billy Joe, safety Ross O'Hanley, defensive tackle Al Dotson, defensive end LaVerne Torczon and flanker Bo Roberson. Earl Faison, complaining of back miseries, was also trimmed after an abortive attempt by Wilson to make a tight end of the adipose 285-pounder.

Robbie contended that Faison was a malingerer and, as such, not entitled to some $60,000 remaining on his three-year contract. The antagonists eventually went to court in a two-year battle settled to Miami's satisfaction. Faison's case was not aided by his record. After one look at huge Earl at Denver, Saban had sent him back to Miami.

During that summer Wilson and Joe Thomas brought in an uncommon variety from minor trades and waiver lists. Dan LaRose, a lineman from Denver, had one eye. Defensive end Bob Petrich from San Diego was a brilliant conversationalist but over the hill as a performer. Preston Carpenter, who had toiled for Wilson in Detroit, was a 33-year-old tight end candidate.

Sam Fleming, a 21-year-old guard for the defunct Brooklyn Eagles of the Continental League, showed up one sultry July day at suppertime. Fleming had come by bus from his home in North Carolina for a tryout. "I applied in March," he said, "and I didn't hear anything except that the camp would open in July."

"Son, tryouts are over," Wilson said. "Why don't you go home and try to catch on somewhere later? Write a few letters."

Fleming started to cry. Wilson began rubbing his neck. "How much is bus fare?" he asked.

"It's—it was $23.70 to come down."

"How much you got?"

"I got $20, Coach," said Fleming, now sobbing softly.

"Here," Wilson said, thrusting out a ten-dollar bill. "What the hell, you got to eat something."

Fleming, who was driven back to the bus depot, cut a forlorn figure, standing at the ticket window with a suitcase as battered as his hopes.

Hercules McElroy reported one morning unannounced. A recent story had pictured the 22-year-old McElroy chomping a dime in half with his teeth, lifting an automobile and supporting a one-ton newsprint roll on his stomach.

"Hercules could be the greatest football player who ever lived," said Ron Laytner, his agent. "Except he's afraid of hurting people. He's fast and tough. He outran a stock car. If somebody will get a sledgehammer, Hercules will lie down and let you hit him in the belly with it."

McElroy was matched against John Roderick, idle in camp while recovering from back surgery. Roderick won a 50-yard race by 10 yards.

"I'm sorry," Wilson told the agent. Hercules never said anything.

The immediate problem, as usual, was at quarterback. Knee and jaw intact, Norton started the exhibition opener against Denver in Akron, Ohio. Wilson was still simmering at Saban over the hurry-up treatment afforded young George, but nobody would have guessed the Dolphins were angry in view of Denver's 2–0 halftime lead. Norton had completed 3 of 15 passes and been nailed by tackle Dave Costa in the end zone.

Stofa then took over, impressively completing 12 of 19 to lead a 19–2 comeback victory. And the next week against Buffalo in Memphis, after rookie Jon Brittenum went 4 for 17 to accumulate 23 yards in the first half, Stofa repeated once again. The rangy blond came on to complete 9 of 15 in the last 30 minutes, including a 16-yard game winner to Jackson in the fourth quarter to clinch a 10–7 victory. "Let's not get too excited," Wilson warned. "We haven't won the Super Bowl."

Indeed, the Dolphins lost their next three exhibitions, the first a 20–19 battle with San Diego before 35,871 Orange Bowl customers at home. Then came losses to Atlanta (27–17) and to New Orleans (20–17) at Charleston, S.C.

Griese, whose estimated $150,000, three-year contract reflected pro football's economies in the first year of the common draft, made a less than auspicious first start in the game against Atlanta. He completed one of six and had two intercepted before Stofa took over, directing a 10-point third quarter to gain a 17–13 lead. But the fourth quarter was Atlanta's. And so was the game.

Despite a bad night against New Orleans, Stofa proved the most consistent of the quarterbacks in camp and was awarded the starting job against the Broncos in the season opener. Brittenum was traded to San Diego, leaving Griese and Norton behind Stofa. Griese, demonstrating poise beyond his 22 years, was in fact right behind.

Wilson retained 10 rookies. He sent Dave Kocourek, the 1966 co-captain, to Oakland for a draft choice and moved Doug Moreau up to a starting spot.

Danny Thomas was absent from the 1967 opener. He had officially withdrawn from the organization and been replaced by Keland. The new general partner had arranged with Robbie to purchase all outstanding stock except for around 12 percent retained by John O'Neil of Miami and the slacks-manufacturing Haggar brothers of Dallas.

"I'm glad that's over," Robbie said of the reorganization. "I hope now we can turn our full attention to the football team."

> I can appreciate that a lot of quarterbacks need three or four years to make it in the pros. But I've never tried. And until I find out for myself, I won't believe I can't make it right now.
>
> —BOB GRIESE

11. *A Drive, a Nine-Iron, a Mingo*

The first four minutes of the Dolphins' 1967 season belonged to John Stofa, "The Cinderella Man" who rebounded from cut lists and three years in the minors to open at quarterback for the team. The rest of the year, for better or worse, was Bob Griese's.

On the first play from scrimmage, Big John cut loose with a 45-yard pass to the redoubtable Auer. Stofa then hit Twilley for six yards and loped the last eight himself, putting the Dolphins ahead of the Broncos by a touchdown with just a minute and 41 seconds elapsed.

Two minutes later the quarterback was writhing on the turf after being low-bridged by Pete Duranko, Stofa's teammate at Bishop McCort High in Johnstown, Pa. Stofa's right ankle was flopped flat on the grass like a rag doll's. "I knew there was something wrong when I heard the ankle crack," Stofa said in Mercy Hospital. "I was stepping forward into the pocket. Denver had the blitz on and somebody knocked the ball away from me. All I could think of was getting back after it. I turned my body but my legs were planted. When it cracked I felt sick. I knew I'd lost my job, just when everything was finally coming together."

The Orange Bowl clock showed 10 minutes, 58 seconds remaining in the first quarter when Stofa fell. Griese knew he was next, for after a promising start, Norton had experienced another miserable training camp. His passes still fluttered and his confidence was gone.

"When they carried John off, I started warming up in a hurry," Griese said. "I felt sorry for John, but I knew I had to forget that and get down to business. It wasn't a question of whether I could do the job. I had to do it."

For a 22-year-old rookie, Griese was frighteningly cool. He had expressed confidence from the start of camp. "I've heard about the difficulties of adjusting from the college to the pro game. It's a stepped-up pace, no doubt about it. In college, weaknesses in the defense could be easily found and exploited. Up here everybody's a lot smarter. I can appreciate that a lot of quarterbacks need three or four years to make it in the pros. But I've never tried. And until I find out for myself, I won't believe I can't make it right now."

This was a rookie talking, but clearly no ordinary rookie. At Purdue the six-foot blond had compiled a .571 passing record—348 completions in 609 passes for 4,402 yards. Against Notre Dame in 1964, he went 19 for 22 while leading the Boilermakers to a 25–21 victory. He credited Bob DeMoss, Purdue's backfield coach, with his development.

Response to crisis matured Griese early. His father died of a heart attack when Bob was 10, and Bob admits he never completely got over it. "I idolized my father. And I guess I've been a quiet person ever since. It was tough on my mother, but she held the family together. And my brother Bill, two years older than I, helped a lot. He gave up his education for me."

After attending Rex Mundi High in Evansville, Ind., Bob entered Purdue with a scholarship. Notre Dame had turned him down, and he repaid Notre Dame on the field.

He did not forget his family. When the Dolphins paid him well for his signature, he established a certain security for his family and sent his 24-year-old brother to Purdue. "It was the least I could do," Bob said.

That Teutonic sense of discipline and duty was matched by Griese's leadership, which was neither vocal nor smacking of corner-lot enthusiasm. He was simply a firm, quiet example.

"I've always had confidence in myself," he said, "and this seems to have helped gain the confidence of others."

When Stofa was carried off, Wilson asked Griese if he was ready. "Yes," was the answer straight out of Frank Merriwell.

"When I entered the huddle for the first time, I had a plan," the quarterback said. "I had only thrown six passes during the exhibition season, with one completion and two interceptions. So I planned to initiate myself slowly. The ball was on our three-yard line, and first I had to get out of there. So I let Joe Auer and Sam Price get me out." Auer and Price gained seven yards each before Larry Seiple, another quiet rookie, who succeeded young Wilson in the punting department, kicked the offense out of trouble.

"On the second series I figured I could start opening up," Griese said. He hit six for seven as the Dolphins drove for a score. The remarkable blond finished with 12 for 19, for 193 yards, two touchdowns and a 35–21 victory.

And that was the end of Miami's quarterback problem. Occasional injuries would sideline the slightly built 180-pounder, but there would never be doubt that Griese was in command.

In that same game Haynes had the best day he would ever enjoy as a Dolphin. He dodged and scooted 151 yards in 12 carries, including a 65-yard touchdown escape and another 3-yard scoring slant to clinch the victory in the fourth quarter.

Wilson's wholesale squad shuffle with the emphasis on youth looked good to the 29,381 whose hopes soared after the Denver victory. And there were 36,272 on hand the following Sunday for Kansas City.

Optimism was followed by adversity. The Chiefs overpowered the Dolphins 24–0, and Griese was not around at the finish. On the second play of the fourth quarter, the quarterback took a blindside head blow from Buck Buchanan.

"I never saw him," Griese said.

"I know he didn't see me," Buchanan said. "I'm glad to know the boy's all right. Their blockers weren't reading us very well and we were all over the kid. But I'll tell you something. That kid was cool."

The following Sunday in New York, Griese injured his right shoulder when defensive end Verlon Biggs sat on the fallen quarterback; later Bob was sent flying against the Jets' bench by cornerback John Sample. He yielded to Norton early in the second quarter. The Jets then proceeded to romp 29–7, as Joe Namath amassed a personal pro high of 415 yards passing by completing 23 of 39 for three touchdowns.

Wilson was never a rigid disciplinarian. In fact, his Detroit teams had been known as party-loving ruffians. But the Lions were experienced and they were winners. Not so Miami. Saturday before the Jets' game, Wilson's Dolphins indulged in wine, women and frolic. As they had before. But this time Wilson got tough.

To prepare for the following Sunday in Kansas City, he conducted an all-out scrimmage, and he also got into a public hassle with Auer over a dropped punt against the Jets. After muffing the punt, Auer had asked assistant coach John Idzik to remove him from the special teams.

Wilson was enraged. "I've never heard of a good pro athlete

who wants to be taken out of a game. If he wants bench time, he'll get it. I realize Joe is a popular player. But I'm running this team and I'll decide who plays football and when."

Auer seemed bewildered by all the fuss. "What the hell, I didn't try to miss the damn thing," he said. "And it didn't even cost us possession of the ball. After all, Ab Haynes recovered it. You'd think the play cost us the ball game, and that Joe Namath wasn't even in town on Sunday.

"I realize the coaches have been good to me," Auer continued, "but I've been pretty good to them, too. I don't think I deserve this. I try all the time. Sometimes it might not seem like it, because I'm not the kind of guy who gets all excited. Last week against Kansas City I took a punt in traffic on the nine-yard line and returned to the 22. I could have let it bounce or stuck up my hand for a fair catch. But I wanted to get us field position. Did anybody say, 'Nice job, Joe,' after that one? No. It's discouraging."

The discouragement was just setting in. With Griese's shoulder smarting and Norton wrestling his familiar confidence problems, the Dolphins picked up Archie Roberts. The former Columbia University star had lingered two years on the Cleveland Browns' cab squad while pursuing medical studies at Western Reserve University. The 24-year-old proved personable, intelligent and unable to help. The Dolphins were shut out a second time by the Chiefs, 41–0.

In a give-and-take after the game, Wilson was asked: "When the Dolphins had the ball on Kansas City's 26 after that poor punt in the fourth quarter, why didn't you give Norton a chance to score instead of putting in Archie Roberts?"

Wilson's answer reflected his mood: "As you must know, the only reason Norton played at all is because of Griese's shoulder injury. Well, Norton had the team on the Chiefs'

35-yard line in the first quarter, their 15 in the second quarter, their 2 in the third quarter and their 25 in the fourth quarter —and we didn't score. I thought it was time to see what Roberts could do."

Replacing Auer on punt returns at Kansas City, Jackson broke his nose. Handsome Frank then replaced Auer in Wilson's doghouse by having his nose set immediately, thus causing him to miss the next game. Wilson felt Jackson should have played out the season before getting the nose job. Jackson had no choice, as it turned out. The operation was ordered by the team physician.

With Griese still out, the Dolphins and Norton were slaughtered 41–10 at Boston the following week. In four straight defeats after the opener, they had scored two touchdowns.

"Man's reach should exceed his grasp," said Emanuel one dull practice afternoon, "or what's a heaven for?" Emanuel could quote Robert Browning, but he was having no more luck than his big-bonus colleague, Norton. And their teammates resented them both. By midseason Emanuel was on the bench while the doughty McDaniel was back in the middle, "where I belong."

The competition between Emanuel and McDaniel intensified when John Bramlett took over the right side in October. Bramlett, a 210-pound round-the-clock terror, had joined the club in late summer after a contract dispute with the Denver Broncos. He acquired the nickname "Bull" when as a minor league outfielder he ran through a fence pursuing a foul ball. After two years in the St. Louis baseball chain, Bramlett left the Tulsa club for his first love, football. "There was no contact in baseball," explained John, who derived unrestrained joy from belting people.

Still another ex-Denver stalwart was 287-pound Ray Jacobs,

a punishing but slow defensive tackle who liked to hunt snakes. Jacobs terrorized guards not only with his brutality but also with the constant wad of tobacco he had learned to squirt about the line of scrimmage. Ray was ponderous, however, and quarterbacks had little to fear after he was finished punishing the blockers.

Namath certainly had nothing to fear the following Sunday. Some 30,049 Orange Bowl witnesses watched their hapless team return from a disastrous road tour to take a 33–14 bombing from the Jets.

Playing the first half only, Namath pegged 13 of 15 passes for 199 yards and two of the touchdowns that produced a 24–0 lead. In contrast, the unfortunate Norton managed to complete 4 of 17 passes for 15 yards. Wilson could take it no longer. Although Griese's right shoulder was still tight, the rookie was put in during the second half. He led the offense on touchdown drives of 61 and 80 yards, throwing nine yards to Jackson and six yards to Noonan in the end zone. It was the first display of a sustained attack since the Denver opener. But it came too late. After five straight losses and consecutive road dates ahead at Buffalo, San Diego and Oakland, the only prospect for the battered squad was the next weekend off.

In September the Dolphins had picked up placekicker Booth Lusteg after his release by Buffalo. Lusteg, a saga in himself, had engaged the inconsistent Mingo in a kicking contest. Mingo, rarely outdone on the practice field, came out the victor and retained his job. But Lusteg stayed around on the cab squad.

After the loss to the Jets, Wilson decided to release Mingo and give Lusteg a chance. Lusteg had been a proficient kicker at Buffalo and could not be any worse than the erratic Mingo. But Wilson asked Joe Robbie not to tell Mingo until the day after Tuesday's scheduled golf outing. "Why not let him enjoy himself?" Wilson reasoned.

Unfortunately, however, news of Mingo's pending departure reached him on the golf course, ruining his game and embarrassing him in front of his teammates. Furthermore, the fact he was waived by Tuesday did not entitle Mingo to his week's salary check of $1,800.

At the golf banquet that evening, Mingo asked his host if he might address the club. Gene was eloquent in the bourbon-and-water ambience. "Play as good as you know how, guys," he pleaded, "and you'll never have to answer to anybody. I know some unkind things have been said about you, but I don't think you deserve it. Just remember to keep playing as well as you can, and the best of luck to you all."

The following Sunday the Dolphins moved into Buffalo's snow and dropped their sixth straight, 35–13. Auer also managed to drop another punt in Buffalo, a town he should never have entered.

The year before, sheriff's deputies had approached Joe with a warrant for his arrest in connection with the farm he lost. Before Auer could explain, he spent the night in jail. Wilson had failed in a daring effort to smuggle his halfback out the dressing-room door. "It's the worst dressing room around," Wilson explained. "No windows."

On the West Coast, the Dolphins set a club record for defeats, eight straight, by losing number seven at San Diego (24–0) and number eight at Oakland (31–17). Griese's protection was as porous as the defense, which had yielded 279 points in nine games.

Wilson's 29th wedding anniversary coincided with the following Sunday's date with Buffalo back in the Orange Bowl. The result: a 17–14 Miami victory in the last two minutes. From Buffalo's 31 with 69 seconds left, Griese fired a down-the-middle strike to Twilley for the winning touchdown.

The Dolphins had a fresh look against Buffalo as Wilson inserted Jack Harper and Stan Mitchell in the backfield to replace Auer and Haynes. And these two remained in the offense at Houston the following Sunday. Dolphin Jack Clancy, who was having a big rookie year, caught seven Griese passes for 126 yards, but the Oilers won 17–14.

Apparently out of the doldrums as Griese began taking charge, the young Dolphins sought to surpass their 1966 record of 3-11. To do this, they needed to win two of their last three games. These were against San Diego, Boston and Houston. All in Miami.

On Sunday Griese fired two touchdown passes and scored a third as the Dolphins produced a 41–24 victory that knocked the Chargers out of the Western Division race. It was the most significant victory yet for Miami and, predictably, was achieved in semiprivacy. Only 23,007 were on hand to goad the Dolphins to their highest point total and third victory of the season.

Harper, whose rapid improvement induced Wilson to dismiss Abner Haynes the week before, escaped on a 37-yard touchdown run. Mitchell scored the fifth touchdown on a plunge, and Lusteg kicked field goals of 14 and 19 yards. Any field goal represented a milestone in those days.

As he had the week before, Wilson started 13 rookies or second-year operatives against Boston. Two of the rookies, Griese and Clancy, were unstoppable in a 41–32 victory over the Patriots, to give Wilson an improved record in his second season. Griese completed 17 of 31 passes for 270 yards. Clancy caught five, matching the AFL rookie high of 60 season receptions by Bo Dickinson of Denver in 1962. The victory also permitted the Dolphins to escape the Eastern Division cellar, now occupied by the Patriots with a 3-10-1 record.

A mob—for Miami—of 31,121 turned out for the season finale against Houston. The Dolphins revived their habit of collapsing before crowds. Griese, who had set an AFL record by passing 122 times without interception, was picked off five times as the Oilers romped 41–10. At game's end, those Dolphins living out of town had their autos packed and waiting outside the Orange Bowl for the getaway.

Griese, already displaying the disciplined detachment of a mechanical man, was a landslide winner for Most Valuable Player, while Clancy's 67 catches set an AFL rookie record. Wilson was encouraged by both the 4-10 record and the achievement of his young players.

Other awards at the squad banquet went to Norm Evans in the offensive line, Ray Jacobs in the defensive line, John Bramlett of the linebackers and Jim Warren of the secondary.

But Wilson had more holes than MVPs. Asked about his future needs, Wilson said: "Well, we could use a tight end, another safetyman, a middle linebacker, a defensive end, a power runner and at least two or three big linemen. Other than that, we're in great shape."

At least the quarterback situation was solved, provided Griese remained healthy. So the day after Christmas, Stofa was traded to the Bengals for Cincinnati's first two bonus rounds in the 1968 draft. "What the heck," Stofa said, laughing, "in a year or two I just might keep a winter home in Miami and another in Cincinnati."

How right he was. Big John's circuitous career would return him to Miami in less than two years.

Another nomad seemed to have found a niche when Gene Mingo was picked up by the Washington Redskins after his Miami Lakes Country Club speech. He promptly kicked field goals of 42 and 35 yards that almost beat Baltimore in a 17–13 battle.

Gene returned to Miami briefly after the Baltimore game to pick up his color TV and "a few other odds and ends" before rejoining the Redskins.

"Hey, Gene," asked Ed Cooke, the defensive captain, "are the uprights wider over in that league?"

"The footballs must be filled with straight-arrow helium," observed John Bramlett.

Mingo was in his glory. "I proved something to myself Sunday. I'm set up in a beautiful apartment. Things couldn't be better," he said.

Three weeks later Mingo kicked a field-goal attempt out of bounds on the three-yard line. "Unbelievable," muttered Washington coach Otto Graham. Shortly after Mingo's Miami visit, he was dismissed by the Redskins.

> This ain't a sober man's game.
> —JIMMY ORR

12. *The Playing Fields of St. Andrew's*

The martini was just right, heavy vermouth. The cigar breathed like a pre-Castro Havana, and the ladies flanking George Chesser were hospitable. Training camp was never like this.

Chesser was reclining his 230 pounds in a soft leather booth of the El Toro Lounge in Boca Raton. An hour earlier he had been blocking multihanded linebackers one-on-one in the nutcracker drill down the road at St. Andrew's. For only the second day in camp, good old George Wilson was getting awfully tough. What had gotten into the coacher in the off-season?

Ah, well, Chesser reasoned. What was it about the Battle of Waterloo being won on the playing fields of Eton? He grinned at this bright thought. His history instructor at Mississippi should have had more patience before flunking him out.

"Ladies," Chesser announced, ordering martinis for all hands, "are you aware that the battles of the Orange Bowl will be won on the playing fields of St. Andrew's?"

Getting no response, he nudged the one on his left who was called Mimi. He got a playful nudge in return, and his moon face beamed. "Sacrifice brings its rewards," Chesser observed, sipping his drink. The ladies giggled.

George Chesser had gone from Mississippi to Delta State College and finally to the Dolphins. In 1966 the tough fullback made the club as a free agent, but spent his time on the special teams while Billy Joe and Rick Casares and Cookie Gilchrist dominated the scene. Chesser carried the football only 16 times. "In 1967, I let my weight get up over 240 a month before camp opened," he explained. "Then I came to my senses, eating nothing but boiled eggs and salad and taking reducing pills."

Chesser reported at 220, but weak from his diet. He just made the team. Cut in September, he remained on the cab squad until injuries to other players moved him back up to the 40 and enabled him to gain another year toward his pension. He carried the football only twice in 1967.

His third season, Chesser believed, would be his big one. He would make his move. But at 230 he was 10 pounds over his self-prescribed limit, and now Wilson wanted him to reduce another five to 215. He needed a respite.

"Here's to beauty," he said to the ladies.

The drink felt bittersweet against Chesser's lips when two Dolphin assistant coaches entered the lounge. Although Wilson was more lenient than most of his peers, liquor was out.

"Boys," he said, gazing in sorrow at the glasses gracing his table, "would you care to meet my cousins?"

The 1968 camp was Chesser's last as a pro.

Chesser was right about good old George cracking down

bit in the summer of 1968, the last term on his three-year contract. Wilson told the squad in its first meeting that poker games would be limited and the lights-out-at-11 P.M. policy would be enforced. "The poker in particular is getting out of hand," Wilson said. "I'm not banning cards altogether. You'd find a way to play anyway. But the stakes are too high, and this has caused some friction."

Wilson continued to regard the evening beer-run with amused tolerance, however. The closest keg to the St. Andrew's outpost was a pizza parlor about five miles from camp. Between the end of afternoon practice around 4:45 and suppertime at 6, those who thirsted arranged a prodigious scheduling feat.

Autos were facing east before the afternoon practice began. Immediately afterward, athletes who appeared unable to walk another step suddenly turned into gazelles, bounding for the locker room. The process of showering and crawling into shirt, shorts and sandals ("Jesus slippers" in the parlance) required about 10 minutes. By 5 P.M. the fleet was rolling.

"There go the beer guys," Wilson would say.

Exactly one hour later, just before the St. Andrew's dining-room door closed, the fleet would rumble back, its crews invariably the last in line for supper.

"Here come the beer guys," Wilson would say.

The coach went into the 1968 season with just 10 remnants of the AFL expansion draft—center Tom Goode, guards Billy Neighbors and Maxie Williams (who had been switched from tackle), offensive tackle Norm Evans, defensive end Mel Branch, defensive tackle Tom Nomina, linebacker Wahoo McDaniel, safety Willie West, cornerbacks Jim Warren and Dick Westmoreland.

There were no crocodile tears, however, because of the

excellent college draft masterminded by Joe Thomas in January. Of seven picks in the first five rounds, four collegians became regulars on the team Don Shula led to the 1972 Super Bowl.

In addition to Larry Csonka, the 240-pound fullback who had broken the rushing records of Jim Brown, Jim Nance and Ernie Davis at Syracuse, the Dolphins grabbed a fifth-round prize from Wyoming in Jim Kiick. The laconic, tough Kiick would team with Csonka to form the most productive running attack in the NFL by 1971.

Others who would become regulars as rookies were Doug Crusan at offensive left tackle and Dick Anderson at safety. Crusan, a 6-5, 255-pound Pennsylvanian, was slow and awkward at the beginning, but as tough as the Monessen steel mills he escaped from on a scholarship to Indiana. The balding Anderson had been a defensive star at Colorado.

The 1968 draft also included a 335-pound lineman named Sam McDowell, Olympic sprint champion Jim Hines, and a sleeper who won a starting linebacking job, Randall Edmunds of Georgia Tech. When McDowell came to camp from Southwest Missouri College he was a study in obesity. "He must have come to camp in a dining car," said Wilson, who was afraid to exercise him for fear the big guy would die of a heart attack. McDowell was sent packing. Hines was not due until fall, after the Mexico City Olympics. But as an eighth-round draftee, the silent Edmunds from Georgia Tech would more than repay the Dolphins over the next two seasons for their modest investment.

The biggest bargain of the lot, however, was a myopic defensive lineman with the alluring name of Manuel Jose Fernandez—alluring because of Miami's burgeoning Cuban refugee population and the need to find more Orange Bowl customers. Only Houston and the last-place Boston Patriots drew fewer customers than Miami in 1967.

Joe Thomas took a chance on Fernandez, signing him as a free agent out of Utah. Thomas had little knowledge of him. But he had a notion that Fernandez might draw the Cubans, even if he only stayed around long enough for the three preseason games in the Orange Bowl.

All three exhibition contests were against NFL opposition —Philadelphia, Baltimore and a rematch with Atlanta, the team that had enabled the Dolphins to top 50,000 in attendance for the first time the year before.

Fernandez could not wave bye-bye in Spanish. Born in the Oakland area, the furthest he got from home was Utah. But from his first menacing week in camp, Manny won a job, and for the next four years would be the Dolphins' outstanding defensive lineman.

He started as the left end opposite Branch. The tackles were Ray Jacobs, the snake-hunter who had had a good year, and the often-injured Nomina, with John Richardson in reserve.

The most interesting battle of the summer focused on the running backs, where Stan Mitchell and Jack Harper were fighting the challenges of Csonka and Kiick. "A better running game will give us a better passing game," Wilson said. "We had to throw the ball too much last year. Everybody knew it was coming. No team can limit itself this way and expect to keep the ball. And as a result we were on defense too long."

The Dolphins were last in the AFL defending against both the run and the pass. So Wilson was determined to establish a running game.

Challenger Mitchell, a quietly droll bachelor from a Tennessee mountain town called Sparta, was aware of Csonka's presence and his No. 1 draft stature. "All I brought were a few T-shirts and a pair of trousers. The way things are goin' around here, I'm gonna keep 'em all packed."

Yet the running back who stirred up the most attention in the summer of 1968 was none other than Joe Auer, who had lost his starting job to Harper the previous November. When Csonka reported belatedly to camp after the college all-star game, he found the personable, imaginative Auer good company. One night they were returning to St. Andrew's from an evening in town. Auer, as usual, was driving his little dune buggy, a topless vehicle built like a jeep. A few hundred yards from camp, the trio rolled over into a roadside ditch. Joe said he had swerved to avoid a possum who came suddenly into the beams of his headlights. "I couldn't hit *any* animal," Auer said. Csonka was unharmed, having landed on Auer.

The possum incident occurred August 22, the night before an exhibition with Boston in Jacksonville. Auer did not make the trip, ostensibly because of the facial cuts, although Joe contended he could have played anyway. The following week Auer went on waivers as an injured player, still protesting he was perfectly all right. "They're trying to railroad me out of camp," said the man who scored the first and last touchdown for the Dolphins in their first season.

Auer's status worried his colleagues. Players incurring line-of-duty injuries are entitled to full pay, but Joe Robbie refused to pay the confused back for the Boston game or the Baltimore exhibition the following week. The catch, it seems, was that rolling over a dune buggy was not considered a line-of-duty hazard.

Meanwhile, Auer hopped a plane to Atlanta and reported to the Falcons as a free agent. That would have been all right as far as the Dolphins were concerned, except Wilson now chose to accuse Auer of taking his playbook along. "I'm fining him five hundred for that," the coach said, citing the same figure Auer claimed he was owed by the club. Wilson added that Auer's exhibition-game status was "in the hands of the commissioner," meaning Milt Woodard, the mild-mannered AFL president.

"As I understand it," Woodard said, predictably, "Auer's injury was not connected with football. It's up to the Dolphins whether they want to pay him or not. As for the playbook, I'll see to that when the Dolphins officially notify me it's missing."

As it turned out, Auer never took the book to Atlanta. He had left it on a table in his Miami apartment, where it was recovered by the Dolphins. And Auer, who played out a fifth season and qualified for his pension with the Falcons, is now a successful businessman in Miami.

Rick Norton, the earnest, gentlemanly Kentuckian, was a tormented young man during preseason training. He yearned to succeed, yet somehow knew he would not. The $350,000 contract haunted his scrupulous conscience. Rick could not read about it without squirming, and it seemed to be constantly in the papers. In 1968 he endured the further abasement of being ranked No. 3 quarterback, behind rookie Kim Hammond and Griese. Hammond was a Florida State University product drafted as a local attraction. But Griese had reduced the competition to virtual anonymity anyway.

> They were trying to get me on a stretcher. Not me. I wasn't about to get carried out of there like a dead man in front of 30,000 people.
>
> —LARRY CSONKA

13. *Paper Cups and Motorcycles*

The 1968 exhibition season was memorable more for its soaring attendance than performance, although rookies Larry Csonka and Dick Anderson demonstrated their abilities immediately. Csonka rammed for 90 yards and Anderson intercepted three passes in the 28–28 opener against Buffalo.

Rookie Jim Keyes, the No. 2 draftee out of Mississippi, blew a 17-yard field-goal opportunity with 15 seconds left. And a quorum of 11,200 at Rochester's St. Thomas Aquinas High School Field soured Robbie on neutral sites. He had been committed to the game, however, in view of Buffalo's trip to Memphis for the St. Jude Hospital exhibition the year before.

But the game at home in Miami three weeks later made Robbie forget about Rochester. "That's when I knew beyond all doubt that our struggle would succeed," he said. The lure of John Unitas and the Baltimore Colts put 68,125 customers in the Orange Bowl the night of August 31. No crowd approaching that figure had ever been recorded by the

Dolphins before. And though Shula's Colts beat the Dolphins 22–13, the fact that they were not humiliated, parlayed with victories over Philadelphia (23–7) and Atlanta (19–13), gave Wilson his first hopeful exhibition season.

It was not conducted without the usual anguish. The record was an uninspiring (for any team but the Dolphins) 2-2-1 because of a 19–17 loss to the Boston Patriots in Jacksonville. Booth Lusteg missed a 30-yard field-goal shot with 15 seconds left. The 29-year-old journeyman was cut four days later.

"Boothie was a great kicker of paper cups," Wilson said, with reference to a habit Lusteg cultivated in practices. Wilson would stare, entranced, at the form and dedication Booth applied to this task.

Lusteg brought dedication to everything he did. As a potential actor born in New Haven, he polished a sterling New England accent. But he played little football either around his home or at the University of Connecticut.

Boothie drifted to New York as a math teacher and was living in Flushing, near Shea Stadium, when he responded to a Jets' public tryout in the Bronx as a kicker. Coach Weeb Ewbank was impressed enough to invite Lusteg to training camp, where he was beaten out by rookie Jim Turner. But he now had the kicking bug.

After two years with the New Bedford Sweepers in the Atlantic Coast League, Lusteg reported to Buffalo's camp for a tryout. He had learned that a kicker's chances are enhanced if he can play another position. So he told the Bills he was a defensive back. Also suspecting that interest might be minimal in a 27-year-old rookie from Connecticut who had no football background, Booth solved that detail by impersonating his brother, who was two years younger and had played football at Boston College.

"And gentlemen," Booth announced, "I know more about the scientific art of placekicking than any man in the world."

It looked like he did. Lusteg won the job and in 1966 was the AFL's second-leading scorer. He kicked 19 of 38 field-goal attempts, 41 of 42 conversions, to finish with 98 points.

Boothie was shrewd enough to invent gimmicks. One of them was circling the football field, in full uniform, before the pregame warmups. Soon Lusteg became so popular that reporters began searching his background; he was quickly exposed as his brother. Or his brother was exposed. In any case, Booth became unnerved. He started missing and was dismissed by the Bills.

He arrived in Miami carrying a little blue bag that was his trademark. In it were his shoes and kicking tee. After Gene Mingo was out, Lusteg finished the 1967 season with seven field goals in 12 attempts and 18 for 18 on extra points. But Wilson regarded Lusteg with more amusement than gratitude. And when Jim Keyes was drafted No. 2, Lusteg's brief candle was out.

When Wahoo McDaniel and Jim Warren, usually among the contract recalcitrants, signed the day before the season opener, the Dolphins surfaced as one big, reasonably happy family. Still there were danger signals. Jack Clancy, the spectacular rookie who had caught a record 67 passes, injured his left knee when decked after grabbing a pass in the Baltimore exhibition. Clancy was through for the year, and Griese lost his favorite receiver.

The Dolphins continued to stumble as the regular season began. Predictably, they lost three straight, all before steadily dwindling home audiences.

With 40,067 viewing the first regular-season game, the Oilers built a 17–3 lead in 20 minutes and coasted. Griese heard the jeers reserved for all quarterbacks as he threw three interceptions. He got very little protection, however, and the ground game Wilson worked at so doggedly in the exhibition season was at best sporadic. Starters Larry Csonka and Stan (Bronko) Mitchell were big but slow.

Of Wilson's other running backs, Jack Harper was sidelined with a pinched neck nerve and Jim Kiick was returning kickoffs with safety Bob Neff. Third-year fullback Sam Price had lost favor. "Bad hands," the coaches said.

Trouble arrived in clusters that week. Mitchell was hospitalized with appendicitis. Safety Bob Petrella broke a thumb, defensive tackle Ray Jacobs was out with a deep calf bruise. And the game of musical linebackers continued with Wahoo McDaniel unseating Frank Emanuel again in the middle. Wilson, who liked Wahoo, had saved his job in camp against a majority opinion that the 30-year-old Choctaw was finished. The indomitable Wahoo had even threatened to leave town and take up full-time wrestling unless the Dolphins sweetened his contract.

For the first time, and only out of necessity, Csonka and Kiick were paired in the backfield against Oakland. The AFL champions (and 33–14 losers to Green Bay in the Super Bowl) attracted only 30,021 to the Orange Bowl while destroying the Dolphins 47–21. Csonka was limited to 17 yards in 12 carries. Kiick, who gained 15 yards in five carries and caught five passes for 41 yards, proved tops among the Dolphins. Jim, a pro from the start, was badly needed. Harper, handicapped by injuries and a 5-10, 190-pound frame, was finished. His pinched neck nerve, similar to the injury that dogged Paul Hornung and eventually retired him, was diagnosed as too dangerous to risk aggravation.

Seven Miami regulars were out in the third game as the Chiefs romped 48–3. Wilson yanked Griese and installed Norton in the second half. Griese had completed 2 passes of

17 and was sacked three times for 35 yards. Physically, the unfortunate Norton fared worse. Rick broke a bone in his left hand.

"I know we're a better team," Wilson insisted. "The big thing now is to get some of these injured guys back. All of a sudden we're going to break loose."

Moreau, Jacobs and Westmoreland returned for the Houston game, Miami's first in the Astrodome. Wilson decided to go with ball control and succeeded, 24–7. Kiick carried 26 times for 104 yards to lead the most satisfying victory the Dolphins had ever achieved. But the satisfaction lasted only one week.

Returning to the Orange Bowl, the Dolphins awarded a tie to the weak Buffalo Bills. With a 14–6 lead in the last two minutes, the Dolphins dropped a lineman and added a linebacker to protect against the passes to come. So a quarterback named Dan Darragh completed 7 of 10 while taking the Bills 80 yards to the end zone, where he hit halfback Gary McDermott with 18 seconds to go. The Bills lined up for a two-point conversion (permissible in the AFL) with Ed Rutkowski at quarterback. Rutkowski then passed again to McDermott for the tie.

Worse than the result was a head injury suffered by Csonka. Larry was not conscious of proceedings from the moment he caught a down-the-middle pass until he realized a photographer was standing on his hand as the fullback lay sprawled behind the bench. He had lost about five minutes.

"I don't even remember going back to the huddle after the pass," he said in Mercy Hospital. "Did I do a decent job on the next play?"

He did. Larry had smacked 11 yards up the middle to the Buffalo five-yard line, where he took another head blow that forced him out of action.

"It feels like a mule kicked me," he said. "Funny thing, though, I can't remember any pain. The first thing I remember is this guy standing on my hand taking pictures."

When Csonka managed to free himself from the foot and the surrounding medics, he insisted on getting up. "The Hunky in me," he said. "They were trying to get me on a stretcher. Not me. I wasn't about to get carried out of there like a dead man in front of 30,000 people."

Bobby Neff, the little defensive handyman who had stuck around on guts for three years, was another victim of the Buffalo game with a wrenched knee. Neff was missed as much for his rustic naiveté as his ability. From a place called Hearne, Texas, Bobby had seen very little of the world. Once, in Oakland, he was kept waiting for a supper date with three teammates who had spent the afternoon across the bay in San Francisco.

"Listen, where were you guys?" Neff demanded when they showed up an hour late.

"We're sorry, Bob," one of them said. "We got held up waiting for the Golden Gate Bridge to come down. The ocean traffic was something fierce."

"Oh," Neff said. "Well, I wish you guys would look ahead to things like that. I'm hungry."

All the Dolphins were hungry by the time they entered Cincinnati for their first experience against Paul Brown's new Bengals. Miami won 24–22 on Griese's scrambling and three touchdown passes, the last a 31-yarder to Mitchell. "Bronko" had recovered from his appendicitis operation just in time to replace Csonka at fullback.

John Stofa, on the other hand, completed just 4 of 10 before being replaced by Dewey Warren in the second quarter. Stofa, whose trade had been panned in the Miami press, heard a steady cascade of boos that bright afternoon in Nippert Stadium. "We catch hell for trading him and they catch hell for taking him," Robbie observed. "It's unfair."

But life is unfair, as the Dolphins rediscovered the following Sunday in Denver. Csonka returned with a 97-yard performance, including a 12-yard touchdown smash that left a swale of Broncos in his wake. Griese completed 16 of 26 passes for 246 yards, including a five-yarder to the recovered Moreau for a touchdown. But the Dolphins blew a 14-point lead in the second half to a prodigious black quarterback named Marlin Briscoe. In relief of Steve Tensi, the 5-10, 177-pound Briscoe scrambled 12 and 10 yards to touchdowns, the second of these in the last two minutes to produce a 21–14 victory.

Wahoo was missing from the lineup in the aftermath of an episode Wilson termed "the last straw." On Friday evening in the Mile High City he knew as well as any, Wahoo was visiting a few familiar haunts with Bob Bruggers, a 24-year-old linebacker who had functioned mainly in reserve and on special teams in his three Miami seasons.

Wahoo had taken a liking to Bruggers, whose style was as silent as his tiny home town of Blomkest, Minn. Bruggers had genuine potential as a 6-1, 230-pound linebacker. But Wahoo saw the youth as a potential man of the world as well. So before very long, the wide-eyed Bruggers was accompanying McDaniel to saloons, the Hialeah Race Course, boxing and wrestling matches. By the time they reached Denver, the pair was inseparable. "He's my faithful white companion," Wahoo said.

The two pals were leaving a Denver lounge, where they'd had a couple of beers, according to Wahoo, for the trip back to the Hilton. But driving a rental, Wahoo backed into another car. He shrugged and started off, only to be accosted by a furious citizen "who came reaching in the window after my keys," said McDaniel.

Wahoo leaped out of the car and admitted that some "shoving" took place. In any case, McDaniel was arrested. The car he had hit belonged to an offduty policeman, and McDaniel turned out to be remonstrating with the man himself.

Wahoo was arrested and charged with malicious destruction of property, attempting to leave the scene of an accident, resisting arrest and driving while intoxicated. Bruggers, who was not charged at all, followed his friend to jail in an attempt to bail him out. Both blew the curfew in the process. At the station, Bruggers phoned Wilson. He needed a little money to spring his friend.

Wilson arrived at the station and discovered that "their tongues were so thick you couldn't understand them," as he said. "And they were having trouble standing up."

Wahoo and Bruggers were dismissed on the spot. End of a long, colorful pro trail for McDaniel, though Bruggers would catch on at San Diego.

As Wahoo rode off into the sunset, a new personality appeared. Monday after the Denver game the Dolphins conducted a mock signing ceremony featuring Jim Hines, at which the Olympic champion, wearing the gold medal he had earned for a world record 9.9 clocking in the 100 meters, was tendered a three-year contract worth an estimated $75,000. The actual signing had taken place the Thursday before in Las Vegas. "Perhaps the safest gamble ever made there," Robbie said.

"Football has always been my first love," Hines said. "But it won't be easy. I went to college on a track scholarship, I haven't played football since high school."

Still, the Dolphins were optimistic. Hines was a product of McClymonds High in Oakland, the athletic proving ground for such as Bill Russell, Frank Robinson, Curt Flood and Vada Pinson among others.

But the more Wilson studied Hines, the more discouraged he became. Before the year ended, the slight 175-pounder earned the nickname "Oops" from his teammates. The football simply seemed to be repelled by Hines' long, wiry fingers. His breathtaking speed compensated somewhat, and he managed to linger two years before Don Shula finally released him in December 1970.

Hines presented a pitiful figure in his three seasons with the Dolphins. From the start, fellow employees resented both his contract and inability to contribute. He was extremely shy and quiet. Nor did Jim ever display emotion or engage in clubhouse camaraderie. As a result he was never generally accepted and walked a lonely path.

At San Diego the week after Denver, Griese put on a spectacular show. He completed 20 of 27 passes for 260 yards while throwing for three scores and setting up a fourth in what Charger Coach Sid Gillman called "one of the classiest performances I've ever seen." But the Dolphins lost 34–28 as their defense collapsed. Worse, Csonka appeared in serious trouble. He had been forced from the Denver game with a recurrence of his head injury. After gaining 61 yards in nine carries at San Diego, Larry was helped to the bench in the second quarter. "I can't understand it, but it's really got me down. I didn't remember a thing until the fourth quarter."

Since the departure of Wahoo, Wilson's linebacking was woefully bad. Emanuel, John Bramlett and Randall Edmunds did not begin to do the job. And the coach blanched but said nothing when he heard a San Diego writer suggest somebody should organize a search party for Miami's linebackers.

Back home before a date at Buffalo, Csonka's head injury was as upsetting as the Dolphins' 2-5-1 record.

"If this keeps up, Csonka will have to reevaluate his occupation," said one Miami neurosurgeon. "Or he may become like a punch-drunk fighter."

Another doctor disagreed. "Most concussions last no longer than 20 minutes and are seldom accompanied by brain-cell damage. It just takes a little while to recover."

Csonka's electroencephalograph reading was normal, but his headaches persisted. Nevertheless, he was determined to practice. Then, the following Thursday night at home, Larry nearly passed out. Unable to keep the mulish Csonka in Mercy Hospital, Dr. Herb Virgin, the team physician, was at least determined he would not play another minute without a special protective helmet. So Bob Lundy, the Dolphins' trainer, ordered such a helmet containing air cells and fluid. The fluid pumped up resistance and worked like a shock absorber.

Csonka was not happy at the prospect. "I'm afraid the thing will weigh me down. My brains are heavy enough already."

With Csonka indisposed, Kiick ran wild in Buffalo's War Memorial Stadium. Jim amassed 111 yards in 23 carries, including a four-yard smash over right tackle Norm Evans to pull out a 21–17 fourth-quarter victory.

From the Buffalo game on, the Dolphins took a rollercoaster ride, behaving either very well or very badly, to finish the season with a 5-8-1 record but the best three-year mark (12-29-1) an expansion team had ever managed.

With no effective middle linebacker and its thin line erased by injury, the defense was inconsistent. John Stofa returned the week after Buffalo to lead Cincinnati to a 38–21 Orange Bowl victory. The following Sunday at Boston, with the cushion-helmeted Csonka back on the field, the Dolphins erupted 34–10. Then came a 35–17 loss at New York, when 38-year-old Babe Parilli fired three late touchdown passes.

Jim Keyes, forced into linebacking duty in New York, tore a leg muscle. In desperation, Wilson handed field-goal chores to the left-footed Doug Moreau, who hadn't kicked competitively since his college days. Keyes was the fifteenth Dolphin of the season to enter Mercy Hospital.

Stan Mitchell became the sixteenth the following week when he broke his big toe in a motorcycle accident that also cost him a $200 fine. "If we needed a motorcycle act, I'd have let Mitch know," Wilson said.

The Dolphins won their first home game of the year, 38–7, against the Patriots, a shell of a team. Still, the victory was not without complications. Griese bruised a knee. And so Wilson decided to "sink or swim" with Norton in the finale against the Jets, who had already clinched the Eastern Division title.

The presence of Joe Namath & Co. brought out 32,843 customers, the most since opening day.

"I'll play as long as it takes to win the game, or as long as Weeb wants me to," said Namath, who on Saturday was opening a Broadway Joe's short-order shop on Miami's swinging 79th Street. Namath jawed into a "Touchdown Roast Beef Sandwich" with gusto. But two years later the place folded.

The Dolphins were in the game until Moreau's 14-yard field-goal attempt in the first quarter struck an upright. Then the Jets went on to win 31–7.

Despite the poor home record (1-5-1) and a defensive breakdown that allowed opponents an average of 25 points, Wilson's 5-8-1 credentials had fulfilled his goal of "improving on our 4-11 1967 season." The Dolphins had the nucleus of an offense with Griese, Csonka, Kiick, Noonan (11 touchdown pass receptions) and the steady Twilley, but they had small defensive muscle.

The pass rush was absent. "One guy, Manny Fernandez, is the only one we can depend on," Wilson said. "And he's a rookie getting double-teamed already." The linebacking was worse. With Wahoo gone, there was no one at middle. Largely because of such weaknesses, the Dolphins had never beaten the strong AFL teams—Oakland, New York and Kansas City. They lost three of four with San Diego, an early power beginning to fade in 1968. Against the top four in three seasons, Wilson's combined record was 1-18. Against the rest of the league the Dolphins were 11-11-1.

But Wilson's contract was now about to expire. Robbie remained silent through the draft and into February, for he was in the midst of another battle, a battle in which the Miami franchise was at stake.

> What happens to a dream deferred?
> Does it dry up
> Like a raisin in the sun?
> Maybe it just sags
> Like a heavy load
> Or does it explode?
>
> —LANGSTON HUGHES

14. *How to Succeed in Business*

In December 1968, Bud Keland tried to fire Joe Robbie as the managing partner of the Dolphins. In fact, Keland tried to eliminate Robbie from the operation altogether. Keland's decision came as a shock to those who thought they knew this mild, pleasant, silent partner, who had begun buying Miami stock in January 1967.

Robbie had been borrowing heavily to stay in business. Interest from his original $7.5 million commitment and at least $4 million more in operating expenses since then were draining everything but his boundless energy. The scrappy lawyer was the most desperate rooter the football team had. Robbie brought bankers to practices to check his collateral on the field. Bob Griese and Larry Csonka and Jim Kiick helped.

Once, in Chicago to seek a badly needed loan, Robbie pleaded his case before a bank director. When he had finished, the director asked him, "If you were sitting in my chair listening to what you have just told me, what would you do?"

"I'd throw me out," Robbie said.

Robbie got his money.

Business began to look a bit better in the spring of 1967. Keland enjoyed having a piece of a football team and wanted more. So Robbie agreed to divide his own holdings in the limited Miami football corporation on an equal basis with Keland. At the same time they acquired the interest of George Gillett.

Gillett had entered the organization with Keland, but soon discovered that Robbie didn't want a business manager. Chuck Burr and Suncoast Sports had cured him of delegating responsibility. Furthermore, Robbie did not get along with the 28-year-old Gillett.

Shortly after Keland and Robbie bought him out, Gillett announced that he planned to take active ownership and control of the Harlem Globetrotters, left rudderless since the death of their founder, Abe Saperstein. Gillett's partners in the $3,710,000 investment were John O'Neil, the Miamian still retaining his share in the Dolphins despite his own differences with Robbie, and Potter Palmer of Chicago, O'Neil's brother-in-law. In a masterpiece of self-restraint, Robbie said Gillett was leaving with the blessings and good wishes of the Dolphins.

Keland's partnership with Robbie was secure. In a formal announcement that September, Robbie made no bones about it. "Bud and I will function with equal responsibility toward the goal of bringing a championship football team to Miami."

In the ensuing year Keland seemed more than content to let Robbie make the decisions. The likable, shy executive appeared at an occasional practice, but otherwise kept his observations to himself.

By 1968, Robbie and O'Neil were enemies. After the first season, Robbie had fired O'Neil from his contrived post of community relations director. O'Neil didn't seem to care. He had a variety of financial interests and seemed happier at golf or the race track than pretending to work. But beneath a carefree exterior, O'Neil smoldered. He was, after all, an original investor; why should he be ignored? O'Neil's attitude emerged in a civil suit late in 1969. He accused Robbie of misusing funds, breach of contractual duties and attempting to deprive him of his rights as a partner.

So Keland, naturally, had O'Neil's encouragement when he moved to oust Robbie and acquire the club in December 1968. The case was put before NFL Commissioner Pete Rozelle to arbitrate. The ownership issue remained in doubt for nearly four months while Robbie feverishly sought more partners and more capital.

George Wilson found himself in the middle of all this when the 1968 season ended and his contract was up. Rozelle had stipulated that until the ownership issue was resolved, neither partner could make an executive decision without the agreement of the other.

"Something's up," Wilson said. "I don't know what it is, but it looks like there might be some changes around here."

Robbie only said, "Under the circumstances, this is no time to make hasty decisions. I have some other business to take care of before I can get into this coaching thing thoroughly."

Keland said nothing, as usual.

In the end, Robbie simply outmatched the subdued Keland. While Robbie knew absolutely everything about his ball club, Keland had spent little time and shown only a small inclination to familiarize himself with the house that Robbie built from scratch.

One incident in particular destroyed whatever chance Keland might have had in Rozelle's eyes. In January 1969 it was established that Keland was an acquaintance of Salvatore

(Sam) Rizzo, a Miami builder whose past connections had been scrutinized by the FBI. Rizzo was a friend of Frank Sinatra's, and both were reportedly hoping to buy into the lineup of the feuding Dolphin partners.

Keland denied any serious financial discussions with Rizzo, also a former racetrack and Nevada gambling casino owner, though he admitted that "Rizzo once said in a flippant way to me, 'If you ever want to sell the Dolphins, let me know.'" But this was enough for Rozelle.

Robbie seemed confident he would surmount the crisis. Rozelle gave him 90 days to find new partners. For two reasons this was an easier alternative than it would have been earlier: realignment of the AFL and NFL into one league seemed imminent, and Joe Namath and the New York Jets had lifted the AFL to respectability with their 16–7 Super Bowl victory over the Baltimore Colts.

Before leaving for the owners' meetings in Palm Springs, Calif., Robbie settled another piece of unfinished business. On March 11, after a "mutual agreement" with Keland, Robbie announced the contract of Wilson and his four assistants would be renewed for the 1969 season.

The coach was far from elated with this one-year renewal and the suspense he had endured to get it. But as he was disposed to do so often in what would become his darkest season in 33 years at the game, Wilson made the best of it. "I'm glad to be back," he said. "We have a good group of players and we've worked hard to get as far as we have. In the next couple of years it could all break our way."

"The progress of a new team is necessarily slow, but it *must* be steady," Robbie added. "The composite three-year record is better than any earlier expansion team. And while the margin is narrow, it does represent progress toward our goal to develop a champion."

Progress, however, had not been fast enough to suit Robbie. There was dissatisfaction with the progress of the younger players. Wilson could handle experienced people, it was said, but as a teacher he was remiss. The Dolphins lacked training in the fundamentals.

Robbie's energies could now be transferred to the Palm Springs meeting of the owners, which ended in a stalemate. The NFL majority favored a retention of the two-league arrangement, while Robbie and Cincinnati's Paul Brown were the early leaders of a group demanding what was rightfully theirs.

"We stand on the merger documents. It's that simple," Brown said. "When we paid our money to get into the league, we were told we would be in the Western Division of the AFL, but not to let that bother us because there'd be realignment in 1970. And we were given a document that says there would be realignment. That's how I presented it to my owners."

The voices of the NFL establishment offered the bone of interleague games within the prevailing two-league arrangement. Typically smug was the late Vince Lombardi's observation that "the American Football League paid $18 million for the common draft and a Super Bowl."

To AFL owners, Lombardi was not the epitome of virtue as extolled by sycophants bent on deifying the coach since his death. At Green Bay and Washington, Lombardi was consistently arrogant and gratuitous toward the AFL, apparently because the league had the temerity to exist at all. Lombardi and his fellow NFL priests conveniently forgot that the $18 million fee paid by the old AFL clubs to the San Francisco 49ers and New York Giants bordered more closely on extortion than "indemnification." The NFL claimed by some sort of squatter's rights' reasoning that Oakland and the New York Jets had no business to muscle in on territory declared untouchable by the 49ers and Giants. Al Capone could not have reasoned it out more clearly while discouraging competition in Chicago.

Lombardi and his budding monopolists also forgot that the AFL had the NFL with its tail between its legs before the merger agreement. A talented sack of NFL stars had been signed, sealed and all but delivered under the commando raiding directed by Al Davis, the AFL commissioner who succeeded Joe Foss for that very purpose.

Robbie needed total realignment. He was painfully aware of South Florida's burning indifference toward such Orange Bowl opponents as Denver and Houston and Boston and San Diego, and even Oakland and Kansas City on a regular basis. In three seasons the Dolphins had averaged less than 30,000 and sold less than 14,000 season tickets on the premise of AFL opposition. Robbie also needed to convince prospective new owners that the Dolphins represented a solid future investment. Only total realignment under the NFL banner would assure potential partners and customers alike that Miami was indeed big league.

Robbie got his way, as usual, but not without a battle. Ralph Wilson, Buffalo's owner who helped lay the groundwork for the 1966 common draft and future agreements, credits Carroll Rosenbloom with finding the formula that eventually would be agreeable to both factions. "Carroll is really the architect of the merger," Wilson said. "Among his suggestions were interleague games starting in 1967, with eventual interleague championship games and the pooling of all television money. Basically, this was the formula we adopted."

On Saturday night, May 10, after the 26 owners had conferred for 36 hours in New York, realignment became reality. Robbie was elated. The Dolphins were placed in the Eastern

Division of the American Football Conference with Baltimore, New York, Boston and Buffalo. "I would have been happy to have either the Jets or Colts in our division. This is absolutely perfect," Robbie said. Baltimore's Rosenbloom, Cleveland's Art Modell and Pittsburgh's Art Rooney agreed to switch to the American Conference in 1970, thereby creating two balanced leagues of 13 teams each.

Five days later, Robbie announced that five prominent Miamians had joined the organization as limited partners. Robbie's triumph was complete. The five who joined Robbie bought out Keland's interest, leaving Robbie sole majority partner with undisputed control of the operation.

Again Robbie had scrambled from the brink of the cliff to ownership security. Just as he had persuaded Danny Thomas to invest in the beginning, and later replaced Thomas with Keland after a chance airport meeting uncovered common interests, Robbie had beaten Rozelle's three-month deadline to find new investors or lose the club.

This time Robbie hit the jackpot through Scott Peake, a Miamian who had done promotional work for the Dolphins. Peake sounded out Sloan McCrea, a prominent local businessman who was not himself interested in a football team but thought he knew a man who was. The man was J. Earl Smalley, a persuasive and energetic citizen of the world as well-known for his effervescence as his investments. Smalley's influence and refusal to waver when doubts arose over the soundness of the Dolphins were mainly responsible for forging Robbie's new deal. Smalley recruited an affluent coalition including Frank Callahan, Harper Sibley, James McLamore and Wilbur Morrison. These five formed the nucleus of the new arrangement.

"Until McCrea spoke with me, I'd had no idea the Dolphins were available for investment," Smalley said. "In fact,

I'd never seen the team play nor had any interest at all in football. Essentially, it was a community-oriented venture. We knew it would be a long time before we saw any profits. And until Shula came along, we never dreamed the team would be so successful so soon."

Outgoing and pleasantly aggressive, Smalley recruited partners with the speed he made friends. In the Palm Bay Club parking lot, not far from the spot Danny Thomas had introduced pro football to Miami from a supine position four years earlier, Sibley was admiring Smalley's sumptuous, bar-equipped camper, dubbed "What a Way to Go." Smalley lived by the slogan.

"It was about 11 o'clock in the morning," Smalley said. "I asked Harper if he wanted to come in with us on the Dolphins. He said he'd think it over and get back to me. By five in the afternoon he called and said, 'Count me in.' We'd had some problems and a few people backed out because ugly rumors were being spread by some anti-Robbie people. But Sibley, Callahan, McLamore and Morrison were with me from the start."

These five, and others who entered later, were worth millions in investments and corporate interests throughout the world. Robbie, however, retained sole responsibility for debts and interest on loans he had amassed the first four years. He also retained responsibility for all decisions outside the coaching realm.

Robbie was jubilant over the coup. "The Miami Dolphins are now a community project as never before," he said. "This is what I've wanted for four years."

> He asked me how big I was and I told him 183, exaggerating a little. He asked me if I still wanted to play pro football and I said, "Does a boll weevil like cotton?"
>
> —JOHN BRAMLETT

15. *Controlling the Press*

On March 24, Nick Buoniconti was acquired from Boston in exchange for reserve quarterback Kim Hammond and outside linebacker John Bramlett. The swap looked too good. Was something wrong with Buoniconti, who in seven seasons with the Patriots was all-AFL middle linebacker five times? A knee injury had restricted his services to eight games in 1968, and cynics suspected the Dolphins were getting damaged goods.

Hammond had shown no more than promise in a year of bench duty behind Bob Griese. Bramlett had been a solid if erratic contributor for two seasons, but at 210 pounds he possessed more bravado than strength. And John's freewheeling attitude and extracurricular activities suited neither Wilson nor Robbie.

Bramlett, who possessed a rare exuberance, would trade blows with anybody, on or off the field. In fact, "The Bull" was facetiously requested by his teammates to wear a bell so they would know when he was in the vicinity. It made no difference to John which color uniform he hit. After winning almost every athletic award Memphis State had to give, Bramlett got a break two years out of college when a Memphis State coach hired by the Denver Broncos looked him up.

"He asked me how big I was and I told him 183, exaggerating a little. He asked me if I still wanted to play pro football and I said, 'Does a boll weevil like cotton?' "

So Bramlett went on a weight program and became a linebacking tiger at Denver before the Dolphins got him in the midst of a contract dispute he was having with the Broncos. Bramlett would continue to menace in Miami. But he also became a discipline problem, and finally it was decided that he should be banished.

To get Buoniconti in the same deal represented a major coup. "I'll never understand why the Patriots made that trade," Joe Thomas was to say over and over again. Buoniconti functioned not only with brilliance in the middle but as an extra coach for the young linebackers flanking him.

The draft that January had produced Bill Stanfill, the Georgia all-American and the nation's premier college lineman. A defensive end, the 6-5 Bulldog captain was a strong pass rusher, and Thomas bypassed Miami's Ted Hendricks to take Stanfill No. 1.

A few other rookies who were to impress that year included 6-7 Bob Heinz, the No. 2 draftee; Eugene (Mercury) Morris, No. 3; and a couple of sleepers—linebacker Jesse Powell (No. 9) and cornerback Lloyd Mumphord (No. 16). But most of the newcomers that ominous July at St. Andrew's were not conspicuous.

Wilson's mood was volcanic. Feeling the pressure of his single-year contract extension, the 55-year-old coach erupted one afternoon in the first of a series of explosions that would contribute to the wreck of a dismal season.

The Whistle Stop Bar in Boca Raton was a frequent source of banter and relaxation for coaches and press. Wilson had a new reporter to contend with that summer, Jim O'Brien of *The Miami News,* and the coach planned to "break him in" properly. Wilson liked reporters to see eye to eye with him, and there were disturbing signs that the curious O'Brien had arrived from Pittsburgh with his own ideas.

The first night of camp, George invited the press to the Whistle Stop for a few rounds of cheer. O'Brien was delighted to join the group. In the salubrious course of events, Wilson initiated a discussion with the newcomer. George outlined his coaching philosophy, his problems and his own attitudes.

O'Brien, of course, was all ears. And his attention increased as Wilson discussed the coaching idols of the era, particularly Vince Lombardi, who had won three straight NFL championships and two Super Bowls before quitting Green Bay in triumph in 1968. "I'm tired of this Lombardi business," Wilson told O'Brien. "Given the same material I will beat him every time. That's because I can get a team up on the day of the game." (Lombardi was a favorite Wilson target after succeeding the late Ray "Scooter" McLean at Green Bay. McLean had been Wilson's roommate on the Bears, and George loyally gave him credit for starting the dynasty Lombardi developed.)

A few days later O'Brien asked Wilson if he could use the material, and Wilson agreed. The subsequent story was snapped up by the wire services and became a national conversation piece, like the "Joe Doakes" appellation that Wilson fired at Don Shula during 1972 Super Bowl week.

O'Brien entered Wilson's doghouse.

"If I thought I could beat Lombardi every time, I ought to be making $100,000 a game or be locked up somewhere," Wilson said. And with that he canceled his daily noon press conferences, saying, "I've been misquoted on a few things lately by guys who apparently don't know much about pro football. So I think I'll just cut out our meetings."

Wilson was also upset by a story that appeared after he slashed 20 rookies from the training camp roster the same day he learned that tight end Jim Cox needed a knee operation and defensive back Bobby Neff would be out indefinitely with a twisted knee. This reporter felt that cutting 20 people after less than two weeks in camp might have been a bit hasty.

"Listen," the coach snapped, "we're through picking up junk nobody wants. We're not an expansion team any more. We're out to win. And remember, I wasn't the guy who brought all these free agents to camp."

Joe Thomas, the guy who did, was furious when the quote was published.

Wilson's "junk" charge centered around a tight-end candidate named Bud Norris, who had been drafted sixth in 1967 out of Washington State. Norris did not set foot on a practice field until 1969. John Idzik, Miami's offensive backfield coach, described Norris as a "hospital case." And the 6-5 redhead had indeed logged more hospital time than the average orderly.

"I never got a chance here," Norris said on being cut. "I'm not blaming Coach Wilson. He knows how to handle a man. But I certainly can't say the same for the front office. All they wanted was to get me healthy again so they could put me on the field and cut me. I got a two-year, no-cut contract and a bonus. Now I'm even having a tough time collecting my bonus."

Robbie exploded, emphasizing in no uncertain terms that Norris had been paid $17,500 by the Dolphins without practicing so much as a minute. "We brought him to camp," Robbie said, "to see if something couldn't be salvaged from our investment."

The Norris case underlined why pro scouts hesitate to sign

even the most promising athlete with a medical problem. Though Norris had won four basketball and three football letters in college, in his senior year he incurred right knee surgery. But Thomas took a chance.

"We checked his doctor and trainer at Washington State," Thomas said. "Both assured us that Norris would be ready for full-time duty when camp opened in 1967."

In April 1967, the Dolphins signed Norris to a $15,000 no-cut contract together with a $7,500 bonus.

"He received the bonus immediately, as well as $5,000 of his contract. He was building a home for his parents, so we helped him out. And we agreed to pay him another $5,000 when he reported," Robbie said.

Between April and July, however, the knee injury was aggravated during therapy. When Norris reached camp he could barely walk.

"We paid him the $5,000 anyway," Thomas said. "We could have refused and even reclaimed the rest of the money because he couldn't pass the physical. But we compromised with him, even though a draftee must come to camp fit or his contract is voided.

"Norris signed the compromise figure, his legal counsel signed it and the Players' Association representative signed it."

Norris underwent further surgery in the fall of 1967, this time by Dr. Virgin, the Dolphins' physician. Both knee operations were paid for by Washington State, where the knee was injured. Norris was then sidelined all of 1968 while his contract was "tolled" (held over) until 1969.

"It was a straightaway deal. He had to make the club," Thomas said.

When Wilson dismissed him quickly, nobody was happy, particularly when Norris instigated the beef. Both Robbie and Thomas understandably felt that Norris had extracted enough cash for not playing.

Poor Wilson then got beat 45–10 by the Minnesota Vikings in the exhibition opener at Tampa. Robbie, who had practiced law in Minneapolis, had wanted desperately to make a good showing against the Vikings. But Wilson, insisting that exhibition games don't mean a thing, substituted for his regulars early "to build depth on the squad"—though it quickly became clear that depth was still missing.

Wilson stuck to his plan of testing the unknowns, to the chagrin of Dolphin fans who watched succeeding losses to the Chicago Bears (16–10) and Philadelphia Eagles (14–10).

The Chicago game was highlighted by a free-for-all featuring middle linebacker Dick Butkus and Larry Little, a 285-pound guard acquired in July from San Diego. In the bench-emptying contretemps, umpire Ralph (Red) Morcroft was bleeding from the thumb and accusing Butkus of biting him. Wilson hoped the fight would lift morale.

But the club kept losing. The Dolphins dropped a 28–21 decision at Cincinnati before returning home before 56,665 and losing to Baltimore 23–10.

Griese had played only sporadically except for the Chicago game, in which he completed just 6 of 20 passes with four interceptions. At Cincinnati, all four Bengal touchdowns followed Griese interceptions that set up drives from Miami's 18, 41, 32 and 29.

Rick Norton, as usual, had nothing but trouble. And aggravating the Norton situation was the fact that Cincinnati had put John Stofa on waivers. Many wondered why Wilson did not claim the local favorite and dismiss Norton.

Wilson was worried. As his old friend Les Bingaman observed more than once that summer, "The boss is not himself." There were problems on the coaching staff. Wilson either kept to himself or huddled with John Idzik. The division left Ernie Hefferle and Tom Keane at loose ends. Bingaman was torn between his loyalty to Wilson and a terrible feeling that "nothin's goin' right. We need to get together, all of us, for a long talk."

Hefferle and Keane were frustrated. Evening squad meetings were brief and sometimes canceled for no apparent reason. And returning from Boca Raton one night, Bingaman failed to reckon with a treacherous 90-degree curve in the unlighted road leading to St. Andrew's. Though Bingo's car was nearly demolished, the big man walked away from it. He had more pressing problems.

Through this uneasy period, Wilson retained the respect and affection of most of his players. "He's a down-to-earth guy you want to get out and do something for," Jim Kiick said. "I've never seen him cut a ballplayer down in public. That tells me something."

Wilson had once taken the time to write a letter to Kiick's father, George, who had played for Bucknell and the Pittsburgh Steelers: "As one father and ex-football player to another," Wilson wrote, "I just want to express our pride here in Miami that Jim Kiick wears a Dolphin uniform."

In the summer of 1968 when black safetyman Willie West acknowledged that the quota system had deprived him of a job with the St. Louis Cardinals five years earlier, Wilson countered in strong terms. "No Negro will be cut because he's a Negro on this squad," the coach said. "And let me add that no Negro will be kept because he's a Negro, either. My job is to find the 40 best football players around here and win games with them." Wilson praised West as "a gentleman who has given 100 percent and a man I admire." West said nothing. Neither West nor most black athletes who earn a living at the game are about to explore the racial situation publicly.

Wilson worked himself into a rage when more trouble followed the five straight 1969 exhibition defeats. Rudy Barber, a reserve linebacker, told the already exiled sportswriter Jim O'Brien that he had been cut because he was black. "Imagine what a story like that does to my family," Wilson said. "I know Rudy Barber and I know he wouldn't have said a thing like that unless he was coaxed into it."

Wilson found reporter O'Brien at suppertime a couple of days after the story appeared. O'Brien had already dismissed the story, but Wilson was smoldering. "I know I've got to win to keep my job, but if I get fired I'll tell you something, punk. I'll have a great big piece of you. You don't have a shred of human decency, putting a thing like that in the paper. And if anything happens to my family because of it, you'll hear plenty. Nobody messes around where my family's concerned. I ought to wipe up the street with you. I'm from a tough neighborhood, and if I was a ballplayer I'd kick your butt."

Wilson began to calm down as the pudgy, 5-8 O'Brien stood his ground.

"I'll say hello to you from now on," Wilson told him softly, "because I'm a gentleman. But that's it."

Back on the field, Coach Wilson's offensive line was further reduced when Larry Little and Norm Evans suffered sprained knees. Then Larry Csonka's headaches recurred. Larry had also managed to crack his nose and blacken his eye against the Eagles. And there was speculation that Csonka was not long for the game. But he was tough and stubborn, playing three quarters of the Cincinnati exhibition with ice stuffed up his nose.

Csonka was held out of the Baltimore game but insisted he wanted to play the final exhibition against Boston. "He's a mule," said Bob Lundy. However, the trainer reported "a questionable abnormality in the bone surface of the skull."

Csonka was restrained from action. In his place, Stan Mitchell gained 30 yards in 11 carries while catching five passes for 75 yards in a 13–0 conquest of the Patriots—the most encouraging aspect of the dismal summer. But this was erased when further X rays disclosed a bone fracture at the base of Csonka's skull. As the Dolphins prepared to open Wilson's "do-or-die" season at Cincinnati, word came that Csonka would be out indefinitely.

> Something's got to go our way one of these days.
> —NICK BUONICONTI

16. *The Worst Is Yet to Come*

George Wilson said he would be "satisfied" with a 7-7 season in 1969. Joe Robbie's goal was "contention" in the Eastern Conference of the final American Football League season.

The opener at Cincinnati was a harbinger of things to come. Saturday night before the game, 29-year-old linebacker Frank Buncom of the Bengals died in his sleep of a massive blood cot on the lung. His teammates were stunned, but came to Nippert Stadium in a punishing mood. They held off a late rally to beat the Dolphins 27–21, and presented two game balls. One went to Paul Brown for his 300th coaching victory, the other to Buncom's widow and six-week-old son.

"About 7:20 this morning I heard this gasping, like somebody struggling for breath," said Ernie Wright, Buncom's roommate. "I looked over and there was Frank, his body heaving. I knew something was terribly wrong.

"I called the trainer and the doctor, but it was too late. Frank just heaved an awful sigh and died there on the bed.

"Later," Wright continued, "I came down to breakfast with the squad and went through the motions. I've been playing this game so long that it's automatic. But this time everybody was silent. I mean, completely silent."

Nevertheless, the Bengals came out swinging and built a 27–14 lead despite rookie Mercury Morris's 105-yard kickoff return. In the final moments a 49-yard pass from Griese to second-year receiver Gene Milton had got the Dolphins to the 22 with 34 seconds to go. But Griese had used all his time-outs and the Bengals ran out the clock by walking leisurely back to the line of scrimmage.

"What reason in the world did we have to hurry?" Brown asked.

Nick Buoniconti, in his first game as a Dolphin, stood on the field as the players were leaving. Tears streamed down the cheeks of the 28-year-old middle linebacker as he screamed at nobody in particular.

The depressing pattern continued at Oakland the following week. George Blanda kicked a 46-yard field goal with 11 seconds left, to win 20–17. One Raider touchdown followed a perfect Griese pass that bounded off the shoulder pads of Stan Mitchell into the arms of safety Dave Grayson, who seized the ball in stride and had a clear path 68 yards to the end zone.

Head in hands, slouched on a dressing-room bench, Wilson was practically speechless. "The Man upstairs says this isn't it, I guess."

At Houston the following week, the Dolphins blew a 10-point lead and were crushed in the second half 22–10. Mitchell was lost indefinitely with a shoulder separation, and Griese spent another afternoon running for his life in the face of blocking breakdowns.

Buoniconti was the last to get dressed. "I don't know, I

don't know," he said, staring around the nearly empty room. "It was this way at Boston in 1965. We knew we had a good ball club but we kept getting beat. Then all of sudden, we began putting it together. Something's got to go our way one of these days."

Jim Riley, who had won the defensive end job opposite rookie Bill Stanfill (Fernandez was moved inside to tackle), spoke up for the defense. "We were just on the field too long. You can't hold them off forever."

Both sides of the Miami line had similar problems in those days. On Griese's scrambling, guard Billy Neighbors protested, "Looky here, if you can hold them out of there three seconds or so you're doing a helluva job. Do you think them bastards are gonna' stand there and let you block 'em all day?"

Trouble was everywhere. Of six kickoff returns by Milton and Morris, the squad's fastest, their furthest progression had been to the 22-yard line. Fumbles and errors of judgment were the cause. Morris muffed one kickoff in the end zone, waited until the horde was in full charge, then finally decided to run it out. He made the four-yard line.

There was nobody to catch punts or kick field goals. Kicker Karl Kremser, a high-strung 22-year-old, had built Wilson's hopes in the exhibition season by making four of six. After three regular season games he had missed four of six.

Another Wilson sore spot was rubbed by sports editor Ed Pope of *The Miami Herald*. Complaints had arisen that Milton and especially Morris, a sprinter from West Texas State who had broken O. J. Simpson's NCAA rushing record, were not being used enough on a team that lacked the speed they could provide.

Addressing his column to the subject, Pope wrote: "It is patently absurd, in the light of Morris's fantastic college career, to denigrate his general talents. . . . Charges of racism seem exaggerated. Yet the suspicion lingers that somehow Wilson lacks the rapport with blacks that he has with whites. . . . Excluding the gradual emergence of guard Larry Little, the Dolphins are the only team in pro football without a black offensive regular."

Such observations stung Wilson, who protested that neither Milton nor Morris had the experience to be regulars.

Wilson did get a break in the home opener, when 35,614 customers turned out and saw Kremser's 39-yard field goal with 5:41 remaining tie Oakland 20–20. Csonka returned to lead the backs with 49 yards in eight carries. Griese continued to have problems. Two interceptions led to both Oakland touchdowns. And then when victory seemed imminent, the quarterback lost his poise. At the Miami 42, Csonka redeemed a broken first-down play, escaping 12 yards to the Oakland 46. Griese fumbled on the next play, but recovered for a yard loss. Next he fired a pass much too high for Kiick, open in the flat. On third down he scrambled back, unnecessarily deep it seemed, then dropped the football. He was hit at Miami's 45, forcing Larry Seiple to punt.

The stream of injuries coursed on. Howard Twilley severely dislocated his left elbow when jolted by cornerback Nemiah Wilson on a pass pattern. The fourth-year receiver was lost for the season.

The week after Oakland, a fan mailed Wilson a horseshoe, which he promptly nailed above the entrance to the coaches' dressing room at Miami Stadium. Then the Dolphins lost two more, 21–14 to San Diego and 17–10 to Kansas City. For six games, all Wilson had to show was the Oakland tie. Against San Diego, Doug Moreau was knocked out of action with a sprained left knee. Larry Seiple was pressed into tight-end duty.

Morris had a big day, including a nine-yard touchdown

sprint, in his first extended opportunity at Kansas City. Perhaps stung by criticism but insisting "it's only fair to Merc that I keep him out until I think he's ready," Wilson bore down on Morris at practice sessions. Over a two-week period the coach gave Morris more personal attention than any Dolphin athlete had received in the previous four years.

Because of the humidity that sticks around Miami in the hot fall months, Wilson wore a towel over his shoulder. When Mercury's hands would sweat before kickoff returns or punt returns or other drills overseen closely by the coach, he would wipe them off on Wilson's towel.

"Merc has all the nerve he needs," Wilson said, permitting himself a grin he rarely displayed his final season.

In the Orange Bowl against a weak Buffalo squad, the Dolphins made a seventh try for their first victory. This would have to be the day. Accordingly, "Victory Sunday" was decreed by Steve Clark, the Miami mayor, after a suggestion by a frustrated fan named Bob Chagnon caught on.

Before 39,837, the Dolphins came through 24–6 in a contest overflowing with fumbles and interceptions on both sides. Jim Kiick, having his second big year, caught a 53-yard Griese pass for one touchdown and bashed one yard to a second. Another touchdown was lost when rookie linebacker Norm McBride was flagged for clipping on Mercury's 55-yard punt return.

The players hoisted Wilson to their shoulders in triumph after the game.

"This is gonna be a hell of a football team," their coach responded. "It's a year or maybe two away from taking everything. We've got guys in the key positions like Griese and Csonka and Kiick and Buoniconti and Anderson. All we need are fill-ins to give us the strength and depth a championship team needs.

"This game coming up Sunday in New York is a big one for us. If we can get by the Jets, there's no telling how many more we'll take this year."

Miami almost got by. They ended crushed 34-31 after a mind-blowing fourth quarter. With Griese throwing three of four passes for touchdowns, the Dolphins led 24-16 in the fourth period. But careless play then lost it for them.

To top it off, Jack Clancy tore a ligament in his right knee, just as it seemed the third-year receiver was on the mend after left-knee surgery in 1968. His six catches for 79 yards were as wasted as was Jim Kiick's 106-yard effort in 15 carries. And after bruising muscles in the back of his left arm, Griese asked to be removed in the fourth quarter. Wilson never forgave him.

Wilson and his four assistants were speechless after the giveaway. The players were betraying their coach with sandlot mistakes.

The worst was yet to come. The Dolphins beat the Patriots 17-16 in the rain and mud of Boston College Stadium the following Sunday, but Griese and Buoniconti were felled by knee injuries. The tough middle linebacker returned on a leg and a half two weeks later, but Griese's twisted right knee finished him for the season. Griese and Buoniconti joined all the regular receivers—Twilley, Clancy and Moreau—on the sideline with Mitchell.

Csonka and Kiick, beginning to be coupled in the same sentence as an entry, were Wilson's last hope in the five games left. It was Csonka who had romped 54 yards over a sloppy track to win the Boston game.

Discipline was waning along with morale. Practices at Miami Stadium, a dingy and dismal place in the best of circumstances, were deteriorating. Les Bingaman, plainly ill at the time, was losing control of the young defensive linemen, some of whom responded by mocking the 43-year-old warrior. Not a pleasant scene to watch.

With Griese and the front-line receivers gone, the offense was hopeless. Norton, apparently forgetting Csonka and Kiick, threw 41 passes the next Sunday at Buffalo. One struck a goalpost with Seiple wide open behind it. The Bills romped 28–3. The Dolphins dropped to fourth place in the East with a 2-7-1 record.

Bill Stanfill's 17-yard touchdown with an interception return was the offense when the Dolphins returned to the Orange Bowl for a 32–7 lacing by Houston. Only 27,218 showed up, but their jeers for Wilson and Norton were loud just the same. Without Griese, Wilson was in a hopeless bind.

Wilson's pique hit a peak Sunday after the Houston defeat. Robbie had scheduled the Boston home game in Tampa instead of Miami, which now looked like the work of a genius. The 32,212 Tampa Stadium customers would never have been matched in the Orange Bowl. One customer was Bill Peterson, the coach of Florida State University and the man rumored to become Wilson's successor. Peterson was in the press box as a guest of the Dolphins.

Like most of the Miami games, this one followed a too-familiar pattern. The Patriots won 38–23, sinking the Dolphins into last place.

Wilson's mental state was mirrored by a post-game blast at Morris. Rarely does a coach burn one of his athletes the way Wilson seared Mercury for a punt-return improvisation in the second quarter. "I'm not going to let the coaches take the blame for something like this," Wilson snapped. "Mercury made a high-school play when he fielded that punt on the five and then backed into the end zone." (Merc said he was "looking for running room.")

"There was no excuse for being tackled and getting a safety

in there," Wilson raged. "We were going good. We led 16–6, but that play turned it around. It set them up for 16 points in just three and a half minutes, and I lay it all on Mercury.

"No, I won't fine him," Wilson responded to a question. "If I was going to fine him, I'd have started a long time ago. You have to go through this, I guess, when you're trying to make pro players out of kids."

Then Wilson found out that Peterson had seen the game from the press box. George launched a tirade directed at Charlie Callahan, the Dolphins' publicist, for allowing Peterson credentials. "Bill Peterson isn't good enough to be a pro coach, and what's more, I just don't care for the man. I don't like any man who sneaks around behind people's backs looking for their jobs. If he wants it, let him come out and say it. Why dillydally and go through back doors?"

Peterson said he was at the game merely to renew acquaintances with Ron Sellers and Kim Hammond, former Florida State athletes with the Boston Patriots. "George is probably right when he says I wouldn't make a good pro coach," said the 1972 coach of the Houston Oilers. "He had a tough job down there. I suppose it was a mistake for me to go to the game at all, but honestly I didn't think a thing about it."

Even the return of John Stofa, the Cinderella Man turned loose by Cincinnati, failed to sway the spotlight from Wilson. And so a special team meeting was held. "With all the heat on Coach Wilson, we thought we better try to do something," Seiple said. "We decided it was time we stopped feeling sorry for ourselves and started playing football instead of hee-hawing around."

Speaking at a banquet that week, Buoniconti told his audience: "When they talk about firing George Wilson I have to laugh. We don't need a new coach. What we need is the second appearance of Christ. Maybe He could work a miracle.

"Wilson is a great leader. He is respected by the players.

Usually you get a coach who knows football but can't get along with the players," Nick added, "or one who is good with the players but isn't that good in football. Wilson is solid. This guy is tops."

Wilson himself got a standing ovation the same week at the annual banquet of a North Miami booster group called the Dolphin Veeps, from the beginning the most consistent loyalists the club had.

When the Dolphins outlasted Denver the following Sunday in the Orange Bowl, 27–24, Csonka made no bones about the motive. "This one was for George Wilson and the coaches," the 240-pound fullback said. "I'm not saying that just because we won. We started out with that intention."

But even in victory there was the taste of ashes. In the last minute of the game, Bingaman collapsed on the sideline, stricken with a heart attack. He remained in Mercy Hospital for the final game of Wilson's coaching tenure, a 27–9 loss to the New York Jets.

In the last encounter of the season, Stofa mopped up for Norton, who was playing his final game. Stofa completed 3 of 15 passes and threw two interceptions. He got a chance to make it closer in the final minutes when he fired a long, perfect pass for Jim Hines in the open. The football bounded off the Olympic champion's shoulder pads, however. And that was Hines' last appearance, too.

Seiple, who separated a shoulder in the Denver game, watched in street clothes with fellow receivers Twilley, Clancy, Moreau, Cox and eight others who had been knocked out since September.

The 3-10-1 record gave the Dolphins one consolation. Only the Chicago Bears and Pittsburgh Steelers were entitled to pick ahead of Miami in the 1970 draft. And that consolation became a windfall in the person of Paul Warfield.

> The right hand should be used once in a fight—to finish it.
>
> —JEM MACE

17. *The Dolphins Lose a Father*

When Joe Thomas waited until age 47 to marry, his reputation as a careful man was not tarnished. Until his resignation a month after the 1972 Super Bowl, Thomas presided judiciously and economically over seven Miami drafts. Most of the young mercenaries in Tulane Stadium against Dallas were Thomas recommendations. In the five drafts before Don Shula arrived, the job of picking and signing the collegians belonged to Thomas.

Even at Minnesota, where he began drafting the Vikings from scratch until Joe Robbie beckoned, Thomas was a lone wolf. A native of Warren, Ohio, Thomas was raised in the strict Christian ethic. One spring during his vacation Joe returned to Ohio and painted the house of his parents inside and out. "I enjoyed it," he said. "It was different. There's nothing like manual labor to relax the mind."

Thomas was a standout end at Ohio Northern in 1943. He was associated with Paul Brown's talented World War II collection at the Great Lakes Naval Training Station. End

Coach Weeb Ewbank was impressed enough with Joe's grasp of the game to hire him later as an assistant at Baltimore.

A temperate Midwesterner who never smoked and seldom drank, Thomas remained at a distance during the often convivial, often bitter George Wilson years, even while Robbie was casting about for a new coach after the disastrous 1969 season. Nor was Joe consulted. He went about his own tasks as always. The successful completion of one of these tasks resulted in the steady, unassuming Thomas becoming gloriously drunk the night before the 1971 draft.

"Judi and I went to the best restaurant in town and I started ordering wine, all kinds of wine," Thomas said. "I can't recall ever being more satisfied with myself."

The morning of the draft Joe brought the happiest hangover in Dolphin history to their downtown offices.

"Look at that board," Thomas directed reporters before the first round started. "That's our No. 1 up there, and you can bet you won't see a name close to it today, or tomorrow either."

The name was Paul Warfield. At the last minute after a two-week round of phone negotiations, Thomas and Robbie had induced the Browns to part with Warfield in exchange for Miami's No. 1 draft pick, who would be Purdue quarterback Mike Phipps.

"We insisted on Warfield from the start," Thomas said. "They tossed some other names at us, but we only wanted Warfield. They told me I must be kidding. But I knew they had high regard for Phipps, and needed a young quarterback against the day Bill Nelsen's knees give out.

"Yet I honestly didn't think the deal would go through until I got a call the day before the draft. When the deal was OK'd, I put the phone down very gently and held it a long time. I wanted to capture the moment."

The Warfield trade was one of four sweeping moves that turned the Dolphins around. That trade and two other coups were instigated within three days of January 1970. Next was the draft itself, which produced four regulars on defense—safety Jake Scott (out of Canada and another coup for Thomas), linebacker Mike Kolen, cornerbacks Tim Foley and Curtis Johnson. The overriding move, of course, was the acquisition of Shula, instigated after the draft and finalized in February. And the fourth major move was Shula's exchange that May of Jack Clancy for Marv Fleming from Green Bay, to give the Dolphins a blocking tight end for the first time.

After the Warfield acquisition Wilson expressed optimism. "My personal feeling is that I will be retained." But privately Wilson said, "I can only hope."

Wilson made a positive psychological contribution to the Dolphins' future in the last AFL All-Star game (which Wilson coached and the East lost 26–3). Nick Buoniconti was the only coaches' choice among the East team. But Wilson invited Larry Little, the beefy guard who had come on to win a regular job that fall. "When Coach Wilson showed that kind of confidence in me," Little said later, "it immediately made me a better player. He didn't have to name me on the team. It was something I'll never forget."

Tom Goode, the durable center, defensive end Bill Stanfill and the reliable Jim Kiick were also Wilson appointees.

Buoniconti was crushed when Wilson was fired on February 18. "I feel like I've lost a father, I really do," the middle linebacker said. Nick thought a few moments. "What did they have to give Shula, half the franchise?"

Most Dolphins echoed Kiick's sentiment: "Wilson treated you like a man." Robbie's attitude was more explicit. "It's

The Dolphins Lose a Father

a factor in George's favor that he enjoys such rapport with his players. But players are not always the best judges of what is good for a team."

Others, however, were less charitable. "Sure, he can inspire," one said. "But what's he ever given us to be inspired with? Our game plans were jokes, and so was our preparation."

The fans were also tired of losing and, for the most part, reacted much in the manner of Archie Stone, Miami's pint-size football ambassador and Wilson's friend from Detroit days. Attending an appreciation dinner for Wilson in April, Stone wore a T-shirt beneath his jacket. Written across the front was, "We Love You George." Turning his back, Archie exposed another inscription: "Go Get 'Em Shula."

By April, Shula was already after 'em. Applying meticulous heed to detail and organization, practically unknown during the easygoing Wilson's regime, Shula compiled dossiers on every athlete he inherited. Much of the material was not flattering. He seemed dissatisfied, in fact, with every phase of the Miami game and particularly the linebacking, Buoniconti excepted.

Kiick and Csonka needed more speed and less weight. Neither side of the line displayed the aggressive quickness Shula demanded. Without a tight end, the off-tackle play was impossible. The receivers were slow. The secondary was uncertain. Griese was inclined to run too much and needed work setting up faster in the pocket.

Thomas, who had expressed many of the same notions in preceding years, saw in Shula a man he could get along with. And Thomas went along even when the new coach announced after less than two months on the job that the Dolphins had joined the BLESTO scouting organization. Shula made it clear to Thomas that his work was not being impugned and that he would retain the scouting authority he had held since 1966, with minor modifications.

Indeed, Thomas that January had produced more than Warfield in the draft. Behind Warfield, five of Miami's next seven choices made the club—tight end Jim Mandich, Tim Foley, Curtis Johnson, Jake Scott and running back Hubert Ginn. In addition, Mike Kolen was a twelfth-round pick.

Mandich was the first to feel Shula's businesslike approach. At a rookie luncheon the free-spirited captain of Michigan's 1970 Rose Bowl team offered a few remarks. "I have observed a number of pretty girls in this area. As a tight end I realize I'm supposed to be catching passes. But considering the young ladies, I have the impression I might be making a few passes as well."

Rising at the speaker's table a few minutes later, Shula turned to the 6-3, 220-pound Mandich with a malicious smile. "I can assure you, Mandich, that when training camp opens, the opportunity for making such passes will never come about. You will be very busy in your off-hours looking for a place to lie down."

Shula had not been on the job a week when he summoned Griese to check the right knee sprained in the mud at Boston. Griese refused to believe an operation was necessary, though more than one physician—including Herb Virgin of the Dolphins—had recommended it. And so he finally emulated another quarterback, Len Dawson of Kansas City, who the year before had suffered a similar knee injury. "I consulted six orthopedic surgeons," Dawson said, "and five recommended surgery. But being a dumb football player, I sided with the guy who said I didn't need an operation."

"The guy" was Dr. Frank Reynolds of St. Louis. Searching for the same solution, Griese also consulted Reynolds and got the answer he wanted. A conditioning program, the doctor said, could restore a damaged cartilage to full strength.

"I went along with his explanation," Shula said. "I was very favorably impressed with Bob. He's a deep thinker, highly conscientious, and he seems really anxious to contribute. Bob also convinced me that his knee was explored and tested the way it should have been."

Next, Shula started hiring assistants. He interviewed Wilson's holdovers but preferred a new staff and fresh outlook. There was also the delicate question of Les Bingaman, still pallid and weak after his heart attack.

Joe Robbie had said in the course of the coaching turnover that "Les Bingaman and Ernie Hefferle [the offensive line coach] will always have a place in this organization if they want it." But Shula had his own ideas about assistants, preferring young men who were prepared to devote long hours to their job. The Dolphins he'd seen on film just made too many mistakes.

A week after he accepted the Miami job, Shula hired Howard Schnellenberger to head his offense and Bill Arnsparger to head the defense. Shula knew both men well as fellow assistants at Kentucky under Blanton Collier in 1959. (Shula ranks Collier just below the One Great Scorer in football acumen.) The 43-year-old Arnsparger had also handled Shula's defensive line at Baltimore, though he had resigned after the 1969 season for his family. A tireless football student during the season, Arnsparger immersed himself in his work to the detriment of everything else. But Shula's persuasion together with an unexplored challenge changed the quiet Kentuckian's mind. He agreed to oversee Miami's defense, a decision that produced amazing results from the start.

"The man knows more defense than anybody I've ever known," Nick Buoniconti said after a few weeks with Arnsparger. "Working with him is a revelation."

Schnellenberger, 36, had coached Joe Namath's Alabama offense to national championships in 1964 and 1965 before joining the pros under George Allen at Los Angeles. Schnellenberger, in fact, had aided Bear Bryant in bringing Namath to Alabama. Soft-spoken and intelligent, the pipe-smoking Schnellenberger would apply a droll wit and a chess master's cunning to his task of coordinating Shula's offense.

Thirty-three-year-old Monte Clark, the youngest of Shula's assistants, was faced with the most difficult job: producing an offensive line. Furthermore, Clark was inexperienced. He had just retired as a tackle after 11 NFL seasons in San Francisco, Dallas and Cleveland. But Collier recommended him, and that was enough for Shula.

"I looked around very carefully for an offensive line coach," Shula said. "I needed to find the right man for a big building job. I always worry about an established player coming into coaching. Many of them are content to stand around and get by on their reputations. I needed a teacher, and Collier convinced me Clark was the man. Hiring Monte may have been the most fortunate move I made."

A 250-pound bundle of nerves, humor and theory, Clark soon had his linemen as busy seeking perfection as he was himself. "Positive feedback" was Clark's term for the satisfaction of hard work, steady improvement and the application of successful blocking techniques.

To tutor the running backs, Shula hired a former college and pro teammate with coaching experience. Carl Taseff, 41, had been a brilliant runner at John Carroll University before he and Shula were drafted by Cleveland's Paul Brown. Both were later traded to Baltimore and functioned together in the defensive backfield.

"I had the advantage, though," Shula said, smiling. "I called the defensive signals and naturally preferred rotating the zone toward my corner. That left Carl all alone against those wide receivers on the other side."

For the defensive line, another problem area, Shula chose Mike Scarry. The 50-year-old Scarry brought 22 years of college and pro coaching experience to a job he attacked with enthusiasm. Scarry had captained the NFL champion Cleveland Rams in 1945 as center and middle linebacker, then performed the same tasks for the All-American Conference Browns the following season, after the Rams moved to Los Angeles.

Shula completed his staff by retaining Tom Keane, the defensive backfield coach and only holdover from the Wilson regime. Keane had been in the same Baltimore backfield with Shula, Taseff and Bert Rechichar in the 1950s. Friendship was not a factor. Keane gained the job only after considerable interrogation and, finally, upon Shula's conviction that Tom would fit into the new operation.

"I'd work all day and spend half the night trying to catch up that first year," Keane said. "It was an entirely different system—and all football the first six months."

Shula made Bingaman a special scouting assistant, and advised him to relax until he regained his health. But Bingo could neither relax nor reconcile himself to a job that amounted to a sinecure. "They didn't know what to do with me, so they handed me this," Bingo said on one of his few visits to the office. The former 320-pound middle guard weighed less than 200, and flesh hung from his big frame in 1970, the last year of his life.

Shula also retained Bob Lundy, the able trainer who had been Friday Macklem's aide in Detroit six years before rejoining Wilson. At 34, Lundy was another tireless worker. So was Dan Dowe, the equipment manager, who also remained with the team.

The rest of Wilson's staff had no difficulty relocating. Idzik joined Don McCafferty's new staff at Baltimore. Hefferle returned to coaching college football at Pittsburgh. Wilson himself took over supervision of a 288-unit garden apartment complex he had invested in at Country Club of Miami.

> As universal a practice as lying is, and as easy a one as it seems, I do not remember to have heard three good lies in all my conversation.
>
> —JONATHAN SWIFT

18. *Don Shula's Ordeal*

"We had a nucleus of talent. But we needed someone to lead us." With these words Bob Griese made it perfectly clear that he was not among the mourners when George Wilson was fired. While Griese liked Wilson, the no-nonsense Hoosier clearly preferred Shula's disciplined and systematic approach.

At 40, Shula possessed the energy to sustain his conviction that the entire field organization had to be changed. Before taking the job, which included stock options, Shula thoroughly explored the Dolphins operation. "I had to know without the slightest doubt that Miami's people were totally dedicated to winning football," Shula said. 'The only way to get a championship team is to build from the bottom up, and to make every physical as well as financial sacrifice necessary to get the job done."

When he was satisfied that there would be no skimping and that he would have an absolutely free hand, Shula plunged into the task. The Miami job contained more potential than the position he had undertaken in Baltimore as Weeb Ewbank's successor. And it was more lucrative. At an estimated $70,000 salary on a five-year contract plus stock options, Shula's deal compared with the ownership agreements drawn up for Washington's Vince Lombardi and Ted Williams.

"I wouldn't be telling the truth if I didn't admit the money and ownership deal were important factors," Shula said. "But neither was decisive, because without a winning ball club, ownership is a liability. I left a sound organization in Baltimore. They treated me well, and I had reason to expect they would continue to do so. Consequently I had to make damned sure I knew what I was getting into."

Shula has made few wrong moves since he was growing up in Painesville, Ohio, a leafy, God-fearing community 30 miles east of Cleveland. As a boy in a hurry, Don once yanked his jacket from a ledge where he had left it during a sandlot football game. He forgot he had placed a brick on the jacket to secure it, and broke his nose as a result. The nose is a prominent feature of his chiseled, square-jawed appearance that mirrors a straight-arrow philosophy.

Shula has always loved athletics and particularly football. At Harvey High he was a star back. And though under six feet and a lightweight, his determination was evident then. "I always seemed to be the organizer," Shula said. "It just came naturally."

Harvey was not a large school, so Shula was not stampeded by college offers. He wound up at John Carroll, a small university in Cleveland's suburbs where the Jesuits were exposing the humanities to a number of unusually large students and uncommonly old veterans on the GI Bill. The large students, it developed, were there for a purpose. While the Jesuits were distracted in the classroom, an ingenious coach named Herb Eisele was building a little football factory under their cassocks.

Shula fit neatly into Eisele's plan. So did Carl Taseff. These two carried the football while John Carroll's squad achieved a giant-killing reputation. Taseff was the athlete, Shula the driver. One night in Cleveland Stadium in 1950, the Blue Streaks, with Shula and Taseff spearheading the offense, upset Syracuse.

After college, while with the Browns and the Colts, Shula filled notebooks with *x*'s and *o*'s and attendant football lore absorbed under Paul Brown and Blanton Collier, Brown's aide at Cleveland, and Ewbank and his staff at Baltimore. Shula assumed the role of field leader and holler guy first as a cornerback for the Browns, then the Colts, and in his last of seven pro years, the Redskins.

The Dolphins soon discovered the new coach was different. While Wilson would occasionally relax an already flexible operation to improve morale, Shula rarely swerved from a timeclock routine. Wilson had his favorites. The new coach treated each man alike.

Shula was fair, honest, tough from the beginning. Neither discipline nor organization had been Wilson's forte. Shula eased up only when the squad was conditioned to the way he wanted things done. Behind his brusque, challenging style, Shula hides a sensitivity and ego characteristic of the achiever. His way is the only way, except on rare occasions. Even then it takes a powerful argument to sway him.

On Sundays, as he had done when a player, Shula ran the game. Wilson believed that each Sunday's performance reflected the week's preparation and the "short list" of preferred tactics that comprised the game plan. "The hay is in the barn," Wilson would say, meaning that coaching is subordinate to preplanned strategy on the day of a game. But Shula had no such conception. "Anybody can prepare a team from Tuesday to Saturday," he said, "and anybody can correct mistakes on Monday. Coaching day is game day. If the game plan isn't working, you change it."

Shula attends Mass daily. His moral convictions are as strong as the fervor he applies to his coaching. And in 1970 he needed everything he had when the integrity he values above all was attacked by Carroll Rosenbloom, owner of the Colts, who was deeply stung by Shula's manner of departure.

No sooner had Shula accepted the Miami job than the Colts accused the Dolphins of tampering. Shula was not their immediate target. Joe Robbie was. The Colts charged that Robbie had neglected to ask for their permission to deal with Shula, and that the stock offer was a lure out of line with NFL protocol since Shula had four years to run on his Baltimore contract.

The Colts were technically correct. Robbie had not bothered with the amenities. Before Robbie began serious negotiations with Shula, Carroll Rosenbloom's son Steve had been notified by Shula, in the absence of his vacationing father. Steve had consented.

On the day Shula's coaching appointment was announced in Miami, Steve Rosenbloom was announcing the coach's resignation: "We're sorry to see Don go, but he's got a chance for ownership that he's wanted a long time. It's our policy that if anyone has a chance to better himself, never to stand in his way."

The observation hardly hinted of anger. But when Steve's father returned, he cut loose. "To me," Rosenbloom stated, "there is no question what they [Shula and Robbie] did. They waited until I was in the Orient to continue their conversations without letting me know."

Rosenbloom added that he knew nothing about what had

transpired until February 18, the day Shula was hired. In other words, Steve Rosenbloom had never bothered to tell his father that they were in danger of losing their head coach, even though Steve had known about the negotiations during the entire month of February.

Rosenbloom struck a surprising chord when asked what he looked for in a head coach. The owner said he looked most of all for a winner, then added: "Unfortunately, we have not had that at Baltimore since Weeb Ewbank left us." Aside from substituting the euphemism "left us" for "was fired" in Ewbank's case, Rosenbloom overlooked two conference championships, one NFL championship and a record for seven Baltimore seasons of 75-26-4, the best in pro football.

The month after he was hired in Miami, Shula encountered his old boss in a hotel lobby. When Shula offered his hand, Rosenbloom turned abruptly and walked off. "I've never had a more humiliating experience," Shula said.

Shula, however, was not implicated either in the original charge by the Colts or later, when Commissioner Pete Rozelle awarded Miami's No. 1 draft pick in 1971 to Baltimore as a penalty for Robbie's indiscretion.

Steadily and almost without South Floridians realizing it, Shula started changing things. He joined BLESTO scouting organization with Joe Thomas's approval—though Shula would have joined anyway. As vice-president and coach, such policy decisions were his. Shula and Robbie then shifted the training base from Boca Raton to Biscayne College, about 12 miles from the Dolphins' downtown Miami offices.

Shula started changing things on the field, too, and getting some revenge against his old team. The Dolphins defeated the Colts in an August exhibition and in their return 1970 regular-season match, then beat them two out of three times in 1971, including the 21–0 humiliation in the American Football Conference championship game. He might have gloated. That he refused to do so testified as strongly for his character as for the agony of silence he continues to endure on those occasions when Rosenbloom insists upon returning to the subject. In fact, the Baltimore owner was so persistent that Rozelle fined him $5,000 and cautioned him to keep silent in 1971. It wasn't enough.

After a November 1971 loss to the Dolphins, Rosenbloom was asked why no young quarterback was being developed against the rapidly approaching day when John Unitas would be gone. The reply was astounding.

"We have Mr. Shula to thank for that," Rosenbloom responded. "When I left for the Orient, my last instructions to Mr. Shula were to draft Dennis Shaw, the quarterback from San Diego State. Unfortunately, Mr. Shula was already committed to Miami at the time, although we did not know it, and he ignored my orders and refused to draft Shaw. And that is why we do not have a young quarterback today ready to step in."

Rosenbloom's statement did not jibe with the facts. Shaw was selected by Buffalo on the first day of the 1970 draft, before Shula and Robbie had had any correspondence whatever.

> Either you live here and have already accustomed yourself to it, or you are going away, and this by your own will; or you are dying and have discharged your duty. Besides these things there is nothing. Be of good cheer, then.
>
> —MARCUS AURELIUS

19. *Summer of 1970: A Conversion*

Pink streaks smearing a black sky were all that was left of the sun as Don Shula's squad moved silently through an after-supper football practice. It was the fourth outdoor drill of the day, Aug. 18, 1970. And the shadowy figures were so obscure that a witness had to wonder how they kept from colliding in the night. Because of South Florida's proximity to the Equator, its twilight is as fleeting as a headwaiter's smile. The practice had begun at dusk. Now, nearly an hour later, these goblins were still puffing through plays. Occasionally a low curse from the mass of moving bodies or an admonition from Shula would interrupt this bizarre rehearsal. "Let's do it once more, everybody. Let's get it right."

Only a few die-hard devotees remained from the crowds that had begun attending practices since it became clear that Shula appeared to be working some kind of miracle at Biscayne College. His Dolphins had won two straight exhibition games without a defeat, and they looked boldly different in the process.

"Hey, Daddy," a small voice demanded. "Who's in the backfield now?"

Since only Shula and the backs could possibly know in the darkness, Daddy issued what seemed a reasonable reply under the circumstances: "Shut up," he explained.

Shula was once asked following an after-supper practice why he didn't outfit his athletes with miner's caps. But the coach did not even grin. He was filled with purpose and he entertained no distractions from that purpose, which was winning football games immediately.

"I'm no miracle man," Shula had said a few months before. "I don't have any magic formulas. I am, however, fairly familiar with the Miami personnel—its strengths and its weaknesses—and my objective is to eliminate the weaknesses and build the strength and particularly the depth so necessary for high-level competition." And Shula meant every word.

"My coaching objective," he said, "is to get the edge in all phases of the game—offense, defense and kicking. The edge comes from experience and confidence. It's not a vocal thing. You must do it on the field."

Now, in the summer of 1970, he was doing it on the field.

Robbie had been generous in contributing to the growth of little Biscayne College. He remains on the board of trustees. And with Shula, he arranged to build a complete practice facility on the 150-acre, 400-student campus, which the Baltimore Orioles now share with them.

By the time practice started in early July, a fenced enclosure contained two freshly grassed football fields complete with 18-inch crowns tapering off from the middle. The crowns were exactly the height of those in the Orange Bowl. Summer practices were open to visitors. In fact, Shula welcomed them, for the businesslike approach he drummed into his squad included selling tickets.

Even before practice began, Shula's employees grasped the idea that life at Biscayne College would be earnest. The coach held "little indoctrination sessions" for rookies and experienced hands separately on consecutive spring weekends. These turned out to include speed and endurance tests in the morning, basic football drills in the afternoon and classroom sessions both morning and afternoon.

"I'm in shape for Wilson," muttered Jim Kiick after Shula's introductory session. "But I'm not ready for this guy."

Nobody was. After handing off during a routine running drill, Bob Griese loped to a halt as his teammates charged the prescribed 10 yards.

"Run it out, Bob," Shula said. Griese nodded perfunctorily.

"Hey, Mr. Quarterback," Shula snapped. "Run it out with the rest of the guys."

Griese nodded emphatically. He knew what the coach meant.

"Come on, Griese, you owe us 10," Shula yelled. "I mean right now."

Shula got his 10 yards immediately. He also impressed everybody that exceptions to the regimen would not be tolerated.

Even Nick Buoniconti, who felt he had lost a father when Wilson was fired, began to change after his first indoctrination session under the exacting Shula. "All the guys know how much I admired Wilson," the 30-year-old linebacker said. "And people are quick to forget that we were nip and tuck with the best in the league before we got wiped out by injuries last year. But this guy is something else. He's so thorough it's unbelievable."

Nick sighed, rubbing the salty sweat from his eyes. "Shula seems to be all right. A lot of organization. A ton of organization, in fact. He has six assistants too. George had four. So the younger guys are bound to get more attention."

Buoniconti was to discover that the "younger guys" would not be the only ones receiving more attention. In two years under Shula and his defensive chief, Bill Arnsparger, Buoniconti was to become a better middle linebacker than he had ever been in Boston.

"They can talk about Dick Butkus or anybody else," said Coach Tom Landry before sending his Dallas team against the Dolphins in the 1972 Super Bowl. "The key to beating their defense is Buoniconti. He does more for his team than any linebacker in the game."

Buoniconti became the roving fulcrum of Miami's defense. And Nick gave the credit to Arnsparger.

But Buoniconti was not there when practice was supposed to open for the experienced personnel on Monday, July 20, one week after the 36 rookies had reported. Nick and John Mackey of Baltimore were in New York, spearheading a battle with the owners to win pension and insurance benefits, which had supposedly been ironed out over the winter. However, the documents had not been signed by the owners, and the players decided to stay out of camp until they were.

Their decision upset Shula more than it did the fringe veterans who were risking unemployment by the delay, because Shula had decided to incorporate his entire system into the Miami framework. Long hours would be needed for the athletes to absorb the changes even under optimum conditions.

After a week with the rookies, Shula knew that less than a dozen had a chance to stick. He was working with lame ducks, for the most part, and he was frustrated. But he never betrayed his feelings.

"I've always believed in making the most of whatever situation arises," he said. "There's no sense dwelling on things you can't do anything about."

When a second week went by with the players and owners still locked at the conference table, Paul Brown closed his Cincinnati camp. "There's nothing more we can do."

Shula did no such thing. And he offered a pithy reason why Biscayne College remained in business: "We'll keep working with the rookies because we may have to play a preseason game with them," he said, alluding to the August 8 opener against Pittsburgh.

"Furthermore," Shula insisted, "it's been a good period of work for a number of reasons. We've been able to get together as a coaching staff, to teach and to get the bugs out of the system. For another thing, the rookies have hung in there. Maybe some of them won't make it, but you've got to admire their tenacity."

The tenacity was extended to the coaching staff. From morning until after midnight, Shula's staff demonstrated astounding durability on the field and in the classroom. Shula's coaches must have constituted the most harassed crew since Captain Bligh's.

The extra time and tutoring paid dividends. Arnsparger found a couple of immediate linebacking prospects in Mike Kolen, the twelfth-round draftee out of Auburn, and a bespectacled, scholarly free agent named Doug Swift.

Swift had emerged from Amherst, where his concentration as a fine arts major outdid his application to football. Ignored by pro scouts who seldom visit schools such as Amherst, Swift decided to try his luck with the Montreal Alouettes in June. He was cut.

Doug's college coach, Jim Ostendarp, gave the Dolphins a call and suggested they take a look at the 6-4, 225-pounder whose potential was never realized in college, by his own choice.

"I liked football," Swift explained. "But I didn't feel a need for the pressure experience at a big school. The big schools feel they have to keep you busy all the time, keep you in a dorm. I might have rebelled. The whole idea is just a little silly and more than a little irrelevant in the education process."

Amherst's version was more to Swift's fancy. Spring drills did not exist. Even during the season, the worthies of Lord Jeff practiced just three times weekly.

"Ostendarp thought I was kind of lazy," Swift said. "He played with the New York Giants and didn't think I'd be willing to put out the work needed to make a pro club."

With nothing to lose, Swift was loose when he reported. He also began hitting everything in sight. There was a devil in him that had never been set free. Furthermore, Shula needed linebackers desperately. Except for Buoniconti in the middle, the coach was determined to find roving types who would fit into the zone defense he had refined to such a state of perfection at Baltimore. Day after day as the experienced players remained out of camp, Shula and Arnsparger grew convinced that the rangy blond with extraordinary intelligence would catch on quickly. Swift rewarded their faith.

Kolen, at 6-2 and 220, brought a reputation as "Captain Crunch" from Auburn and showed from the start why the sobriquet was applied. All the quiet, gentlemanly Kolen had to do was absorb the system. Like many self-effacing athletes, he became a demon on the field. Kolen and Swift dominated the early scrimmages.

Another rookie standout was Curtis Johnson, a 6-1, 195-pound cornerback who captained a Toledo University team that never lost a game in his college career. The No. 4 draft pick, Johnson's speed and aggressiveness convinced Shula that he could dispense with Jim Warren, who had guarded the Dolphins' left corner from the start. Before camp opened, Shula had traded right corner Dick Westmoreland. The coach felt that while both were qualified if not spectacular performers, they were rooted in habits too deep to change. He preferred teaching the Shula zone to younger and presumably more adaptable men.

A later arrival turned out to be the best prospect of all at a position that had gone practically untended since Willie West retired after the 1968 season—free safety. Dick Anderson had been used there in 1969, but the strong and not-so-swift Colorado product was out of position. Shula had determined that Anderson would operate at strong-side safety, where his range on pass coverage would be less sweeping and his proclivities as a hitter would better serve the defense.

When rookie Jake Scott arrived in the last week of July from Canada, the free-safety dilemma was solved. Scott was 25 years old, cold as a gigolo and absolutely dedicated to football. The most poised rookie to enter the NFL since Pete Rozelle. Joe Thomas had drafted Scott seventh, despite an option year remaining on his Canadian contract. An All-Southeastern Conference safety at Georgia, Jake had left the university with a year of eligibility remaining. "I wanted the money," he explained, "and I had a good offer in Canada."

As a rookie for the Vancouver Lions, Scott seized 42 passes playing flanker. And the following year his picture appeared on the cover of the Montreal brochure after the Alouettes obtained him in an early 1970 trade. But he remained unsigned at Montreal and requested a release from Coach Sam Etcheverry. "When I was drafted by Miami, that's all I could think about," Jake said. "I wanted very much to play in the NFL. Besides, I'm a safetyman, not a flanker. And Montreal's safetymen were set."

After four months of negotiating with the Alouettes—and finally clearing a transfer through the CFL commissioner—the Dolphins got Jake to Biscayne College. But not without paying the Alouettes $50,000, the equivalent of Scott's value.

On the first practice day, Shula knew he had found not only his free safety but also his punt returner. At Georgia in 1968, Scott was runner-up in the nation on punt returns. "But I wasn't about to do that in Canada," Scott explained. "No fair catches allowed. I didn't make enough money to play flanker and return punts."

So "Crazy Jake," as his reckless habits led him to be called, not only caught punts for the Dolphins but returned them with frightening abandon. The 6-1, 185-pound bachelor never missed a game in two years, despite separating a shoulder early in the 1970 season and breaking bones in both hands toward the end of the 1971 campaign.

Bright as these rookies looked, however, Shula remained stymied until the owner-player negotiations at last were settled on August 3, the Monday before the Saturday night exhibition opener with Pittsburgh in Jacksonville. When the rest of the squad did show up, Shula scheduled a week of preparation unprecedented anywhere. Practices twice daily are the scourge of training camps. Shula started with three daily practices and worked up to four.

"I believe that when you're in camp, you should be learning about football, either in the classroom or on the practice field. Nobody should be standing around," Shula said. "And the only way to keep everybody busy is with a tough schedule. This is a young group that should be adaptable to hard work. Well, we're going to work."

Shula began instilling his new system with astonishing results. Those who could not keep up were quickly dismissed. But the brighter rookies held on well, showing to advantage the extra work they had undergone while the experienced performers were out of camp.

Paul Warfield did not arrive until Thursday, two days before the opener, as contract talks were still in progress between the Dolphins and his agent, Ed Keating of the Mark McCormack firm in Cleveland.

Keating came to camp for a discussion with Shula, but the coach could not be bothered, as much as he wanted Warfield in camp.

The gifted receiver at length appeared "under protest" but willing to work. Shortly thereafter, the persistent Keating arranged a four-year contract with the Dolphins worth more than $250,000.

Mercury Morris became an early victim of evening practice. Sprinting for a short, flat pass in the dusk, Morris collided with second-year linebacker Dale McCullers. Mercury hemorrhaged a thigh so severely he needed 14 drainage holes plus tubes inserted into the wound. He would not be ready until October.

After 48 hours of Shula's first camp, Larry Csonka and Jim Kiick were shuffling toward the lunchroom. Neither back seemed able to lift his feet. "You," said Csonka, as I met them halfway. "You and your goddam Shula."

Csonka was among the coach's special projects. From a strapping 250 pounds he weighed at the May "indoctrination" session, Larry had shed 15.

"A true Hungarian, nothing but work," Csonka said of Shula. "I know another one. My father. When my old man told us to build a barn in 30 days," continued Csonka, a native of rural Stow, Ohio, "it meant we'd damn well better have the thing up in 28 days."

Shula was charging $10 a pound overweight, based on figures he had prepared after first viewing the bulk of his squad in the spring.

"At least I'm below my limit," Kiick said. "I haven't the strength to lift a fork."

All this might have caused problems among an older group. But only two of 1969's regulars who survived Shula's first camp—center Tom Goode and guard Maxie Williams—were over 30.

Marv Fleming, in his eighth year after seven at Green Bay, was among the hustle leaders, being accustomed to hard summer labor under Vince Lombardi. "Come on, Norm, you and me, Baby, you and me," Fleming would exhort Norm Evans as the right tackle and tight end broke thousands of huddles and came up to the line together.

"What a winner," Shula said, watching Fleming. "For the first time this team is able to run the off-tackle play."

Buoniconti, the senior defensive member in point of service, had built his pro career on hustle. The squad was perfectly if painfully tuned to Shula's exacting timetable. But Shula needed positive results. And, fortunately, the results came quickly. Pittsburgh was beaten 16–10. The following Saturday night in the Orange Bowl, 60,460 curious customers turned out to watch the Dolphins defeat Cincinnati 20–10. The next victim was San Francisco, 17–7. No Miami team had ever won three exhibition games in one summer, much less three straight.

Baltimore was next. The fuss created by Carroll Rosenbloom and the Colts had South Florida nearly as stirred up as Shula's instant success.

Bubba Smith had taken a shot at his old coach that July. "I don't think he understands black men," said the 6-8, 290-pound defensive end. "Me, for instance. I can't function right when somebody is always hollering in my ear."

The Dolphins didn't believe it. In Miami that first summer, Shula treated blacks and whites indiscriminately. Even his room list was integrated. Warfield and Griese, for example, were roommates. Shula made everyone work.

"Once he hollered at me from the other end of the field," Csonka said. "I thought maybe my pants were falling down, I was losing so much weight. Or that my kid had run out on the field.

"Hell, he was yelling because I was six inches out of position. He said, 'How do you expect to get an angle on a linebacker from over there?' Six inches—that was 'over there' to Shula. He's really something.

"But I'll tell you something else," Csonka said. "For the first time, I really think I know what I'm doing."

Guard Larry Little, another special weight project, went down in a massive heap the first day of practice. Larry appeared to have been hit by an elephant gun.

"He was standing there next to me," said Monte Clark, the offensive line coach, "and all of a sudden he was gone. Flat on his back."

Larry was borne off on the rear of a station wagon, but was back the next day. There was no time for relaxation. Dropouts simply fell too far behind.

Tom Goode broke a wristbone in August. The tough catfish raiser from Mississippi had not missed a game in four years. He fell behind.

Wherever Shula saw holes, he tried to shore them up by trades and by perusing waiver lists. As the team with a 1969 record bettering only Pittsburgh's 1-13 mark in the American Football Conference, the Dolphins had the second pick of players dismissed by rivals.

Football players entered and left the Biscayne College

camp in numbers reminiscent of a Marx Brothers' comedy at the height of its door-slamming congestion. But this wholesale shuffling as well as the evening practices and constant meetings were paying off.

Joe Robbie was in a state of euphoria. "If we beat the Colts it'll blow the lid off this town."

They beat the Colts 20–13 before a capacity house of 76,712, who were partly accommodated on temporary bleachers lugged in from Biscayne College.

That victory represented a milestone. In no preceding year had Miami's season-ticket sale climbed more than 3,000. By 1969 a high of 17,478 had been reached, while the average attendance climbed to a modest though still red-ink 34,688. But after Baltimore the skeptics began buying. Some 26,161 season tickets were sold, and average attendance in Shula's first year boomed to 62,877.

Saturday after Baltimore, the Dolphins took their first defeat, 26–21, at the hand of quarterback Sonny Jurgensen of Washington. The game was played at Tampa and followed the death of Vince Lombardi the day before, a tragedy that seemed to inflame the Redskins as Frank Buncom's death had affected the Bengals in Miami's 1969 opener at Cincinnati.

Still paring his squad through trial and error on the field, Shula next squirmed through an error-laden 20–17 loss to Atlanta. But the defeat helped make up his mind. In the final cut he swept the squad almost clean of the 1966 expansion holdovers and other veterans he felt could be replaced by rookies. Youth was the password.

> Once my Uncle Al substituted in the cannon for my father, who was ill. My uncle came out all right, but he missed the net and hit the ferris wheel. He broke about every bone in his body, but fortunately recovered.
>
> —BOB KUECHENBERG

20. *No Miracle Man*

Shula opened the 1970 season with 20 new faces, a turnover of nearly half the 40-man roster and 7-man taxi squad.

Billy Neighbors, the stubby, popular Alabaman who had lifted squad spirits in the depressing years, had retired after the 1969 campaign. "Spanky" had been fun, particularly while airborne. From 30,000 feet up, Neighbors charted the course of eels moving across the nation from a starting point somewhere in the Grand Bahamas.

"Lookee there," Billy would alert a rookie traveler. "See those eels down there? Well, they crawl all the way to California *and back*. That there's a phenomenon been goin' on for centuries."

Nobody but presumably Neighbors ever saw these eels. But as Billy pointed out on the practice field, "Nobody ever saw pain, either. But you can damn well be sure it's here."

Why the eels were going to California remained another mystery as incredulous as Neighbors himself, a shrewd stockbroker in the offseason but a confused guard. Tom Goode, the center, would find himself whispering assignments to his buddy as they approached the line of scrimmage.

"Checkoffs were something else with old Billy," Goode said. "I'll sure miss telling him what to do."

After a practice lecture by Ernie Hefferle, the offensive line coach, Neighbors protested one hot August day at gnat-infested Boca Raton. "Listen, Ernie, just because I'm a dumb football player doesn't make me a dumb human bein'."

But Billy was an old 29 when he retired, after a distinguished career at Alabama and in the AFL. He represented another era in Miami. And Shula's transition became obvious when previous untouchables were released one after another.

Rick Norton and Frank Emanuel, representing $750,000 worth of expense, went packing that summer, as did Jim Warren. Wide receiver Jack Clancy, cornerback Dick Westmoreland and safety Tom Beier also departed in trades.

Jim Hines, whose hands would never grow accustomed to a football, was demoted to the cab squad and later released. Fleming's acquisition for Clancy made Doug Moreau expendable, as did the presence of No. 2 draftee Jim Mandich. Moreau never had a chance. After two knee operations within four months in the winter of 1969–70, Doug would never be the same. He retired.

Goode never played again for the Dolphins. Knee complications arose after the broken wristbone, and Tom went on injured reserve. He was later acquired by the Colts, however, and had a happy ending to his nine-year career. Tom snapped the football for Jim O'Brien's field goal that defeated Dallas in the 1971 Super Bowl. So he went home to West Point, Miss., and his catfish with an extra $25,000 and a championship ring.

Replacements came through trades and the waiver-list shuttle service operated that summer by Shula and Arnsparger, who concentrated on two new conference entries from the NFL, Baltimore and Cleveland. Both teams had talent to spare.

Carl Mauck, a center who was to fill a sore need in December, and linebacker Dick Palmer were plucked from the Colts. From the Browns came guard Jim Langer and defensive back Dean Brown, both of whom were moved up from the cab squad when injuries struck in late November.

From San Francisco on an oversight, Shula grabbed 6-6, 265-pound offensive tackle Wayne Moore. Dick Nolan, the 49ers' coach, had by accident included Moore on his last, no-recall waiver list. A year later the 27-year-old Texan was challenging for a starting job when a knee injury finished him for the 1971 season. "I consider him one of the fine line prospects in pro football," Shula said.

The most romantic of the newcomers was a walk-on named Bob Kuechenberg, a Notre Dame product who had been drafted fourth but dismissed by Philadelphia in 1969. From there, the balding young guard briefly visited Atlanta's camp before he wound up with the Chicago Owls of the Continental League.

Kuechenberg gained a tryout from the Dolphins and, like Doug Swift, profited from the extra time afforded newcomers while the veterans hassled with the owners. Still, Kuech was a lightweight up front at 6-2 and barely 245. He was waived, went unclaimed and was retained on the taxi squad. When injuries finished both Maxie Williams and Bob DeMarco in late November, Kuechenberg stepped in to finish the season as regular left guard. And nobody moved him in 1971. Kuechenberg displayed exceptional speed—and a tenacity inherited from his father, a human cannonball at carnivals and circuses in the Midwest. His advice to Bob was simple: "Go to college or be a cannonball."

"That cannonball stuff can be tricky business," Bob said. "You need exact timing. Once my Uncle Al substituted in the cannon for my father, who was ill. My uncle came out all right, but he missed the net and hit the ferris wheel. He broke about every bone in his body, but fortunately recovered."

Uncle Al's experience helped make up Bob's mind about college, just as the family's durability helped the 22-year-old survive frequent vocal barrages from Shula. "All in the interests of improving Kuech," said the coach.

Bob took it all in good nature. "Coach Shula says I'm almost eligible to be inducted into the Hall of Shame for being the first lineman responsible for 1,000 yards in penalties." Kuechenberg was immensely likable from the start.

Besides Kuechenberg and Swift, three other free agents came from nowhere to fill jobs. The largest was Frank Cornish, an affable, 285-pound defensive tackle released after four seasons with the Chicago Bears for being too slow, by Coach Jim Dooley's standards. But Shula needed a big man to shore up a light-brigade defensive line. Neither Manny Fernandez nor John Richardson, the incumbent tackles, weighed 250. Bob Heinz, a 6-6, 270-pounder, was only in his second season and needed to develop the aggressiveness attendant to experience.

The smartest of the free agents was Ted Davis, a linebacker first signed by Baltimore in 1964. After three seasons he was sent to New Orleans in the expansion draft, where he spent three more years. Davis knew Shula's zone and performed ably as a fourth linebacker in 1970, though his 215 pounds limited his potential.

The free agent with glamor was a sawed-off, left-footed,

sidewheeling soccer kicker named Garabad Sarkis Yepremian, who at 26 was a man without a country. Of Armenian parents, Garo was born on the Mediterranean island of Cyprus, making him a British subject. In 1950, after Britain withdrew from that land to let the Turks and Greeks argue for possession, Garo's father fled to London searching for a new home for his family.

In England, Garo was managing Worsteds, Ltd., and also playing soccer when his older brother beckoned from America. After trying but failing to gain a soccer scholarship—he had no high-school diploma and the regimental NCAA demanded one—the brothers Yepremian started to write pro clubs. Krikor became an untiring agent for Garo.

They had luck at Detroit, where Garo's strong instep made an impression in tryouts. Four days after reporting to the Lions, he was kicking off in a game he did not understand. Nevertheless he had a good 1966 season, with 13 field goals including an NFL-record six in a victory over Minnesota. But Joe Schmidt replaced Harry Gilmer as head coach in 1967, and the 5-7, 170-pound Yepremian was not Schmidt's idea of a football player. He lingered on the taxi squad for the next three seasons, while weaving ties in his basement for subsistence money.

"I was pretty discouraged at the time," said Garo. "But I was convinced I could be a kicker."

Though he spoke four languages, Yepremian was unable to convince anybody of his left-footed prowess. So Edwin Anderson of the Lions wrote to Shula and suggested he give the earnest Cypriot a tryout.

Yepremian was astonishingly good from the start. But Shula had an obligation to Karl Kremser, a nervous youth who had done well enough as a 1969 rookie to deserve a shot at retaining his job. Of his 13 field goals in 22 attempts,

Kremser had not missed on eight opportunities inside the 30.

Shula explained this to Garo, who was content to bide his time on the taxi squad. Garo's accuracy, however, particularly from long range, had shaken the impressionable Kremser from the start of camp. And when he missed a routine shot in the season opener at Boston, Karl was as good as gone.

Except for Warfield, Fleming and DeMarco, the offense was familiar. Howard Twilley, managing to stave off competitors for the fourth straight year, opened at wide receiver opposite Warfield. Among Twilley's challengers was Willie Richardson, who had caught 178 passes in seven seasons for Shula at Baltimore. The tackles were Norm Evans and Doug Crusan, the guards Larry Little and Maxie Williams, the center Bob DeMarco. The quarterback was Griese, the running backs Csonka and Kiick.

The defense had been radically altered to include rookies Mike Kolen, Doug Swift, Curtis Johnson and Jake Scott. Kolen and Swift flanked Nick Buoniconti behind the line. Johnson was at the left corner opposite Lloyd Mumphord, the second-year pro who had displaced Dick Westmoreland. Scott was at free safety, with Dick Anderson the strong safety. Only the front four of Bill Stanfill, John Richardson, Manny Fernandez and Jim Riley remained unchanged.

In the opening game of the season the Dolphins absorbed a 27–14 defeat at the hands of the Boston Patriots. Shula was crushed, and Monte Clark, the high-strung offensive line coach, was sent to the hospital for a blood-pressure checkup.

Griese was sacked eight times, a record for a Boston team that had seldom displayed such aggressiveness in the past. Furthermore, the Dolphins blew a 14–3 lead in the last few minutes of the first half. Shula was simmering after the game, which had been played in ancient Harvard Stadium. One bright reporter, disturbed enough after the winding climb to the press box and the jockey's accommodations, collared a fellow cynic en route to the loser's dressing room. "Shula was right," the reporter said, disgusted. "He's no miracle man."

Florida's writing contingent was all ears while waiting to be admitted to the dressing room of Harvard's Dillon Field House. And the walls of old Dillon are as thin as they are storied. Inside, unaware that every discouraging word was overheard, Shula berated his routed troops. Among other staccato observations, he advised them that their performance would make them objects of ridicule in South Florida.

After opening the door to the wretches outside, Shula erupted all over again when he learned the size of his audience. Bernie Lincicombe of the Fort Lauderdale *Sun-Sentinel* reasoned with him. "What the hell, Coach, look at it this way," Lincicombe counseled. "They've been objects of ridicule for four years."

Even in the awful circumstances, Shula bit his lip to remain properly grim. Among the coach's likable traits is a rigid honesty with himself and others. He broke up laughing while recalling Lincicombe's line later.

Monte Clark, the offensive line coach, was inconsolable for two weeks after the debacle. "The adrenalin was flowing just as though I was still playing," Clark said. "I couldn't help it. The first game is so very important in a season. I was a wreck."

Clark's state on the sideline deteriorated with the progress of the game, particularly when Griese's protection broke down and the quarterback was flattened. "I thought I was a complete coaching failure, a bust. I saw July and August and September go down the drain."

Buoniconti, Miami's player representative, had a different problem: The squad was summoned to sing Christmas carols and he was in charge. The idea was to place an album in the home of every red-blooded season ticket-holder, and all 26 NFL clubs were called on to enlist choirs. Buoniconti recruited his vocalists and led them to the recording studio. But he refused to allow coverage of the event. "No way," Nick said. "After the performance we put on in Boston, how do you think The Man [Shula] would react if he saw a picture of us singing? And how do you think we'd feel ourselves?"

Nick was probably right. Members of the audience who heard the show swore there was a suspicious tremolo in the left side of the offensive line, which was getting blamed for almost everything else by the South Florida fans. "Same old Dolphins," went the refrain.

But the critics were muffled, Clark's blood pressure eased a bit and the choir sighed in relief the following Sunday at Houston. The Dolphins beat the Oilers 20–10 on the cement-like floor of the Astrodome.

Carrying over his bad luck from Harvard Stadium, Kremser kicked footballs everywhere but between the uprights in a Saturday drill. Shula, waiting for an excuse to activate Yepremian, did so on the spot.

Little Garo was a hit from the start, punching field goals of 31 and 42 yards between Griese touchdown passes of three yards to rookie tight end Jim Mandich and five yards to the indomitable Twilley. Shula used Mandich with Fleming in a seven-man line near the end zone. Braced for the run, Houston's defense left Mandich to his own designs in the end zone.

"I want to thank you very much," Yepremian said after the game. And this became a trademark of the prematurely bald 26-year-old with Continental manners.

Bill Arnsparger's defense was identifying itself as a "rubber-band" operation that yielded but seldom snapped. The Oilers outgained the visitors in total yardage, 307 to 284.

However, the game may well have been won in the first quarter. On first down at the Miami one-yard line, safeties Scott and Anderson sprang up to stop fullback Hoyle Granger. On second down the same pair halted running back Woody Campbell. And when Johnson fumbled on third down, the Oilers had to settle for Roy Gerela's 10-yard field goal. Arnsparger's defense continued this way right up to the 1972 Super Bowl.

Clark's offensive line redeemed itself. Griese, preferring to roll out ("moving pocket" style), was left pretty much undisturbed as he completed 10 of 17 passes for 138 yards.

Prior to the home opener against Oakland, the Orange Bowl attendance high for an AFL visitor was the 48,108 who came to see Joe Namath's New York Jets in December 1969. But 57,140 came to see the Dolphins beat Oakland 20–13, and to sit through a second-quarter storm reminiscent of Harvey Hester's Seahawk days. The new Poly-Turf turned white under sheets of rain, but drained to mere dampness by the third quarter; the ground crew had neglected to pull sideline plugs that would have allowed the water to quickly flow off the crowned artificial surface.

The Dolphins didn't care, however. They had never beaten Oakland in six prior tries. And before the deluge struck, a beautiful maneuver by Warfield convinced his colleagues the game would be theirs.

Early in the second quarter, Griese dropped back to pass from the Oakland 49. Wide to the quarterback's left, covered as usual by two defenders, Warfield darted into the secondary on a zigzag course. Paul left cornerback Willie Brown rooted with a stunning outside fake, then scampered across the grain through the middle of the Raider secondary. Seizing Griese's pass at the Oakland 40, he hustled goalward in that bounding gait of his that had produced 44 touchdowns in five seasons with Cleveland. At the 25, however, Warfield appeared trapped by two defenders in front of him and a third coming on hard from the rear.

Without losing cadence, Warfield ran in place a few steps and then did a 360-degree pirouette. He landed in full stride and fled untouched to the end zone. This was Warfield's introduction to Miami. After an awed moment of silence, the Orange Bowl erupted in a standing ovation.

Only Sam Skinner, the Falstaffian black journalist from the West Coast, appeared unaffected by the move. "Nothing new," Skinner observed. "We call it the 'Police Spin.' The brothers use it to elude the cops."

Warfield reacted with his usual equanimity. "It happened instinctively," he said. "There's really nothing to elaborate. But I'm pleased the crowd reacted so warmly. It made me feel I belonged."

Warfield caught a second touchdown pass from Griese, and Yepremian contributed field goals of 47 and 40 yards to finish the Raiders.

Two more barriers fell the following Saturday night in New York. Warfield and Twilley caught touchdown passes and Yepremian soccer-styled field goals of 37 and 11 yards as the Dolphins defeated the Jets 20–6. It marked the first time a Miami team had won three straight regular-season games and the first time the Jets and Joe Namath had been beaten in nine tries.

Namath, the swinging bachelor, serves as an interesting American symbol, a long-haired hard-hat in tune with the rebellious young. From the moment he was signed to a $427,000 contract by showman Sonny Werblin, Namath lived the role. He was a hero straight out of Victorian melodrama, possessed with courage and timing and swagger. Manhattan was overwhelmed. Joe embodied Hemingway's definition of courage: grace under pressure. At first he was almost a caricature out of O. Henry, a rube bringing sophisticated Manhattan to heel. But he is now losing ground as his thrice-opened knees threaten to erase him momentarily from the public consciousness.

Griese is Namath's antithesis. Only a few know the terms of the contracts he has signed (estimated at $50,000 to $80,000 a year) to guide the Dolphins since 1967. Very much a family man, Griese attends Mass every Sunday, works at real estate in the winter and operates a profitable summer camp for boys. He is difficult to know personally. "I'm an ordinary Joe," is Bob's explanation. "I've been built up to be something I'm not. Still, I think I have a right to a personal life."

Bob is not physically gifted. He throws quickly but lacks the powerful arm of a Namath or Lamonica, a Bradshaw or Plunkett. Griese succeeds by using mind and body. He is spectacular as a scrambler.

"I've got to make it right now," Griese once told a friend. Yet while Namath was hurling 62 passes for 397 yards, trying to do it himself in a 29–22 defeat the following week by Baltimore, Griese was continuing the pattern that would characterize Shula's offense.

At Buffalo Griese turned the brunt of the attack over to Csonka and Kiick. The 26-year-old quarterback had done the same against Oakland and Houston, calling only 18 pass plays in each instance while using 32 running plays against the Raiders, 44 against the Oilers. Griese now had the balanced attack George Wilson could not produce, and he was making the most of it. Griese called 35 running plays and 26 pass plays as the Dolphins dominated the Bills 33–14.

Csonka smashed for touchdowns of five and four yards. Warfield escaped for a 43-yard touchdown pass. And the incredible Yepremian hit field goals of 46, 42, 47 and 30 yards. Garo's instep was beginning to discourage defenses.

Csonka, trimmed to 235, was reaching the potential predicted by his agent two years before. "Larry will soon overshadow Griese," said Alan Brickman of Syracuse. In five games, including four straight victories, Csonka and Kiick had forged a combined 545 yards rushing. Kiick added 218 yards on 16 catches. The "complete athlete," in Shula's phrase.

Everything was coming up roses as the Dolphins returned to Miami tied with Baltimore for the AFC East lead. Joe Robbie confidently predicted the crowd would surpass 70,000 for Sunday's game with Cleveland. He was right. An unprecedented sellout of 75,312 represented a high for a regular-season game.

Historically, however, the Dolphins lived up to standard. Just when success seemed within arm's reach, Miami succumbed to the Browns 28–0.

The following Sunday, Shula returned to Baltimore for the first time in enemy clothing. He was applauded and cheered by the usual full house of 60,240 at "The Asylum on 33rd Street." The crowd became even more jubilant as the Colts stampeded the Dolphins 35–0.

The futility continued the next Sunday at Philadelphia. The Eagles, who had played 16 games without a win, ran up a 24–0 bulge on the Dolphins in three quarters. Griese was removed for John Stofa, who had been called upon previously to mop up against Cleveland and Baltimore. Now, after Griese's offense had been shut out for 11 straight quarters, Stofa got the Dolphins on the board by directing a 17-point fourth quarter that included touchdown passes of 52 yards to Warfield and 27 yards to Willie Richardson after Yepremian's 24-yard field goal.

All that accomplished, however, was a third consecutive defeat and a clamor to get Griese out of there for the Cinderella Man.

> I knew it was my joint burning down. But why bother the poor firemen at three o'clock in the morning?
> —CHARLIE WREN

21. *An Indestructible Heavyweight*

Bob Griese, the hero of the early season, was the traditionally dishonored figurehead when the Dolphins returned home to try to break their three-game losing string in the game against New Orleans. The "We Want Stofa" club was revived and clamoring during the week that Shula was making up his mind about which quarterback to use. Complicating Griese's situation was a hip injury he had suffered against Philadelphia, plus the seven interceptions in the losses to the Browns, Colts and Eagles. In the end, Don Shula enunciated his practical if unpopular decision: "Griese is my No. 1 quarterback."

Predictably, the fair-weather fans avoided the Orange Bowl. Only 42,866 came out to watch the Dolphins emerge with a 21–10 victory. Griese rewarded Shula's confidence by completing 15 of 19 passes for 225 yards without an interception.

The Colts were next at the Orange Bowl, and those of little faith returned to form a 67,699 crowd that exulted in a 34–17 Miami victory. Jake Scott, who had been returning punts with reckless abandon all season, escaped 77 yards to a first-quarter touchdown, and the Dolphins were never headed.

Griese startled the defense on a draw in the second quarter. From the Baltimore 15, the quarterback retreated as if to pass before scampering straight up the middle for a score and a 14–3 lead that set off a grandstand uproar which continued unabated for the rest of the afternoon.

Shula made no attempt to hide his elation in the dressing room. "This one has to represent our finest accomplishment yet." But the dressing room was uncommonly quiet, for the game ball had been dedicated to the memory of Les Bingaman.

Bingaman had died of a heart attack the Thursday night prior to the game. George Wilson's defensive line coach had been failing steadily all year. But his death at 44 saddened everybody who had known the gruff and gentle giant. The game ball went to Betty, his wife, and two-year-old Lester III. Bingo had feared little Les would never make a pro because "the kid is smiling all the time. Somebody put him through a smiling machine."

Manny Fernandez and his colleagues on the front four—Jim Riley, John Richardson and Bill Stanfill—left after the Baltimore game for McKenzie, Tenn., where Bingaman was to be buried the next day.

"It's hard to explain a game ball unless you know Bingaman," said Buoniconti, who had led a vicious defensive effort with 10 tackles. "We had no choice. We had to give the ball to Betty and her boy. There was so much love for the guy on this club. Love, that's the only word for it."

Bingaman, "born on a mountain top in Tennessee," cultivated a poignant and gleefully coarse sense of humor in his massive frame. Sitting in a "saloon" (never a lounge) near his southwest Miami home, armed with a stein of draught and a jar of fiery peppers, Les delighted in learning what he called "that pretty poem," which he went over line by line and draught by draught.

> Me father was a gentleman,
> And musical to boot;
> He used to play piano
> In a house of ill repute;
> The madam was a lady,
> A credit to her cult;
> She liked me father's playin',
> And I was the result.

Though Bingo would roar at the punch line, he was mostly a quiet man much given to brooding. He was virtually unbeatable at dollar poker, and was an avid antique collector who outsharped many a dealer for a prized relic.

Among the funeral home visitors was Charlie Wren, whose St. Petersburg Beach saloon Les had called home in 1966. "Look at him," Charlie said. "He don't look nothing like he did four years ago. He reminds me of McGuinness. Les would love that story."

McGuinness was a buck-and-wing hoofer Charlie had befriended when he operated an "honest speakeasy" on 47th Street in New York. "Al Jolson used to warn me," Charlie said, "to tell McGuinness to slow down. I tried to, but he wouldn't. He finally got himself a job in a Ziegfeld show and killed himself rehearsing in front of the mirror."

Charlie had left New York shortly after Prohibition. There had been talk he set fire to his own joint, which Charlie disclaimed. Standing beside Bingaman, who had never believed Charlie's innocence, he exonerated himself again. "I walked around the corner with a friend," Charlie said, "and we both seen smoke coming out of a building on 47th. My friend yelled, 'Look, Charlie, ain't that your place?'

"I said, 'Aw, don't bother the poor firemen at three o'clock in the morning.'"

> As for the rest, to come to the conclusion
> Of this true dream, the telescope is gone
> Which kept my optics free from all delusion,
> And show'd me what I in my turn have shown;
> All I saw farther, in the last confusion,
> Was, that King George slipp'd into heaven for one;
> And when the tumult dwindled to a calm,
> I left him practising the hundredth psalm.
>
> —LORD BYRON

22. *High Road to Muddy Oakland*

It was Monday night, November 30, in Atlanta. Sportscaster Howard Cosell's eyes were moist and he was sniffling in the television booth with Don Meredith and Keith Jackson. The Dolphins and Falcons were matched on Monday Night Football, and hero Cosell was taking a vocal mauling from a few neighboring wits in Atlanta Stadium.

"Here's a bottle, Howard!" one taunted. "Have another drink!"

"Hey, Howard, bundle up! You might catch cold!"

Cosell reacted with wounded indignation. The week before, in Philadelphia, he had last been seen at halftime, bundled up and obviously indisposed. Meredith had offered no clearer explanation to the viewers than simply remarking that Howard had left for the night.

"I wouldn't have *thought* of leaving," Cosell protested. "I had a *severe* cold."

On the field things were going from bad to worse for the Falcons. Even without Paul Warfield, who had broken a rib against Baltimore and was sidelined indefinitely, the Dolphins were asserting physical superiority against an outfit that prided itself on muscle.

Larry Csonka was fierce while elbowing for 108 yards in 19 carries. Mercury Morris, gaining confidence each week after his training-camp thigh injury, dashed 76 yards in six spot carries and added a 49-yard kickoff return. The Dolphins stayed mainly on the ground as Jim Kiick's one-yard touchdown dive plus field goals of 43 and 9 yards by Garo Yepremian produced a 13-0 halftime lead.

After the home team made it close in the fourth quarter, Griese staged his finest clutch performance of the season. He directed an 80-yard drive that consumed nearly nine minutes and resulted in Csonka's one-yard plunge for the clinching score with time nearly gone. Twice on third-down plays Griese scrambled out of apparent traps to hit Marv Fleming and then Howard Twilley for first downs. Don Shula called it "our most important sustained drive of the year." The 20-7 victory gave the Dolphins a third straight win, a 7-4 record and a shot at the AFC post-season playoffs.

The depth Shula had bargained for in his waiver and cab-squad manipulations had paid off. Bob Kuechenberg went all the way at left guard replacing Maxie Williams, who had moved over to center when Bob DeMarco was injured in the Baltimore game. Karl Noonan, who sat behind Warfield for nine games, grabbed a 51-yard touchdown pass from Griese to seal Baltimore's fate. And when Williams was hurt, Carl Mauck took over for the balance of the season. On defense, big Frank Cornish in the line, Ted Davis at both outside linebacking positions and rookie Tim Foley in the secondary all contributed in reserve roles.

With the Baltimore game the Dolphins began operating as though possessed. Against Boston the following Sunday before 51,032, most of whom had never seen a Patriot except in Revolutionary War reproductions, the Dolphins exacted vengeance, 37–20, for their opening-game defeat.

The next Sunday, playing the crippled New York Jets, Yepremian's instep was the difference as the 5-7 Armenian left-footed field goals of 40, 13 and 21 yards in a 16–10 victory. Garo's 21-yarder, which just about sealed things with 41 seconds left, set off a frenzied roar from 75,099 Orange Bowl witnesses. The fifth straight victory also established a Miami record.

The sixth straight was accomplished with ease. Two Kiick touchdowns, another by Csonka and a 21-yard catch by Twilley helped to amass a 31–0 halftime lead over hapless Buffalo before another huge crowd of 70,990.

The Harvard Stadium cynic was wrong. Shula had indeed accomplished some kind of miracle with a team that had been provoking laughter or tears only a year before. The 10-4 record was second in the East to Baltimore's 11-2-1. But only two other clubs in the NFL (Minnesota, 12-2, and San Francisco, 10-3-1) finished with better records. And so, as the second-place AFC team with the best record, the Dolphins gained their playoff trip in the "wild card" category.

Wild card was right. After being shut out for 11 quarters and losing three straight in midseason, the Dolphins had won six in a row down the stretch, four of them without the injured Warfield and two other regulars in the line. Even Carroll Rosenbloom was impressed. The Baltimore owner called a press conference, partly to explain that he was guided more by emotion than by reason in his prior descriptions of Shula as a "pig" and a "loser of big ones."

Shula's miracle, as indeed Miami fans saw it, was wrought

by his personality, drive and positivism. The coach literally changed the thinking of an outfit that had won 15 of 56 games in their first four years. From a team that wondered how it would lose on a given Sunday, Shula's Miami team never doubted that it would win.

After the victory over New York which virtually clinched a playoff trip in December, Shula nervously sipped coffee and bemoaned a missed defensive assignment abetting the Jets' only touchdown. "We gave it to them, just gave it to them," Shula muttered.

Curt Gowdy, sleepless after a transcontinental leap that included tubal forensics in Oakland and Miami on consecutive days, shook his head in bewilderment. "How does he act when he loses?" Gowdy wondered.

Howard Twilley walked by grinning like a bumpkin on Saturday night. Twilley's relentless blocking and able hands overcome a slowness afoot and lack of size that cause football students to wonder why nobody can beat him out of a starting job. Shula openly admires Twilley. Except, being Shula, he would trade Howard in a minute for a more talented athlete.

Against the Jets, Twilley had seized 11 passes for 131 yards and two touchdowns while blocking with a demonic viciousness.

"Twilley," Shula demanded. "What the hell are you doing out so late? Don't you know it's almost 10 o'clock?"

Twilley just grinned.

"Look, Howard," the coach said, "if you can't find anything to do, why not go out and crack back on a linebacker?"

The personal touch is among Shula's most effective qualities. He and his staff lived in the Biscayne College dormitories among the players. Shula knew the first names of all the players' wives. He knew that Scott's mother as well as Maxie

Williams' mother were intense football fans. And Shula made certain they were kept posted.

On the Orange Bowl sideline during the Jets' game, Shula gave Lloyd Mumphord a stem-to-stern chewing out for the cornerback's careless coverage on a pass that sailed out of bounds. "You're giving him far too much to the outside," the coach yelled. "You've got Jake Scott to help you inside. Dammit, Lloyd, get out there closer to the sideline where you belong." All this over an incomplete pass. At a post-game party a few hours later, Shula hurried across the room when he saw Mumphord and his wife leaving. Calling both by their first names, the coach bid them farewell as fondly as though they were leaving the country.

After qualifying for the playoff trip to Oakland, Shula immediately announced that the squad would depart on Christmas Eve. "I've always found it better to leave for the West Coast a couple of days early," he explained. "It's a long trip, and this way we can work out Friday and Saturday." To Shula, December 25 was the Friday before Sunday's game.

Warfield, his broken rib tightly wrapped, returned for the Oakland game. But Manny Fernandez, the only consistent pass-rusher of the front four, separated his shoulder in a freak practice collision with Larry Seiple in December. Fernandez gave it a try, but he was so grotesquely strapped that he resembled Quasimodo, and could not function effectively. Still the Dolphins had surmounted injuries en route to Oakland and were confident that their success would continue.

This was in contrast to Paul Brown's Cincinnati team. The Bengals had squeezed into the playoffs with an 8-6 record and were up against the Colts in Baltimore, an unenviable assignment. "Our kids are happy to have come this far," Brown said before the game. "We consider our season a tremendous success, win or lose."

Shula offered no such opinion. "Everything we've worked so hard to achieve is on the line in this game," he said. "We have only one thought—to win."

On a field oozing with mud, Miami's Super Bowl aspirations were erased in two quick second-half developments after Warfield had produced a 7–0 lead by grabbing a 16-yard toss from Griese in the end zone. Oakland's Fred Biletnikoff evened up the score with a 22-yard touchdown catch of a Daryle Lamonica pass.

With the score tied in the third quarter, the wet football slipped as Griese aimed at Warfield, behind Willie Brown. The wobbler landed in the cornerback's hands, and Brown dashed 50 yards down the sideline to score. The clincher came early in the fourth quarter. From his 18, Lamonica faded back while enjoying fatherly protection. Rod Sherman was in full stride when Lamonica let it go. The receiver caught the pass just out of cornerback Curtis Johnson's reach and kept moving. The play covered 82 yards and finished the Dolphins.

Griese then hit Willie Richardson for seven yards in the end zone, but it was too late. The impudent Dolphins had finally been knocked out, though not before giving 54,401 customers their money's worth.

Few Miami players had anything to say after the 21–14 loss. "I'm still proud of these ballplayers," Shula said. "They came a long way and they can look back on their efforts with the pride of winners."

> Like almost every professional football player, I'm simply not a one-dimensional figure.
>
> —JERRY KRAMER

23. *Butch and Sundance*

From the day they met, Larry Csonka and Jim Kiick were an entry. As 1968 rookies, they became roommates after arriving from the College All-Star game at the Dolphins' Boca Raton camp.

Drafted No. 1 after a great year at Syracuse, Csonka was the object of attention that summer. Yet before the first interview had begun, he pointed to a supine figure dozing on a cot in the corner of the room. "Listen, guys, I want you to meet Jim Kiick," Larry said. "You're going to hear from him." The figure on the cot rolled over, waved an arm of sleepy greeting and sat up curiously on the edge of his bed.

"Too fat and too slow," was the observation of Norm Van Brocklin, All-Star coach against the Green Bay Packers, in keeping Kiick seated behind Csonka and Lee White.

"He also said I had a lousy attitude," added Kiick, a self-deprecating character who transmits a false impression of listlessness. "I suppose it was my fault. I'm not a big holler guy, and unless you play for Southern Cal or UCLA in the West, nobody in the East knows you from Adam."

Van Brocklin was not impressed that Kiick had been an all-conference tailback at Wyoming for three straight years, amassing 1,714 yards on 431 carries and another 600 yards on pass receptions.

Kiick didn't make much of an impression his rookie summer. He might have been overlooked entirely if not for a no-cut contract and the fact that first-string running backs Stan Mitchell and Jack Harper were injured in September.

The no-cut had its drawbacks. "My own fault, though, for listening to my wife," he explained. "She had this thing about security."

Alice and Jim's lawyer double-teamed him into signing a two-year arrangement in the $15,000–$17,000 range. This prevented him from claiming the raise he strongly merited from his 1968 rookie season, when he gained 1,043 total yards and was voted the club's outstanding rookie.

"I spend money pretty fast," Kiick noted. "But I didn't get much to spend those first two years. I got an $8,000 bonus for signing, but that went out the window. Hell, I don't want to hustle around scraping in the offseason."

Csonka, Kiick's most consistent booster, managed to get his footloose pal a public relations job for a frozen-food trucking firm. But Kiick quit after one winter. "I guess I should be grateful to Larry for recommending me. Except I wasn't cut out to go around shaking hands with people I don't even know."

In many ways Kiick was born for pro football. Jim's friends wonder what he will do when his body betrays him, as he has been the most durable of Dolphins. In his second season Kiick functioned in a manner that amazed George Wilson. In one game, on November 30, when the Dolphins were going nowhere but down, Kiick went all out—ignoring a shattered big toe, a pulled ankle tendon, a punctured elbow, a dislocated hip and a broken finger on the right hand.

As a rookie he made the AFL East All-Star team. "I couldn't believe it," he said. "I didn't think I was good enough for the *Mad* magazine team. Being recognized at your profession is an honor you don't forget," said Kiick, seriously for a change. "I don't let anybody kid me about that. There's nothing like earning the respect of the guys you work with."

Jim got his raise in 1970, the same year Csonka came on big after two frustrating seasons of head injuries. The pair totaled 1,532 yards (874 from Csonka) of the 2,082 the Dolphins gained on the ground. In addition, Kiick's 28 catches for 703 yards trailed only Warfield. Jim scored 12 touchdowns, a club record, and proved himself worth every cent of a $34,000 contract that held him until spring 1971.

In late 1970, Kiick and Csonka were captivated by the film "Butch Cassidy and the Sundance Kid." On the basis of Csonka's wry contention that "Kiick is always getting me into trouble," Larry cast himself as Robert (Sundance Kid) Redford while Kiick assumed the role of Paul (Butch Cassidy) Newman. They began feeding one another lines from the script. "We got so we didn't have to finish a sentence," Csonka said. "One guy would know right away what the other guy was talking about, like pig-Latin."

At Los Angeles, Kiick was buried beneath a swale of Rams including Deacon Jones and the Olsen brothers. He looked up, saw Csonka staring balefully at him, and paraphrased the film's recurring line: "Listen, Kid, find out who these guys are. We ain't coming back *here* again."

"Hell, you think about football, and it's a gruesome game," Csonka explained. "Who really wants to go out on Sunday and get his brains beaten. It's unnatural. So Jim and I decided we'd get all the enjoyment out of it we can. Maybe we're nuts, but little things like the Butch and Sundance stuff help. Even though we're both getting pretty sick of it."

Like Shula, Csonka possesses a Hungarian adamance and biting wit. Behind black eyes is a mixture of mischief and humanity that make him a most likable individual, proud of his toughness and yet disappointed that his brawn had been celebrated above all else.

On a visit to Syracuse before his freshman year, Larry was told by a lineman named Gary Buggenhagen that he could develop forearm strength by banging his arms against solid objects. Larry immediately started working on the walls of the family's Stow, Ohio, homestead.

"Take him," Larry's father implored Coach Bernie Schwartzwalder. "Please take him before he knocks the house down."

But Csonka is a gentle giant whose human side seldom gets a chance to emerge. "I hate being classified as some kind of animal," he says. "I don't enjoy pain. I'm no sprinter. So I have to use what I've got to gain every inch. Does that make me a brute? Don't get me wrong, I love football. I just don't like so much of the bull surrounding it."

Offseason, Csonka separates himself from the squad. "I see enough of the guys during the rest of the year," he explains.

The rollicking Csonka and Kiick created only a routine stir when they announced in June 1971 that they had secured the services of the Mark McCormack agency to handle their affairs. Csonka's contract, a three-year agreement at approximately $30,000 a year, was also up. Dissatisfied with the renewals the Dolphins had offered, they decided, through agent Ed Keating, to hold out as a team.

"I'm no bargainer," Kiick explained, "and neither is Larry. We don't want to haggle. But we know we're worth more than we're being offered, so we decided to get an agent." The McCormack firm has an unquestioned reputation. Its clients include Arnold Palmer, Jack Nicklaus, Dave McNally, Jean-Claude Killy and Paul Warfield.

Shula was angry when the pair refused to report to camp while unsigned, on the grounds that injuries would destroy their bargaining power. "They have an obligation to be in camp. It's in their contracts," the coach insisted. He imposed a fine of $200 on each back for every day they missed.

The coach had been hit with another blow earlier. Joe Theismann, the Notre Dame quarterback and Miami's No. 4 draft choice, suddenly signed with Toronto after verbally agreeing to play for the Dolphins. So Shula signed George Mira to compete with John Stofa for the backup job behind Griese. The move was popular. Mira had been a scrambling hero at the University of Miami before getting lost behind John Brodie in San Francisco. But Shula had misgivings, for Mira, after pressing to be traded, had gone from the 49ers to Philadelphia to Baltimore without making an impression.

While Csonka and Kiick held out and the bargaining grew acrimonious between Ed Keating and Joe Thomas, Shula began to believe his summers were snakebit. He had planned to vary the power attack supplied by Csonka and Kiick with the breakaway potential of Mercury Morris in a three-back offense. Morris had gained 409 yards in 60 carries the previous year for a 6.8 average. But with the other two absent, Shula was stymied.

Csonka and Kiick began to feel guilty. "We know we can't stay home indefinitely," Csonka said at one point. But they kept to themselves and let Keating joust with management.

Finally the backs could stand it no longer. "Hell," Kiick said, "we'd have played for nothing." After a two-week holdout, costing each man $2,800, Csonka and Kiick returned "for the good of the team."

The night after reporting, both players signed contracts in

the Miami Heart Institute where Thomas was laid up with hepatitis. The McCormack affiliation was worth its salt, even after the 15 percent fee. Similar contracts for the two players totaled more than $150,000 each spread over three seasons, plus incentive bonuses.

Their $5,600 total fine was later matched by Joe Robbie and paid into a fund for Greg Stead, a paralyzed athlete from Edison High in Miami.

Reversals continued as Otto Stowe, the No. 1 draft choice whose speed and pass-catching abilities Shula was counting on to take the pressure off Warfield (Twilley, as usual, had to prove himself), suffered a seizure and was rushed to the hospital. Stowe returned a few days later, after tests had determined that nothing was amiss with the rookie who had broken Big Eight receiving records at Iowa State. Then Morris severely sprained an ankle. It seemed that the three-back offense was doomed.

The exhibition season fit the same uncertain theme. Orange Bowl crowds topping 60,000 watched the Dolphins lose the opener to Cincinnati 27–10, then tie San Francisco 17–17. Next came a 10–7 loss to the Packers in Green Bay.

Panic was not evident, however. Shula no longer needed to sell tickets, and he was experimenting with his inexperienced employees. The following Saturday night the Dolphins defeated Detroit 28–24, with Griese going the distance before a home crowd of 63,082.

Mira won the second-string quarterback job by default. Stofa, who appeared to be running ahead, was walloped amidships by Washington linebacker Jack Pardee. John suffered a painful hip dislocation that reduced him to injured-reserve status—until he was traded to the Denver Broncos in November for a draft choice.

Mira enjoyed a good night against the Redskins in a 27–10

Miami victory to even the exhibition ledger going into the sixth game at Minnesota. The 61,202 Washington crowd gave the Dolphins a four-game Orange Bowl average of 61,452 and made them one of the most lucrative cities in the NFL for preseason capers.

But Shula remained worried about his squad, particularly after a 24–0 chastening by the Vikings. "We've been inconsistent to say the least. Either we play extremely good or extremely bad. I honestly don't know what to think of the schedule ahead of us."

Another matter of concern was a broken bone in the right wrist of Nick Buoniconti. The 30-year-old defensive plug had fractured it against Detroit and wore a cast to the season opener at Denver. "I'm a celebrity at last," Nick said, waving the cast. "I broke the same bone Namath did."

Buoniconti insisted on playing, but Shula took no chances. Instead, he traded a No. 2 draft pick to Cleveland for Bob Matheson, an experienced linebacker who became a valuable asset.

Three other defensive regulars missed all or part of the summer exercises. Curtis Johnson was idle all six weekends because of a hemorrhaged thigh. Johnson never did regain the left corner. However Tim Foley, another of the excellent 1970 rookie crop reaped by Joe Thomas, came on strong at the position. Foley, too, had missed the 1970 exhibition season because of an ankle injury.

At 6-1 and 195, Johnson was too hefty and too quick to be out of work for long. By October the silent Toledoan had ousted Lloyd Mumphord from the right corner, and remained a fixture all year.

Jake Scott, whose 290 yards with 27 punt returns had helped earn Dolphin Rookie of the Year honors in 1970, sat out the last four games with a severely sprained ankle.

The ankle stayed with Scott all season. But as with a shoulder separation the year before, Jake was literally needled into action every Sunday when the regular season began. "It's just a little old ache," Scott said of the ankle. "My mother would kill me if she saw me layin' down on the job."

Manny Fernandez sat out the first four exhibitions recuperating from shoulder surgery, then bounced back to be voted the Dolphins' outstanding defensive lineman for the fourth straight season.

On offense, guard Maxie Williams and tackle Wayne Moore were eliminated because of back and knee injuries respectively. This proved the end for 31-year-old Williams, a six-year pro and one of only two Dolphins remaining from the 1966 expansion draft. The other was Norm Evans, 28 and in his prime at right tackle.

After Stan Mitchell was reserved with an ankle injury, just three others remained from the original squad—backup safety Bob Petrella, substitute receiver Karl Noonan and the indomitable Howard Twilley.

The potential of top draft choice Otto Stowe, who opened the season opposite Warfield until Twilley took over as usual, helped convince Shula that 32-year-old Willie Richardson had run his course. Rehired by Baltimore, Richardson never regained his form of the late 1960s. The Colts dismissed him after the season.

Though such rivals as the Colts and Jets in the AFC East knew first-hand that Shula's Dolphins would be formidable, few established NFL firms really believed the doormats from Miami had come of age despite the 10-4 season in 1970. Besides physical precision instilled by Shula, the Dolphins also had a quarterback advantage. Joe Namath was again indisposed and so was John Unitas, who had ruptured an Achilles tendon playing paddle-ball early in the year. Their absence left Bob Griese without a peer in the East. The efficient Griese had completed 58 percent of his passes in 1970 while throwing less often in deference to a running game that led the AFC. The "No-Name Defense," which was gaining identity through its lack thereof, had led the AFC with a 228-point low.

The four-a-day practices and continuous skill-busting sessions were impositions of the past. They had served their purpose. Dr. Thomas Tutko, a San Jose State psychologist who supervised spring testing the pros resent so deeply, said Shula's squad scored highest of the NFL squads he tested in "motivation."

Shula's practices are models of the Latin dictum *repetitio est mater studeorum* (the mother of achievement is repetition). A calisthenics session is invariably followed by agility and quickness drills. These are triggered by a coach moving a football. And if a player moves so much as a split second before or after the ball, the drill is repeated.

Shula's camp is more mental than physical. The practices are designed to teach and perfect. Plays are repeated until the head coach is satisfied, and usually this takes a while. For the most part, Shula prefers to save the hitting for Sundays. His stress on conditioning, however, is responsible for the remarkable scarcity of crippling injuries.

In his second season at the helm Shula stressed the ground game, enforced by Csonka and Kiick and the distraction Warfield's menacing presence posed in the enemy secondary. Warfield was also the perfect lightning bolt when the ground game got sticky. The wispy receiver caught 11 touchdown passes and scampered 996 yards, exceeded only by Bob Hayes of Dallas.

No longer were the offensive linemen required to fall back and pass-block while Griese unloaded 30 or more times a game. "It's really fun," said right guard Larry Little, who was to make all-pro in his fifth season. Trimmed to 265 and now possessing the speed to go with the motivation Sid Gillman had not been able to find, Little constituted a one-man gang leading Csonka or Kiick or Morris on sweeps.

"The Monday morning after Little got finished with us," said cornerback Earlie Thomas of the Jets, "our whole secondary was in the training room."

Little is a selfless and charming individual despite his menacing mustache and massive frame. Larry was in the van of a black group that initiated the Gold Coast Summer Camp in 1970. The camp was founded, its brochure now reads, "on the premise that the best place to institute constructive social refinement is with our youth." Enrollment was free.

But Little and company could not afford a brochure or anything else except time when the project first began. The ghetto kids slept in tents near the Miami Beach dog track. Providing food was something else. Little's group kicked in its own money until this was exhausted. Joe Robbie, impressed, then staked all hands to a meal and later announced that in future years the Dolphins would underwrite the camp's expenses with proceeds from an annual intrasquad game. The following year the site was moved to the dormitories and spacious grounds of Biscayne College.

Little became a South Florida hero. Tragedy entered his life when Larry's brother was killed in a ghetto argument two days before the Gold Coast benefit scrimmage. But Larry participated. "I couldn't stand off from something I believe in."

Little's number 66 also stood out on the same offensive line that finished the 1970 season in Oakland's mud. The only "new face" was Bob DeMarco. At 33, the canny center regained his starting job with an excellent summer performance he extended all the way to New Orleans.

Marv Fleming was pressed hard by Jim Mandich at tight end but retained the position on the strength of his blocking. No gazelle in the secondary, the pigeon-toed Fleming was never noted for talent as a receiver. "If you win, it makes no difference how many passes you catch," was Marv's reasoning, straight out of Vince Lombardi's book at Green Bay.

For insurance Shula acquired Wayne Mass, released by Chicago after three seasons there, to back up offensive tackles Norm Evans and Doug Crusan. "Cannonball" Kuechenberg remained at left guard.

Bob Heinz and Frank Cornish gradually gained more playing time than John Richardson at right defensive tackle. The rest of the front four remained intact—Fernandez at left tackle, Stanfill at right end, Jim Riley at left end. Assistant Mike Scarry, intent on improving a rush that dropped passers only 18 times in 1970, worked these men hard all summer.

Except for cornerback changes involving Foley and Johnson, the rest of the "No-Name Defense" stayed put. Buoniconti, Doug Swift and Mike Kolen were the linebackers, with Matheson and third-year pro Jesse Powell gaining considerable playing time behind them. Scott and Dick Anderson were the safeties.

The youth of the squad made it difficult to crack. Only three draft choices landed on the active 40—Stowe, linebacker Dale Farley and defensive end Vern Den Herder. The cab squad included two rookie free agents, quarterback Jim Del Gaizo and defensive tackle Maulty Moore. An experienced free agent was regained in Jack Clancy, whose 67 catches had set an AFL record for the Dolphins in 1967. Released by Green Bay and later by Atlanta, the injury-harassed Clancy was cabbed as an additional receiver when Richardson left.

Running backs Terry Cole and Charlie Leigh were obscured by Csonka and Kiick, as was Morris himself. Mercury returned kickoffs but spent most Sundays fidgeting unhappily on the bench. Except for poor Mercury's nerves, however, this was only fitting; 1971 was the year of Butch Cassidy and the Sundance Kid.

> At the battle of Pharsalia, Pompey was blamed for halting his army to await the enemy on foot. Caesar condemned this measure as not only tending to lessen the vigor of the blows, which is always greatest in the assailants, but also to dampen the fire and spirit of the men; whereas those who advance with impetuosity and animate each other with shouts, are filled with an enthusiastic valor and superior ardor.
>
> —PLUTARCH

24. *Tiptoe Through the Poly-Turf*

The Dolphins landed in Denver for the 1971 opener together with the earliest snowstorm in the Mile High City's recent history. But Sunday turned bright and warm—and miserable after a fumbling 10–10 draw with an outfit that wasn't going anywhere. "We did everything we could to lose the ball game, so I guess we should be grateful for the tie," said a truculent Don Shula in the dressing room.

When asked why he had removed rookie Otto Stowe for Howard Twilley in the second half, Shula snapped, "What do you mean, 'why'?" Then, carefully modulating his tone, he said, "Because I thought Twilley had the experience to get open. Stowe wasn't catching any passes."

Fortunately Paul Warfield was. He caught six for 146 yards, including a slant-in toss in the last three minutes that covered 31 yards and furnished the tying touchdown. This pattern of Warfield cutting across the middle was to produce consistent yardage all year. President Nixon was later to advise Shula that he thought this pattern would go against Dallas in the Super Bowl.

Warfield's heroics in Denver were neutralized by four Miami fumbles, including a last-minute muff on a punt return by Jake Scott at the Denver 23. A rarity for Scott. "I relaxed a little and let my arm get away from my body," said Scott, who had returned 18 yards and was struggling for more with three Broncos. "All I had to do was signal for a fair catch and let Garo kick a field goal." Maybe. Yepremian had already joined the error brigade by blowing field-goal shots from 41, 36 and 35 yards out.

In his first pro game at Detroit, against Shula's Baltimore Colts, Garo kicked off into the end zone. "I stood there and admired its beauty," the sawed-off Armenian said in his precise, missionary-school English. "Then I saw several of them [Colts] coming after me. It occurred to me that these men wanted to hurt me." Garo, who knew nothing at all of the game, wheeled about and scampered back to the Detroit bench as fast as he could.

The crowd and even the players burst into laughter, and Garo never outlived the scene in his three years with the Lions. Alex Karras, of course, rode him unmercifully. "These little runts aren't football players," Alex observed. "They sit there on the bench, never get their uniforms mussed and come in for a few seconds. Then they run off squealing, 'Hooray, I keeck touchdown.' Nuts. They ought to be outlawed from the game."

Karras had company after Denver. Among Garo's unflattering correspondence the next week was a letter with a man's tie drawn on it, the type Garo's family made and sold so successfully in Miami. On the tie was the inscription 10–10. Underneath it was written, "Go back to Cyprus, bum. We don't buy this kind of tie." But Garo's confidence never wavered. Against Buffalo the following Sunday he banged field goals of 15, 46, 13, 9 and 48 yards in a 29–14 Miami victory. Garo was himself again. "I want to thank you very much," said the balding 27-year-old who requested jersey number 1 "because I intend to become the best kicker in football."

While Garo redeemed himself, Kiick slashed 108 yards, Csonka 103 in 20 carries apiece. Larry also emerged with his ninth broken nose. "A guy stuck an arm straight out and I rammed into it. I never did have a sense of direction," Csonka said. Larry's broken nose upset the squeamish Marv Fleming. "Blood was dripping on Marv's shoes in the huddle," Zonk said. "He looked down and all of a sudden his eyes got very big. So I tried to be more considerate. I let it drop on Kiick's shoes. He likes it. Makes him think he's been in a ball game."

The Dolphins emerged from Buffalo to play an Orange Bowl burlesque with the New York Jets. The farce marked the beginning of the end for the artificial Poly-Turf laid down only the year before to lure the Super Bowl to Miami. The game against New York included 59 pratfalls on both sides, dutifully recorded by Shula's coaches peering at the films Monday morning. Not so incidentally, the Dolphins lost 14–10, and with a 1-1-1 record were hardly in enviable position for a championship run. Shula was as peeved over the loss as he was at the carpet eroding in the tropical climate.

So was Joe Robbie. Robbie and Shula were on record as opposing Poly-Turf when economy-minded City of Miami commissioners voted to accept the American Biltrite Rubber Company's low bid. Monsanto's AstroTurf or Minnesota Mining and Manufacturing's Tartan, both tested, had been their preference.

Monsanto and 3M each offered comparable bids: $335,610 for AstroTurf, $339,975 for Tartan. But American Biltrite, just branching into the synthetic rug field, came up with a $205,933 offer and reduced it another $50,000 in return for the Massachusetts company's sign being displayed on the Orange Bowl scoreboard. The low bid accepted in April 1970 guaranteed Poly-Turf's playability for five years. If the rug proved a failure, it would be replaced "to the satisfaction of and at no cost to the city."

Poly-Turf passed its first season's test without incident, except for complaints arising from the heat it generated on the Orange Bowl floor. A thermometer inserted among the synthetic blades before the Cleveland game in October recorded 140 degrees, as high as the instrument registered. Complications began arising after Baltimore defeated Dallas in Super Bowl V. A giant NFL insignia had been painted at midfield with oil- and aluminum-based chemicals. The City of Miami's stadium crew was still struggling to scrub this off the rug in May. By the time the detergents had succeeded in removing the artistry, the rug's bright green newness had faded to a bluish pallor.

Howard Twilley, who keeps a close eye on the field because of the sharp cuts he must make to compensate for his lack of speed, foresaw problems in August 1971. "The stuff is falling apart. It's getting slippery and it's coming off on my shoes," Twilley said.

After New York the focus shifted to Cincinnati, where the following Sunday, on AstroTurf, the Dolphins managed to beat the Bengals 23–13. But Shula was not proud of the performance. "We went in hoping to contain them, which we didn't do," the coach said, citing 214 yards gained by Paul Brown's swift but erring outfit. "They got a lot of yardage, but to hell with yardage," Nick Buoniconti snarled. "They didn't get many points." Griese hit touchdown passes of 43 yards to Warfield and 4 yards to Twilley, both on third-down plays. Yepremian sideswiped field goals of 19, 36 and 16 yards, the latter finally assuring the victory with four minutes left.

The following Sunday against the New England Patriots—the newly tagged Bostonians—the Poly-Turf was exposed to another tumbling act. That Miami romped 41–3 was traceable in part to the extra care they took on the crumbling, slippery rug, as the Dolphins fell only 24 times to the Patriots' 31. Okeechobee Joe, a cartoon character offering daily newspaper homilies on the local or national scene, suggested: "If the grass in the Orange Bowl keeps layin' down, they ought to call it Polly Adler instead of Poly-Turf."

American Biltrite officials, stung into action when city commissioners voted to suspend monthly payments on the four-year financing plan, sent a crew to maintain the rug. But this was a stopgap measure. The matted blades were curried with brushes and the surface was vacuumed as well as hosed down before every game. Company representatives blamed the rug's erosion on poor maintenance by the city. The city manager countered with yet another blast. "They haven't even sent us a service manual!" Early in 1972, American Biltrite lived up to its guarantee and replaced the carpet.

The Dolphins disliked artificial turf for economic as well as physical reasons. Lockers at Biscayne College resembled small shoe stores as the athletes bought six or more pairs for every different surface. Bills soared (only a few NFL teams furnish footwear), particularly for backs and receivers.

Artificial turf is hardest on big men who fall hard. "God help us," Csonka said after one game, "if they don't do something about those damn rugs. I don't know how long I can stand this kind of punishment."

After Boston, Shula was feeling more hopeful about his squad and the 3-1-1 record they carried into Shea Stadium for their rematch with the Jets. He was rewarded with a 30–14 victory, while Butch Cassidy and the Sundance Kid achieved star status in New York.

"Butch ran like the sheriff was chasing him," Csonka noted, referring to Kiick's 121 yards in 17 carries. Larry himself smashed for 137 yards in 20 carries. It was the most productive Sunday afternoon of their interwoven careers. And both credited Larry Little's blocking exploits. The 265-pound guard consistently wiped out the corners, enabling Csonka and Kiick to turn them repeatedly.

The front four, strengthened by the emergence of big Bob Heinz, added four more quarterback sacks to the seven they had recorded against the Patriots. Bob Davis, struggling for the injured Namath, was the victim. Once Dick Anderson stormed through on a safety blitz and stole the football from the bewildered Davis. Dick had a score to settle. In the 14–10 Orange Bowl loss, he had inadvertently allowed a punt to brush his shoulder and be recovered by the Jets in the final minutes. The blunder led to the winning touchdown. But after the steal an observer noted, "Now they won't have Tricky Dick to kick around any more."

"We ought to play in this state all the time," said Kiick, goaded on by friends from his native New Jersey, for whom he had bought 110 tickets. The month before Kiick and Csonka had each topped 100 yards in Buffalo.

The soft, wet field and the light rain were ideal for the power backs. "I love it," Kiick said. "There's something that's no good about finishing with a clean uniform on artificial turf. It's like playing football in your living room. And I love doing well in New York. If you make it here, it's a big thing."

The victory was the third straight for the Dolphins and meant first place in the AFC East when Baltimore was beaten by Minnesota Monday night.

At the Pasadena Hilton in the smoggy brown suburbs of Los Angeles, where the Dolphins stayed the following weekend, Shula's squad was a curiosity. Here was this old AFL team with guys like Crusan, Johnson, Heinz, Kuechenberg, Swift, Kolen, Scott, Foley—who were these guys?

Csonka was a doubtful starter right up to the pregame medication ceremony, when a six-inch needle carrying Novocain was plunged into a golf-ball–size swelling above his right knee.

Csonka, at half speed, and Kiick, also a knee victim, were held to less than 100 yards combined by the Rams. But when the running game stalled, Griese cranked up his flying machine. He and Warfield caught the secondary napping on an improvised pass pattern resulting in an early 74-yard touchdown play. Deacon Jones had leaped offside a split second before the ball was snapped. Griese scrambled to his left in the confusion. "When I saw Bob scramble, I changed my pattern," said Warfield, who had started across the middle before veering back to the outside and taking the lob in the open.

An 11-yard touchdown pass to Twilley and Yepremian's 20-yard field goal produced a 17–0 lead after three quarters and identified the Dolphins to the silent dismay of 72,903 customers.

Yet the visitors were hanging on at the end, after a one-yard touchdown smash by Larry Smith and a 45-yard scoring pass from Roman Gabriel to Jack Snow in the fourth quarter. Yepremian then hit a 40-yard field goal with three minutes left that made a touchdown necessary if the Rams were to win it. LA did manage to reach the Miami 31, before

Buoniconti bobbed up to drop Willie Ellison in his tracks on a fourth-down, short-yardage situation. The intrepid lawyer, clutching the game ball afterward, called it "the biggest and best victory in Dolphin history. This is my first game ball under Shula, and I'll tell you something. You're never too old to appreciate it."

The Dolphins returned to the Orange Bowl for a month of four wins in four games, establishing a club record of eight straight victories. And the team now began attracting a new type of fan—the teeny-bopper, the paunchy Walter Mitty complete with Dolphin jersey, the handkerchief-waver, and other victims of the "We're No. 1" syndrome synonymous with success-worshipping America.

> A little neglect may breed great mischief; for want of a nail the shoe was lost; for want of a shoe the horse was lost; and for want of a horse the rider was lost, being overtaken and slain by an enemy, all for want of a little care about a horse-shoe nail.
>
> —BENJAMIN FRANKLIN

25. *Blackouts 1971*

Joe Robbie rarely falters when confronted by big decisions. The successful exploration of the Orange Bowl bonds, the hiring of Joe Thomas, the recruiting of partners and bankers, the acquiring of Don Shula—all reflected the mental agility of the Dolphins' president. But trivial matters, unattended, frequently mushroomed into crises that might have been avoided. Nobody in the Dolphin office paid much attention, for instance, when in the spring of 1971 a schedule conflict was discovered. Baltimore at Miami was scheduled for 4 P.M. on Saturday, December 11, as part of a nationally televised doubleheader. On the same night at 8 P.M., Florida A&M was to play in the Tallahassee school's annual Orange Blossom Classic. The game was a December fixture in the Orange Bowl and had precedence over the pros.

The Classic was usually held on the first Saturday of December. However, the date was set back a week to avoid a conflict with the University of Miami playing the night of December 4. So the Dolphins were on a collision course with Jake Gaither, Florida A&M's venerable athletic director who represented a father figure to black athletes throughout the state. Jake had sent many an athlete to the pros, and until recent years, when integration progress enabled black athletes to enroll in schools formerly closed to them, Gaither's Rattlers were on a par with Eddie Robinson's brilliant Grambling Tigers.

Since Gaither had worked with the pros for years, neither Robbie nor Commissioner Pete Rozelle seemed concerned over the December 11 conflict. Months passed without any change, although several City of Miami officials expressed worry. The kickoffs were just four hours apart. How could the Orange Bowl be cleaned up, the crumbling Poly-Turf be curried and dampened down to accommodate both events?

By autumn Rozelle was worried too. Gaither was making uncooperative noises in Tallahassee. "We are not going to lose money to accommodate the Dolphins," Gaither replied when asked to change his date. Jake was then invited to the Waldorf-Astoria for a weekend in Manhattan and a deal. "A representative of the NFL," he said, had offered $25,000 in cash, $15,000 in radio-television advertising, two scholarships worth $1,500 each and 3,000 tickets to the Miami-Baltimore game. In return, he was asked to switch his starting time or date so that NFL's doubleheader could be preserved.

At the Waldorf, Jake said that he decided to join in the spirit of the surroundings. Sipping champagne, the Florida A&M athletic director demanded $100,000. Nobody took his glass away, but from then on the situation deteriorated. Gaither went down to $75,000 but refused to consider anything less, particularly the Miami-Baltimore tickets. "What in the world am I going to do with 3,000 tickets? Scalp them? We're running a university. We're not in the ticket business."

It was difficult to pin blame. Rozelle passed the buck to the Dolphins for neglecting to inform the commissioner's office of the Classic date prior to the NFL's schedule release. "How many pro games are scheduled on a Saturday in December?" Robbie countered.

Rozelle finally bowed to Gaither. On October 12 he switched home dates between Miami and Baltimore. The December 11 game would be played in Baltimore. The Colts and Dolphins were moved to the Orange Bowl on Sunday, November 21. The switch gave the Dolphins the entire month of November at home, something else the NFL had hoped to avoid.

"It's perfectly all right with me," Gaither said, and then pulled another card. Because the televised game was still too close to the Classic kickoff and the National Collegiate Athletic Association has a rule enforcing local blackouts in such conflicts, Gaither said he could not permit NBC to show the Miami-Baltimore game in South Florida.

As the Dolphins kept winning and interest became feverish, Gaither's decision hit the fans in their most vulnerable spot—right in the tube. The AFC East championship might very well hinge on Miami's December 11 game at Baltimore.

Again, Rozelle underestimated his man. The commissioner expressed confidence that Gaither would change his mind as he had in the past when NFL doubleheaders were nationally televised on December Saturdays. "I've been accommodating the National Football League, the Dolphins and television for three or four years, and all I got out of it was a polite thank you," Gaither responded. "I'm not inclined to extend them any favors. Particularly the Dolphins. I feel they haven't treated me right in the whole thing.

"The pro game will last three hours," Gaither added, "and I'm afraid that after everybody watches it, nobody will want to come downtown for our game."

Gaither, encouraged by the NCAA, stuck to his guns despite mounting pressure from Dolphin fans growing frantic as the December 11 date grew nearer.

Frustration was compounded as the Dolphins kept winning. The Orange Bowl stretch run began November 7 with a 34–0 slaughter of obliging Buffalo, the first shutout in club history despite a 364-yard yield by the defense. Kiick's knee kept him idle. But Morris was turned loose and responded with 116 yards in 13 carries, including a 45-yard touchdown dash. Wasting Mercury's talents on the bench seemed an extravagance, but Shula was understandably reluctant to break up Csonka and Kiick.

When Pittsburgh came in on November 14, Shula's *wunderkinds* were seeking to match their record 1970 string with a sixth straight victory.

As usual, there were worrisome factors. First was the fact that Steeler Coach Chuck Noll's team was 4-4, tied with Cleveland at the top of the AFC Central Division. Offsetting this was the restricted mobility of Terry Bradshaw, Pittsburgh's precocious quarterback, who had sprained his left ankle in a 26–9 victory over the Browns the week before.

Shula's quarterback situation looked even worse the day before the game, however, as Bob Griese became nauseated during a brief drill at the Orange Bowl. Griese the introvert let it pass until around suppertime, when he continued to feel sick. He finally phoned Dr. Herb Virgin, who sent him to Mercy Hospital. Griese remained there overnight for tests. "Somebody kept waking me up and turning me over every two hours," the quarterback said. "I couldn't get a decent wink of sleep."

Apparently the cause of Griese's discomfort was something he ate. He was released Sunday morning, kept down a soft-boiled egg, and reported for duty. But he was weak, his eyes were glazed, and Shula decided to start George Mira.

Mira was helpless except for a short drive leading to Yepremian's 43-yard field goal. And while the Dolphins were stalled, the Steelers put up two touchdowns on Bradshaw passes of 30 and 28 yards. Behind 14–3, Shula turned to Griese.

When No. 12 loped onto the Poly-Turf in the second quarter he was greeted with a roar. On his first series Griese fumbled the ball away. A few minutes later Bradshaw threw his third touchdown pass, a 16-yarder to Ron Smith. The Steelers led 21–3. In eight minutes and 42 seconds the Steelers had scored more points on the "No-Name Defense" than any prior opponent.

Then Griese led an 80-yard march of his own in seven plays, capping it with a 12-yarder to Paul Warfield. And with 1:52 left in the half, the Griese-Warfield combo struck again, this time for 86 yards, their longest connection of the season. As in Los Angeles, the ingenious receiver turned a broken pattern to advantage. "I was supposed to be the decoy on a screen to Csonka," Warfield said. "I got out about 15 yards, turned and saw Bob start scrambling to his left. I had started across field but instinctively headed upfield when the pattern collapsed and Bob began running. He saw me immediately. It's the receiver's job to adjust patterns."

The short-sleeved mob was warm in the 80-degree temperature, but Griese remained calm and cool. After every offensive series, he pulled on a light jacket and sat on the bench. "I took every second of rest I could," he explained.

On the first play of the fourth quarter, from the Miami 40, Griese and Warfield gave their admirers something more to howl about. Paul took a perfectly led pass in stride at the Pittsburgh 15 and proceeded to his third touchdown, and eleventh of the season.

Griese had emerged from the hospital to bring the Dolphins from 18 points behind to the 24–21 victory. "I still don't know what was wrong with me," Bob said later in the locker room. "But I must be all right now. I'm hungry."

"The championship teams come from behind," the coach said, holding court in another corner of the jubilant room. "Today we proved we have the stuff." Shula remembered the occasion all year, even after qualifying for the Super Bowl with a pair of spectacular playoff victories. "The Pittsburgh game was the one that made us believe in ourselves," Shula said. "We kept our poise and came from 18 points behind. If I had to go back over the season, I'd point to that game as the one that gave us faith in ourselves."

Then came the Colts, and the war that was supposed to have been waged in Baltimore until Jake Gaither grew stubborn. Interest had peaked. The Orange Bowl was festooned with white handkerchiefs and crammed to the upper corners.

The Dolphins beat the Colts 17–14 in a battle Buoniconti called a street fight. Again the Dolphins came from behind, after a 78-yard drive directed by the 37-year-old fox, John Unitas. Jim Kiick got the touchdown back by crashing a yard into the end zone midway in the third quarter. Both Kiick and Csonka were prospering with superb blocking up front. And Griese was also getting excellent protection against Bubba Smith and his menacing colleagues.

Less than two minutes after Kiick's score, Unitas made a rare mistake. Deep in his own territory, he dropped back to pass. His receiver slipped on the Poly-Turf. "I saw him go, but I couldn't hold back," the quarterback said. "The ball slipped off my fingers as I was trying to arrest the motion."

His wobbler was intercepted by linebacker Doug Swift, who returned 12 yards to Baltimore's 10, setting up Fleming's first touchdown catch in two years as a Dolphin. Linebackers Mike Curtis and Ted Hendricks were confused on the coverage. Each expected the other to drop with Fleming. As a result, Marvelous Marv was alone when he squeezed Griese's pass. "I'm no Paul Warfield," Marv said. "But I'd like to be known as a tight end who can catch as well as block."

A discouraging afternoon for Unitas ended when he was shaken up while blocking Mike Kolen on an end-around play. Earl Morrall in relief led a tying touchdown drive, but the Dolphins did not seem concerned. Up front, Cannonball Kuechenberg, 33-year-old Bob DeMarco and the rest of Monte Clark's precise gang were moving the Colts around. Finally, after a fourth-quarter thrust to the Baltimore 13, Yepremian won the game with a 20-yard field goal. In beating the World Champions, the Dolphins gained 168 yards rushing against a defense that had permitted an average of less than 70 yards in its first nine games.

Howard Cosell, more eloquent than he'd been a year before in Atlanta, returned with his ABC retinue to look at the Dolphins and the Bears on Monday night, November 29. The Cicero of circuitry was stunned. While the Dolphins were amassing 446 yards in the 34–3 debacle, all Howard could manage was: "These Miami Dolphins are manhandling the Chicago Bears as one seldom sees the Chicago Bears manhandled."

Griese fired touchdown passes to Marv Fleming, again, and to Csonka. The Sundance Kid smashed for two other scores while gaining 104 yards in 16 carries to lead the team to their eighth straight victory. Impressive under the circumstances was the fact that Chicago came in needing the game. Miami, however, signaled the Bears' collapse. They went straight downhill from there, and Coach Jim Dooley was fired by George Halas after the season.

With a 9-1-1 record and an apparent stranglehold on the

East title, the Dolphins closed their four-game home stand laughing and headed for a date with New England at the Patriots' compact new stadium in Foxboro, Mass.

Ceremonies before the game honored the Pats' all-time team of the 1960s, which included the Dolphins' Nick Buoniconti. Upton Bell, the Pats' general manager, described the scene briefly. "The trouble with this setup," observed Shula's old pal from Baltimore days, "is that our all-time team is out there in civvies. Miami's all-time team is in uniform."

A tragic sight affected Buoniconti and other Dolphins who remembered Ross O'Hanley as an original Miami expansion draftee from the Patriots. O'Hanley never played a game for the Dolphins. A severe thigh bruise in camp at St. Petersburg Beach in a collision with rookie Ben Rizzo finished him for the 1966 season. He retired the next year. A brilliant Boston College graduate, O'Hanley was a mathematics teacher at Boston English High before progressing to the state attorney general's office as an aide. At 32, O'Hanley was struck down with a brain tumor.

The night before the ceremonies at Schaefer Stadium, his reflexes gone, O'Hanley fell down a flight of stairs at his home. But he showed up for the affair. His head swollen grotesquely but his mind still clear, Ross inched across the field aided by a friend.

The Patriots turned Coach John Mazur's well-conceived offense into a 34–13 rout of the heavily favored Dolphins. Mazur deployed three wide receivers, scrapping a tight end and forcing the secondary to adjust its zone coverage. The score reflected Miami's inability to adjust. Jim Plunkett, the brilliant rookie quarterback, forced Miami's safeties into one-on-one coverage and took advantage of this surprise element to enjoy a field day with his former Stanford target, Randy Vataha.

Miami's offense was hurting. Griese's left shoulder was stiff and there were three Dolphin fumbles. One of these was ascribed to Kiick, but Griese conceded that his inability to function naturally on the handoff contributed to the lost football. It was Kiick's only muff all year. When Csonka fumbled a handoff that struck his knee in the first quarter of the Super Bowl, it was Larry's only lost fumble all year. (The backs carried a total of 447 times in 17 games through the Super Bowl.)

Two fumbles, both lost to the Patriots, were committed by the usually surehanded Hubert Ginn on kickoff returns. The Patriots turned them into an early lead and never looked back. Vataha caught seven Plunkett passes for 129 yards and two touchdowns.

"We talked about the game clinching the playoffs for us," Shula said. "We certainly should have been ready. We wanted it for many reasons, but wanting is not enough. Now we must do the job ourselves." So the winning string had come to an end; ahead lay Baltimore.

The Dolphins couldn't do it. Given a second chance in his Memorial Stadium dustbowl, Unitas controlled the game while leading the Colts to a 14–3 victory and regaining first place in the East by a slim margin. With one game to go, Baltimore stood at 10-3, Miami at 9-3-1. But the resurgent Patriots came through again, salvaging a championship for the Dolphins even as they had apparently wrecked Miami's chances in Foxboro. On the last day of the season the Patriots dumped the Colts 21–17 while the Dolphins were walloping Green Bay 27–6.

The surprising turnabout effected by the Patriots caused cynics to believe that the Colts had performed at less than peak efficiency in their final game, as the "wild card" playoff spot, whose opposition would be a mediocre Cleveland team, seemed more comfortable than the date awaiting the East champion at Kansas City.

The Colts indignantly denied this. As Coach Don McCafferty pointed out, the loss to New England took away the home-field advantage the Colts would have gained for the AFC championship game.

The loudest protest came from South Miamians blacked out of the game in Baltimore. A few made the trip. Others took off for motels outside the 75-mile blackout area caused by the NCAA's and Gaither's insistence on protecting the Orange Blossom Classic. Most fans, however, squirmed unhappily to Rick Weaver's radio description of Unitas eating up the minutes while engineering touchdown drives of 81 yards in 18 plays and 87 yards in 16 plays.

His left shoulder still stiff, Griese was ineffective and unsure of himself on the few occasions the Colts were not controlling the action. The quarterback's frustration was reflected when Baltimore's aggressive patrons poured it on Shula at game's end. As the visitors filed toward their dressing room, beer cups and other debris flew from the grandstand. Shula shrugged it off. "They were the same way when I was here," he said. "They're just an enthusiastic bunch." But Griese was testy. "Lots of these people work in factories or somewhere for $80 a week. What they say or do doesn't bother me."

Dolphin fans back home divided their animosity among Rozelle and Robbie and Gaither. Robbie had overlooked the conflict in the first place. Rozelle had blandly let months pass before acting. Gaither had stood by "on principle" after his $75,000 indemnity request was refused by the NFL.

Ill will from the Baltimore blackout lingered through the AFC championship game, when of course the demand for tickets far exceeded the supply. Another Miami blackout was imposed. Efforts to remove it were renewed, but Rozelle stuck to NFL policy with historical justification.

The Green Bay victory assured Shula of a goal he had sought, playing the conference championship game at home. And the game against the Packers was memorable for individual accomplishments as well. Csonka became the first Dolphin to top 1,000 yards rushing. The action was halted so the Sundance Kid could collect the football as he surpassed the four-figure mark. "What if he loses yardage on the next play," mused George Ratterman, in the NBC booth. "Does he have to give the ball back?"

Yepremian's size $7\frac{1}{2}$ shoes propelled field goals of 26 and 27 yards, and three extra points. His 117-point season total won the NFL scoring championship by three from Washington's Curt Knight.

Griese's 13 completions of 21 passes for 122 yards gained the AFC passing title and quarterback percentage crown. Jim Riley, who had kissed the Poly-Turf the month before when a Pittsburgh safetyman's slip caused him to fumble a punt, romped over the carpet to sack Bart Starr three times and help the front four finish with 34 quarterback sacks, nearly double their 1970 total. Lloyd Mumphord and Curtis Johnson, active in spoiling field-goal attempts all year, collaborated again against the Packers. Mumphord slipped around the corner to make the block. Then Johnson seized the bounding ball and sprinted 47 yards to a touchdown. The "No-Name Defense" completed a season in which it allowed just 174 points, an average of less than 13, and 54 less than its 228-point yield the year before.

With a possible conference championship now looming at home, the outlook was as sunny as the Florida weather. There was only one hitch. To reach the title game, the Dolphins had to get by Kansas City. And the Western champions were clear favorites on their home field.

> Call hallelujah, call amen, call deep thanks.
> The strong men keep coming on.
> —CARL SANDBURG

26. *Christmas in Kansas City*

The weather in Kansas City added to the Dolphins' sense of security. Though fog obscured the Missouri River and coated the city, the day was warm. And when the sun emerged in early afternoon and the thermometer read 63 degrees, the tropic-oriented visitors felt at home.

Howard Twilley was observing his twenty-seventh birthday, Larry Csonka his twenty-fifth. And in the spirit of the Christmas season, Don Shula had relaxed the reins the night before. From six to nine o'clock there was a party thrown by Joe Robbie. All the athletes so disposed had a few beers. The reporters, priests, minority owners, wives, children and close friends were invited. Even Shula seemed willing to let down and enjoy an hour of banter, although the game dominated his thoughts.

When Shula left Baltimore after presiding over the only mediocre season (8-5-1) since his first in 1963, a few Colts were glad the tyrant was gone. Don McCafferty, Shula's former aide and successor at Baltimore, is called "The Easy Rider" and is publicly cherished by his troops, but only in pianissimo relief to the harsh brass motif conducted by his predecessor. The complaining Colts began to resent life under Shula when the victories stopped coming automatically, despite the same painstaking heed to detail and sacrifices imposed on them when they were succeeding.

The compulsory 9:30 convocations for beer and sandwiches Saturday nights on the road, for example, are timed exactly right to destroy the evening for the curious and the thirsty. Moreover, as one victim of the 9:30 snack noted, "If you reach for a third can of beer, the coaches look at you funny." But few hired hands quarrel with the coach's dictum that "our only function on any trip in any town is to perform to the best of our abilities on Sunday afternoon."

Now it was Kansas City, a playoff game and Christmas Eve. So Shula made sure his mercenaries had paid their respects to the party by nine. Tomorrow would be a long day —though no Dolphin or Chief could have realized how long it would be when the slim Norwegian Jan Stenerud's kickoff soared far over Mercury Morris's head to bound off the wall behind the end zone.

Nearly six quarters later, after 82 minutes and 40 seconds of awful suspense, pro football's longest game was won by its smallest player. A 37-yard kick by Garo Yepremian rose into the electrically lighted darkness and ended the ordeal with a 27–24 Miami victory.

Stenerud, acclaimed the game's premier kicker despite Yepremian's NFL point leadership, had blown a 32-yard field goal that would have broken the stalemate with 31 seconds left of regulation time. The Dolphins had rushed the kicker frantically. Lloyd Mumphord, in fact, said the ball had sailed right through his outstretched arms. But Stenerud, pale and remorseful in the dressing room afterward, offered no excuses. "I just missed it," he said. "I feel like hiding. These fellows play like the devil all day and half the night and lose everything because of me. I don't feel like playing football ever again."

Stenerud was bent on faulting himself, but the game contained many stunning turnabouts. Bob Griese, his bruised left shoulder aching dully but intact, brought the offense from behind three times to send the battle into overtime. "I couldn't believe it was happening," said Willie Lanier. "The third time particularly, I just never thought they could come back."

They did, though, because the Chiefs could not contain Paul Warfield, who humiliated their secondary with seven catches for 140 yards.

Lanier, the middle linebacker, keyed relentlessly on Larry Csonka. "Every time I looked up, Lanier was on top of me," Zonk said. "It's tough enough to go up against a grizzly bear, but it's impossible when the grizzly is smart." Still, Zonk wound up with 86 yards in 24 carries.

Kiick, working full time with Csonka, produced another 80 yards. Using only two backs in such pressurized circumstances caused Mercury Morris to remark bitterly after the Super Bowl loss: "Shula has lost faith in me."

And Marv Fleming, the blocking specialist, grabbed four passes for 37 yards, including a big one. Chastised all year for his unconscionable habit of jumping offside, Fleming barged through a herd of end-zone bodies to snatch Griese's five-yard snap throw over the middle. The catch served to tie the contest a third time with 96 seconds left when Garo's conversion made it 24–24.

But the finest performance of all came from Ed Podolak. The 24-year-old Iowan kept the Chiefs in command. He totaled 350 yards while doing practically everything. He carried 17 times from scrimmage for 85 yards, caught eight Len

Dawson passes for 110 yards, returned three kickoffs for 154 yards and two punts for a bit more. After Fleming's end-zone catch and Yepremian's tying kick, Podolak turned the Dolphins' mood from elation to despair. He sprinted right up the middle, found an opening in the wedge and escaped down the sideline with nobody in front of him.

Curtis Johnson had not given up, however. Sprinting across field on the dead run, the cornerback silenced the roar of 50,374 partisans with a desperate lunge that jolted Podolak out of bounds at the Miami 22-yard line. Playing the percentages, Coach Hank Stram then maneuvered for the field goal that sailed inches to the right.

It was the second big play of the game for Johnson, whose sensitivities had been tormented all year by the 82-yard bomb that escaped him "by less than an inch" and proved decisive in 1970's playoff defeat against Oakland. "It's all part of the game, I know," said the 23-year-old Ohioan. "But people don't understand that."

In Kansas City, Johnson came through with an interception that changed the course of the game. All year the Chiefs had been thriving on Dawson's passes to the brilliant Otis Taylor. Leading 10–7 and driving in the second quarter, Dawson unloaded to his favorite receiver, cutting across field deep into the zone defense. For a few moments Taylor appeared open at the 10-yard line. Then up jumped Johnson to intercept the football, and Dawson never tried the pattern the rest of the game. "I was protecting the zone for just such a pass," Johnson said. "They had been doing a lot of cross-field stuff and we'd worked hard on it in practice all week."

Johnson had turned three games around with brilliant individual efforts in 1971. Yet not until the Kansas City interception and the play on Podolak did the Oakland image of Daryle Lamonica and Rod Sherman begin to fade from his mind. "I actually dreamed about that play," Curtis said. "It stayed with me through the winter, through training camp and through the season. Now maybe it will go away."

Johnson also contributed seven tackles, second only to Nick Buoniconti's nine. Johnson's seventh was another saver. In the first 15-minute sudden-death period, Dawson hit fleet Elmo Wright over the middle. The quarterback's 63-yard bomb to Wright in the fourth quarter had set up Podolak's three-yard second-touchdown run and a 24–17 lead for the Chiefs with 6:46 left.

Wright once again seemed to have running room at midfield, until Johnson appeared and flattened the little receiver at the Miami 46. That pass represented the last hurrah for the Chiefs. Three plays later, tackle Bob Heinz tipped a Dawson pass at the line of scrimmage, Jake Scott intercepted and the Chiefs did not threaten again.

The tenacity of Miami's defense and the Dolphins' three comebacks to tie had worn them out.

The Chiefs had gone ahead halfway through the first quarter on Stenerud's 24-yard field goal, the only one he would make in four tries. He missed a 29-yarder when pressured by Jim Riley's charge in the second quarter, and had a 42-yard effort blocked by the ubiquitous Buoniconti and Mumphord in the fifth quarter.

Starting slowly, because "we can't seem to stand prosperity" in the words of Csonka, the Dolphins took a second blow when Lanier picked off a misfired Griese pass and returned it 18 yards to the Miami 35. Podolak then scored his first touchdown seven plays later on a short screen pass from Dawson. The first of three Stenerud conversions gave the home team a 10-point lead within 12 minutes and encouraged the Romans in Municipal Stadium to call for a rout. The Dolphins had never beaten Kansas City in six tries.

But on the last play of the first quarter, Griese lobbed a perfectly led pass to Warfield over cornerback Emmitt Thomas's head along the sideline. Paul plucked the football on the run, danced along the sideline and made 35 yards to the Kansas City 21. Two plays later, Marvelous Marv Fleming caught the first of his clutch passes, over the middle for 16 yards to the four-yard line. A minute later Fleming helped the offense reach the one by virtue of a half-the-distance penalty. Safety Jim Kearney was flagged for tripping Marv in the end zone.

Csonka took care of the last yard, and the Dolphins were on the board three minutes into the second quarter. Johnson's interception on Taylor blunted the next Kansas City drive, as the defensive vigilantes under Bill Arnsparger limited Taylor to three catches for 12 yards.

The defense also made a breakthrough that led to a half-time tie. Larry Seiple had boomed a 50-yard punt for Mumphord to sprint under and nail Podolak in his shadow at the eight-yard line. Two plays later, huge, affable Frank Cornish, the 285-pound tackle who had been released by Shula in September and rehired in October after a month spent "fishing and thinking," enveloped Podolak coming up the middle. Not content merely to smother the small man, Frank also stripped the football from his grasp.

Dick Anderson recovered the loose ball at the 12 with a minute left. A pass to Warfield gained five, but two others to Howard Twilley failed before Yepremian's 14-yard field goal evened the match with 13 seconds left in the half.

Podolak took Yepremian's second-half kickoff out to his 25, and from there Dawson stayed mainly earthbound in a 15-play march that consumed nearly 10 minutes and resulted in a 17–10 lead when fullback Jim Otis dived over to score.

Facing extinction again, Griese in the next 20 minutes

staged the most impressive passing performance of his five-year pro career. He stood cool in the pocket, linemen blocking like savages, while completing four straight in an eight-play, 71-yard push culminating in Kiick's one-yard lunge. En route, the quarterback popped passes of 24 and 6 yards to Twilley, 23 yards to Warfield, and 6 more on a sideline flip to Kiick who reached the one. Butch Cassidy needed two tries to penetrate the wall turreted by 6-7 Buck Buchanan and his foursome, including Curley Culp, Aaron Brown and Marv Upshaw. They could lift a golf course. But Butch finally made it off his left tackle, with a minute to go in the third quarter and the natives growing uneasy over the visitors' refusal to wilt. This was not the same outfit so accommodating in the past.

Two turnovers early in the fourth quarter increased the anxiety. Linebacker Mike Kolen smashed Wendell Hayes with a vicious face-on shot. Buoniconti recovered the discharged ball at the Kansas City 47. Six plays later, Griese had the Dolphins threatening to go ahead for the first time when he scrambled 12 yards to the 17. But he paid for the escape. He was slammed to earth on his tender left shoulder by Bell and linebacker Jim Lynch. Two plays later Lynch intercepted Griese's soft pass at the nine. The steal ignited the Chiefs, who hurried 91 yards in seven plays to regain the lead. Podolak went in behind right tackle Jim Tyrer and guard Ed Budde with only 6:46 remaining.

Once again the Miami cause looked hopeless. But Griese struck back, with a 13-yard pass to Fleming at the Miami 42. And then came a heart stopper. On a flanker-around maneuver that had been succeeding all year, Paul Warfield dropped the football. However, Bob DeMarco was watching. The 33-year-old center snatched Pauline from the tracks just as the Chiefs were bearing down on her.

Next Fleming tipped a pass intended for Warfield, open in the middle. The ball seemed to hang in the air before finally landing incomplete amid a clutch of red shirts. Griese, faced with a third-and-13 situation, came right back to Warfield over the middle for 18 yards and a first down at the Kansas City 43.

Less than three minutes remained when Griese encountered another third-down situation. This time, at the 38, he zipped a sideline pass to Warfield. The play gained 26 yards as the two-minute whistle blew.

Griese came right back with a sideline shot to Twilley for seven yards. The quarterback dropped back again. The Chiefs were on him, but he dodged to his left and fired a fastball over the middle. Fleming squeezed it in the end zone. Griese had completed six of seven passes in the drive, including the last four in a row. The game was slated for overtime.

After 20 minutes of sudden-death struggle, Griese remembered the "Csonka Special," a play in which Larry goes off the weakside tackle on a counter against the blocking flow. At his 35 on second down, Griese thought the play would work. He was right. Both Lanier and Lynch went for a fake flip to Kiick, running behind left guard Bob Kuechenberg, who had pulled to his right. At the same time Csonka and Larry Little, who had delayed a second before veering to his left, formed a 500-pound tandem charging unmolested to the left. Csonka proceeded 29 yards before he was ganged down at the Kansas City 36. Csonka and Kiick then added six more positioning yards to set it up for Garo.

"I knew I would make it," Yepremian said. "I barely missed the 52-yarder [at 12:21 of the fifth period]. After coming so close, I was positive I could not fail on anything less than 50 yards. DeMarco made a perfect snap, and Noonan held the ball just right."

Noonan, on seeing the kick was true, raised his arms to signal a score and began jumping around madly on the grass. Hands on hips, Griese stared at Noonan a few moments as though he were watching a stranger. Then the quarterback began laughing uncontrollably.

> The woods are lovely, dark and deep,
> But I have promises to keep,
> And miles to go before I sleep,
> And miles to go before I sleep.
>
> —ROBERT FROST

27. *The Ultimate Confrontation*

At the Orange Bowl ticket windows, fans sweated out intolerable lines for hours. Some camped overnight. The throng that filled Miami International Airport when the Dolphins returned from Kansas City signaled a week of bedlam. They were joined by thousands of kids and similarly afflicted juvenile adults running riot. People grabbed the athletes and anybody who looked like one in a scavenger hunt as repelling as it was impressive. The homecoming was more of a pop-culture happening than a welcome.

Though Shula often displays bursts of impatience with his employees, the patience he displays with even the most obnoxious fan is amazing. His Biscayne College training camps, open to the public, are crowded to the point of upsetting the athletes. But Shula stands signing his name and answering questions he would chastise reporters for asking.

After struggling through the airport mob with his son Dave, Shula reached his car to find the battery dead. Undaunted, he hitchhiked to his Miami Lakes home about 12 miles to the north. "I knew we'd have no problem getting a ride," he said. "There were fans all over the place. I invited the people who took us home in for a drink."

After Shula's guests had left, the coach got his first of two calls from President Nixon. They had corresponded before.

"Before he was President he wrote me a letter I still cherish," Shula said. "It was written after Baltimore's Super Bowl loss to the Jets. He said he knew how I felt because he'd been down that road before. But this time he just wanted to congratulate us."

The next day Shula enjoyed his first Sunday of relaxation since September. "We've got some pretty beat guys," Shula said. "Thank God for the extra day we have to prepare for the championship game."

The coach watched Baltimore subdue the Cleveland Browns 20–3 in the AFL companion piece to Miami's upset at Kansas City. It seemed that the Dolphins and Don McCafferty's Colts had spent the weekend setting up another confrontation. "I had the feeling the Colts would win," Shula said. "I'm happy we're playing the game here at home in front of our fans."

Not everybody was happy. The annual Orange Bowl game involving Nebraska and Alabama was scheduled New Year's night, hours before the AFC championship game. And in the splash the Dolphins created, the Orange Bowl Committee was far from jubilant. Its showpiece was reduced to a curiosity by the pros.

The mood of the customers seeking tickets deteriorated from impatience to anger. Patrons were massed in disorderly, seemingly endless lines for the privilege of paying $15 (chairbacks), $12 (sideline) or $8 (end zone) for seats. All were season ticket-holders, who had the option of buying an additional ticket for every two tickets they held during the season. And since more than 46,000 season tickets had been sold, only a few seats remained for public sale. In the end, scarcely anybody was satisfied.

"I'm sick over what happened," Robbie said. "It will not happen again." But it happened again the following week while Robbie and the Dolphins were in New Orleans for the Super Bowl. Thousands of fans in football-berserk South Florida clamored for tickets despite television. This time the rhubarb could not be helped, although the Dolphins unwittingly ignited the confusion by announcing in a letter to season ticketholders the "good news" that 10,000 seats would be available to them at Tulane Stadium. Except by the time the 15 Dolphin owners, plus the coaches, players, press and others privileged to buy them were satisfied, only about 7,000 tickets remained. And these were sold in less than an hour.

Robbie could not win. He was blamed for the blackout at Baltimore, even though the petulant NCAA was more culpable, and he was blamed for the mysterious disappearance of $15 Super Bowl tickets even though the game was available free on television. And circulating a misleading "good news" letter to more than 46,000 season ticketholders hopelessly afflicted with Dolphinitis was just bad public relations.

No NFL organization had succeeded so abruptly, yet Robbie was unable to savor achievement. Few who professed enmity for Robbie had met the man; or if they had, made an effort to understand him. Employees feared his wrath. When Joe Thomas turned down a three-year contract renewal as personnel director and Charlie Gesino also left the club in the winter of 1972, both deeply troubled over deteriorated relations with Robbie, the only survivor from the original front-office cast was Charlie Callahan. The easygoing, 56-year-old publicist earned the title of "The Last Man."

If the tough-minded Robbie was disturbed over the defections, he showed no sign. He descended from independent, adventurous stock. His father spent most of his eleventh year on a journey from Baka'a Valley in Lebanon to Sisseton, S.D. Standing before Canadian immigration officers in Montreal, the moneybag his mother had strapped to his waist nearly empty, the boy tried to understand what he was being asked. Since he was slipped out of Lebanon in 1905 to avoid conscription by the ruling Turks, the boy needed all his ingenuity. Sailors had handed him over to friendly innkeepers in Marseilles, Liverpool and other strange ports.

"Your name," the officials demanded, pointing to his chest. "Your name." He understood. "Arabi," he said.

An official wrote down "Robbie," thereby admitting Joseph Arabi to the Western World with a new name.

When he jumped on the AFL longshot in Miami, he applied characteristic fervor. Robbie always made it clear who was running the railroad, even though the Dolphins' outlook was bleaker than Penn Central's until Shula arrived. Robbie was criticized for insisting on full management control since he was totally inexperienced at the task.

"Every coach, every scout, every business manager wants to be general manager," Robbie said. "I told every damned one of them when they applied that until this enterprise was satisfactorily financed and operating, I wouldn't divide management responsibility with anybody. I had to retain this authority myself."

Though he often blundered in the area of human relations, only an enlightened businessman could have persevered as Robbie did. If his guest Orange Bowl preachers invoking parallels between football and life infuriated captive audiences before every game, his football team eventually soothed them. If his brush-offs and aggressive style were hard to take, his acquisitions of Shula, Griese, Csonka, Buoniconti,

Scott and Warfield were not. Robbie never traded a star for money, and in fact displayed financial recklessness by hiring expensive but spent comets such as Cookie Gilchrist and Earl Faison when he could not afford them. Robbie boasts justifiably that "no Miami Dolphin has ever played out the one-year option clause in his contract."

Dolphinitis, a disease familiar in established NFL cities but hitherto unknown in South Florida, was evident in epidemic proportions during the AFC championship game against the arch-rival Colts.

Tom Matte and Norm Bulaich, Baltimore's regular running backs, were out with leg problems. The Dolphins would seem to have an advantage there, even though chunky Don Nottingham, the tough rookie tagged "The Human Bowling Ball," had been playing impressively. His backfield mate would be Don McCauley, a second rookie who the Colts had drafted No. 1 out of North Carolina with the pick obtained from Miami in the Shula snatch.

Knowing the Colts so well, Shula blanched at the word "advantage."

"Any time you talk about playing Baltimore, you never use the word 'advantage,' " he said. "The Colts have great quickness and great size. You have to be conscious of their defense and of people like Bubba Smith and Ted Hendricks. Here are two guys, both 6-7 and extremely quick and strong. On field goals you can't put too much emphasis on blocking Smith, or Hendricks will shoot the gap. If you concentrate on stopping them both, safety Jerry Logan will penetrate another gap. In all phases we'll have to take care of our individual areas and be strong. We'll get pushed back a little, but the idea is to hold."

Shula wanted very much to break on top. "They took command in the first half last time. Unitas was perfect. He completed 12 of 13 passes, and the only one he didn't complete was dropped. In the second half we did much better defensively, but we couldn't score. That's always a problem when Baltimore gets on top, penetrating that great defense."

To score first, Shula and defensive boss Bill Arnsparger decided to keep the linebackers closer to the line of scrimmage instead of deploying them into the deeper passing zones. If the linebackers could anticipate the screens and quickies Unitas liked to aim at his running backs, this slight change of tactics might furnish an element of surprise.

"For the rest of us," said cornerback Tim Foley, "the job was to get back upfield as quickly as possible. In other words, react to the ball."

The game started at 4:35 in a cooling drizzle with dusk coming on. Conditions were ideal. The mist wasn't even enough to raise the umbrellas Miami football fans are seldom without.

Shula got his wish early. On Miami's second possession, second and five at its 25, Griese faked a handoff to Csonka. As he did, Warfield started downfield. The play-action froze Rick Volk, the safety on Warfield's side. "Csonka and Kiick are great runners," Warfield explained afterward. "And I'm pretty sure Volk was fooled by the play-action. Griese, with those quick hands, is about the best I've seen at faking. Volk is aggressive. When he started to come up after Csonka, I had the feeling I might get free. I knew it when I saw that Volk did not rotate to his responsibility [Warfield]. And when he did, it was too late."

Griese unloaded. Warfield took the pass at midfield and scampered the rest of the 75-yard route unimpeded. Yepremian kicked the extra point to give Shula his 7–0 lead.

Then the change in linebacking tactics began to show. The short passes Unitas had used to puncture the Dolphins in

Baltimore were not available to him. With his backs covered by linebackers, he had to hesitate while searching elsewhere. By then he was being harassed by the front four of Fernandez, Heinz, Riley and Stanfill. Three times they leveled the quarterback outright, an exceptional feat since the Dolphins did not blitz the entire game.

When Unitas was forced to passes of medium or long range, the zip was not there. He was often off-target and sometimes his passes fluttered. But Nottingham and McCauley were not idle, and on one second-quarter drive it appeared the Colts would succeed. Unitas led a 72-yard march to the Miami nine-yard line, fourth and less than two. Disdaining a field goal, he sent Nottingham bowling into the line. But Buoniconti, the cork in the current, was there. Nick rose up to drop Nottingham short. The Colts never penetrated that deeply again.

They battled into the third quarter. Griese, playing conservatively, passed hardly at all. He threw only eight times the entire day. Unitas, struggling to gain control of the game, was more and more tempted to cut loose. And finally he did. The maneuver resulted in finishing the Colts and furnishing the handkerchief-waving partisans with a sight Shula called "the most spectacular defensive play I've ever seen."

Unitas unloaded a long pass for wide receiver Eddie Hinton, sprinting into Miami territory with Curtis Johnson in close pursuit. When the high pass arrived at the Miami 38, Johnson went right up with Hinton, getting a good piece of the football and knocking it forward in an arch.

Dick Anderson was there. "I saw that Johnson had Hinton covered," the safety said, "and slowed down to stay out of the way. Curtis went up and batted the ball right back to me. I started to my right, got a few yards over midfield and saw Colts all in a bunch. So I went the other way, to my left."

When Anderson veered across the grain, he started picking up blocks from everyone. The effect was devastating. "My eyes were popping as I ran," Anderson said. "I saw people landing on their heads. Boomp, upended, like that. Fantastic. I've never seen so many people on their heads."

The instant Anderson made his sharp cut, Jake Scott scythed Tom Mitchell, the Colts' tight end. Next, Mike Kolen somersaulted wide receiver Ray Perkins. By then Anderson had picked up an escort of Foley and Doug Swift. "I found a wall set up like a punt return," Anderson said. "I knew I was still a long way from the end zone, but by that time I could see running room."

As Anderson crossed the 30, Foley sent a Colt flying. The son of an affluent family from Wilmette, Ill., Foley plays the game for fun. And he was all excited. "I knew who it was I blocked, all right. It was guard John Williams. I know because I was just wild about getting the chance for a shot at him. John had been laying into me pretty good all day."

With Foley gone, Anderson picked his way along behind Heinz as Swift leveled pursuing guard Dan Sullivan with a crackback block.

Crossing the 20, Anderson saw Unitas. "A picture flashed through my mind," he said. "I'd seen Unitas knock people out of bounds many times when he was the last man. I didn't want that to happen, so I cut back toward the inside again." Heinz took care of the rest, belting Unitas while the 38-year-old quarterback was trying to reverse his field with Anderson. The final cutback also caused Bob Vogel, the 250-pound tackle, to lose his equilibrium and tumble to the Poly-Turf as Anderson chugged by into the end zone.

On the sideline and twisting with every block, Shula was ecstatic. "I was prouder of that play than any I've seen in football," he said. "I thought Anderson was going to get maybe four or five yards. Then you could see the blocks form.

What a sight. That's what real football is all about. It's a spur-of-the-moment thing. You can't work on something like that. People just have to want to do it."

Anderson, the balding, 25-year-old son of a Boulder, Colo., chemist, had dispatched Baltimore's championship hopes and Super Bowl aspiration on the spot.

Griese and Warfield applied the *coup de grace*. On a third-and-two call at the Miami 45, a play that might be expected of Unitas, Griese strung another one out to his favorite receiver on a down-and-in maneuver. Again the quarterback had caught the defense coming forward with a play-action fake to Kiick. Gathering in the pass at Baltimore's 20, Warfield stopped cold to let Volk and cornerback Charlie Stukes sprint by. Then, after looking around "to assess the situation," Paul planted his right foot, did a three-step pirouette similar to his "police spin" against Oakland the year before, and proceeded around Volk and Stukes for 15 more yards to the Baltimore five before the enraged Mike Curtis caught up from behind and knocked the artist out of bounds.

The middle linebacker only delayed the third touchdown. On the next play Csonka followed Larry Little and tackle Norm Evans through a gaping hole to the runner's right. Zonk scored standing up.

The 21–0 victory marked the first time in 97 games and seven seasons that the Colts had been shut out.

Baltimore sought no alibis in the championship game, though center Bill Curry offered an explanation of their offensive problems. "I couldn't find Buoniconti," Curry said. "That's their whole defensive scheme, to keep blockers off Buoniconti and let him make the play. If I get to meet Buoniconti, it's a different story. Not because I'm better, but because I'm bigger than Nick."

Curry's thinking was the same applied to Miami's defense

by the Dallas Cowboys two weeks later in New Orleans. The Cowboys, however, made it work. Center Dave Manders and guards Blaine Nye and John Niland led a blocking attack designed to keep Buoniconti out of the picture. And without Nick to help, Miami's left side was particularly vulnerable to the well-escorted running of Duane Thomas and Walt Garrison, who romped for 169 yards in 33 carries. The Cowboys amassed 252 total rushing yards and controlled the football to the extent of running up 23 first downs. Both set Super Bowl records.

Manders had met Buoniconti before, in a 17–14 Michigan State victory over Nick's 1961 Notre Dame team. "Nick is no Dick Butkus," Manders said. "He's not as strong and he's not as tall. Nick is quick though, and probably reacts faster than any middle linebacker. Watching the screens teams have tried against the Dolphins, I saw that Nick was usually the first one there. And with his small body, he does a devastating job. He's a reckless player and a gambler. You've got to outwit him."

After Kansas City and Baltimore, a Super Bowl encore was almost too much to ask. Miami's "No-Name Defense," so often the key to success all year when Griese's offense stumbled, simply could not accomplish the whole task against Dallas. In Super Bowl VI the Dolphins succumbed to Dallas, 24–3.

Later in the dressing room, Robbie moved silently among his coaches and players, trying but apparently unable to offer the encouragement he still felt. Finally, eyes moist and almost to himself he said, "We have promises to keep." Then he added even more privately, "And miles to go before we sleep."

> We just got killed. They killed us but they didn't whip us. We'll be back.
>
> —JAKE SCOTT *in New Orleans*

28. *Gree-Gree Gertie's Revenge*

Monday morning, in the lobby of the Fontainebleau Hotel, coaches and players milled around, waiting for the buses and looking vaguely guilty. The shellshock of the Tulane Stadium dressing room had given way to dull disgust.

Mercury Morris had been the first to register his feelings on Sunday. All season long Morris had been a distant third running back behind Butch Cassidy and the Sundance Kid. Mercury was the quickest, most artful dodger of the three, yet his labors were pretty much restricted to returning kickoffs. In New Orleans the ebullient, outgoing Morris had been upstaged by the silent, sullen Duane Thomas, Mercury's teammate and blocker at West Texas State where Morris set a career NCAA rushing record of 3,388 yards.

After the Super Bowl, Morris decided to have his inning. Placing a chair in the middle of the locker room, Mercury made himself accessible to the torrent of reporters in the first few delicate minutes. Most Dolphins—if they were not Griese or Warfield or Shula—sulked in their stalls.

Naturally, the reporters converged on the available Morris,

who let them know right off that his speed might have altered the outcome. "But the only time I got off the bench was for kickoffs and 'The Star-Spangled Banner,'" he said. "I guess it was three times all afternoon."

Mercury's complaint did not go unnoticed by Shula. After Merc's rap session, the coach took him aside and delivered a brief, sharp lecture of his own. "I can understand an athlete being disappointed over not playing," Shula said later. "In fact, it shouldn't be any other way. But if he has a complaint, I'd like to hear about it first. I know he's disappointed. But we got here with Csonka and Kiick. All year our running game has depended on Csonka and Kiick as blockers, not just runners.

"When Csonka runs to the outside, Kiick helps make the play work because he's big enough to block the defensive end or linebacker. Actually, our outside running wasn't bad, except we didn't have the ball much. In the first half we only had it 8 minutes to their 22 minutes.

"Still, when Garo's field goal got us on the scoreboard in the second quarter I felt we could come back. We'd played poorly in the first half, but I thought we'd start moving."

The halftime score was 10–3. For the Cowboys, Mike Clark's nine-yard field goal was followed by Lance Alworth's seven-yard touchdown catch of a Roger Staubach pass. Alworth had beaten Curtis Johnson to the corner flag with an inside feint and sharp outside cut before taking Staubach's perfect toss.

"When they moved right through us for that third-quarter touchdown," Shula said, "we couldn't recover. That was the drive that finished us." The coach was referring to a 71-yard, eight-play assault completed when the brilliant Thomas swept three yards past Buoniconti and Anderson to score standing up. Buoniconti was out on his feet.

Months later, Nick said, "I must have seemed very vague in my answers after the game. But I really didn't have any answers at the time. I still can't remember when or how I was hurt."

"Late in the fourth quarter, Nick was trying to encourage the defense on the sideline," said linebacker Bob Matheson. "He told us to get it up, that the score was 10–3 and we were still in it. What the hell, the score was 24–3. The bells rung for Nick the whole second half."

Cowboy center Dave Manders and guards John Niland and Blaine Nye were Buoniconti's principal problems. "They waited for me to commit myself," he said. "Then the blocker on either side would take me in the direction I was headed anyway, and the back would make his cut the other way. It was totally frustrating, and it must have been worse during the part I don't remember.

"What happened in my case, I think, was too much concern about all their formations and not enough about the type of blocking in their line. I guess none of us paid enough attention to their blocking style. They didn't knock us out of there. They just screened us off, split our defense." In view of the Cowboys' painstaking preparations for Buoniconti, however, there is no evidence that their blocking action in New Orleans was available on film at all. In any case, Nick got no help from his colleagues in containing Thomas or Garrison.

Reporting for 1972's summer camp at Biscayne College, Buoniconti understood what Cornell Green had said the year before. "In July we start thinking of winning the Super Bowl," said the Dallas safety who had been in post-season action five straight years before winning the NFL championship.

"I don't think about winning our division or conference

championship or *getting* to the Super Bowl," Green said. "I think only of winning it. Once you've been there you don't settle for anything less."

In his search for answers, Buoniconti got his best explanation from Willie Lanier, the ultimate middle linebacker. Lanier had battled the Dolphins at their best in the 82-minute, 40-second playoff classic Christmas Day in Kansas City.

"Looking back, I really enjoyed playing that contest," Lanier told Buoniconti, "for the sheer competitiveness and suspense of the thing. Winning is important, of course. But you should derive some enjoyment from the game or you shouldn't be in it. And very few people can look back on an experience like that game.

"By the same token," Lanier said, "you guys were so intent on getting to the Super Bowl—and it was such an uphill, exciting climb—that once there, your minds weren't really focused on winning it. For you it was almost an anticlimax."

In March 1972, Nick received a letter from Ross O'Hanley, his former teammate at Boston and the expansion draft Dolphin whose woeful physical condition had shocked his friends during the Schaefer Stadium ceremonies prior to Miami's loss at Foxboro a few months earlier. "He wrote to thank me for helping him get total disability," said Buoniconti, the Dolphins' player representative and an activist in the NFL Players' Association. Before Nick could reply, O'Hanley died at 32.

"I was still thinking of what to say to a guy like that, when he died," Nick said. "What courage he had, refusing to feel sorry for himself even a minute."

When the Dolphins returned to Miami after the New Orleans defeat they needed all the courage they could muster to face yet another airport reception by the faithful. Bob Griese, Paul Warfield, Larry Csonka, Jake Scott, Larry Little and Bill Stanfill were luckier than their colleagues. They went directly to the Pro Bowl in Los Angeles.

The last straw in New Orleans had been Chuck Howley's fourth-quarter interception and 40-yard return to set up the final Cowboy touchdown. Howley, who was superb at outside linebacker, admitted that he was obsessed with a vengeance motive, not against the Dolphins but a New Orleans busboy.

When Dallas played the Saints in October, Howley and George Andrie had dinner at Kolb's, the German restaurant on St. Charles Street. The busboy recognized his guests and told them New Orleans would win because the Cowboys were choke artists. "This kid was something else," Howley said. "The waiter finally came over and told him to haul out. But before he did, I got hot and so did George. I told him, 'I'm not saying what will happen tomorrow, but I guarantee you this, kid. We'll see you back here in January. And I want to hear the song you're singing then.' "

Howley stayed out of Kolb's after the game, which the Saints won 24–14. "But I've been thinking about that punk ever since," the linebacker said. "And I was really looking forward to coming back."

New Orleans also had a special meaning for Monte Clark, the Dolphins' offensive line coach. Once, as a tackle with the Cleveland Browns, he had been there to face the Saints. En route, Coach Blanton Collier warned the Browns to beware of being lulled into complacency by the lavish hospitality of their hosts.

"So we arrived, and immediately I got this lonely feeling. The buses weren't even there yet to take us to the hotel. Eventually," Clark said, "they showed up. But the weekend was dismal.

"Somebody put a voodoo doll in Bill Nelson's room," Clark

continued, referring to the quarterback whose surgical knees are like Joe Namath's. "The doll's name was Gree-Gree Gertie. And she had pins stuck in her knees. The fans in that city are something else. Imagine the tender-hearted soul who jabbed the voodoo pins in poor Bill's knees."

Nobody to the Dolphins' knowledge fashioned a voodoo doll in Miami's colors. But Gree-Gree Gertie struck anyway.

She appeared to affect Griese as much as anybody, although Csonka took the rap for a first-quarter fumble. "I had a hole as big as a truck," Zonk said, "but I never got control of the ball. I took my eyes off it and glanced a split second at that beautiful hole. If I hadn't fumbled it might have been a different ball game entirely."

But Howley's interception was the most discouraging turn of events. Griese couldn't get anything moving against the quick strength of the Dallas front four and the range of Tom Landry's well-drilled linebackers. Griese's fate was signaled on the last play of the first quarter. He had tried to scramble out of a broken pass pattern, but he found Andrie and Larry Cole on the other end cutting off his outside escape routes. Then defensive tackle Bob Lilly smashed through to dump him for a 29-yard loss.

A few "neutral" press box observers even cheered Griese's misfortune, for his prevailing attitude of aloof politeness had soured some reporters. "What's the matter with him?" was a frequent question. The answer: Griese takes some knowing.

After the season, the all-pro quarterback's home town of Evansville gave him a day, as did Kiick's friends in Lincoln Park, N.J. Griese's reaction was typical. "It was embarrassing," he said. "I mean, it was premature. Look, it was wonderful of those people and great for my mother. She even bought a new dress for the occasion.

"But there I was, sitting and listening to all those people say nice things about me. And all I could think was, This is what they do for you at the end of a career, not the start of one. I still have so much to do that it just doesn't seem right."

Griese's plight can be understood by every athlete who has demands made upon his time. He was determined to limit his speaking appearances. "I'm elated that people want me. It shows they think a lot of me," Griese said. "But I want a good family life with Judy and my sons. You must draw the line someplace. What good is money if you have to ignore such things? And I really don't enjoy making appearances and speeches. I'm much more comfortable sitting off in a corner with two or three close friends. I just don't like crowds."

Buoniconti was among six Dolphins who paid in surgery for 1971 labors. He was hospitalized for a bone graft on his right wrist, injured in August and protected by a cast all season. Jake Scott the all-pro safety, needed operations to repair broken bones in both wrists. "We just got killed," Jake said of the Dallas ordeal, in which he broke his second wristbone. "They killed us but they didn't whip us. We'll be back."

Defensive tackle Manny Fernandez underwent knee surgery in April for an irritation that refused to heal. George Mira had bone chips removed from the right elbow that idled him most of the 1971 training camp. Mira's position grew shakier when Shula acquired 37-year-old Earl Morrall on waivers from the Colts in spring. In 1968, Morrall had replaced ailing John Unitas and was NFL player of the year under Shula.

Larry Csonka and Jim Kiick both had surgery, Csonka for bone chips in an elbow, Kiick for an assortment of troubles including broken bones in both feet. Jim played with the Dolphin basketball team until he broke the bone in his right foot. It was then that X rays determined his left foot contained a minor break as well. Nor was Carl Taseff spared. Playing basketball with Shula, the backfield aide snapped an Achilles tendon.

And neither was President Nixon spared. He received the "Bonehead of the Year" trophy from the Dallas Bonehead Club for his suggested slant-in pass to Paul Warfield against the Cowboys. Warfield got nowhere with the pattern in New Orleans.

Two more original Dolphins departed before the 1972 training camp opened. Guard Maxie Williams and fullback Stan Mitchell retired, leaving just four from the 1966 St. Petersburg Beach cast: Norm Evans, last of the expansion draftees; Bob Petrella, whose intelligence and versatility enabled him to survive six camps as reserve safety despite National Guard training commitments each summer; Karl Noonan, the free agent whose no-cut contract during 1966 training camp extended indefinitely; and Howard Twilley, still beating off challenges in his seventh pro season.

All the Dolphins and members of their families ended an exhilarating year on an appropriately humble note. Otto Stowe, the rookie wide receiver, had contracted hepatitis at Minneapolis in the exhibition season. By New Orleans, the disease had reached the infectious stage.

Everybody associated with Stowe and the squad was obliged to bend over for an immunization shot.

Index

Allen, George, 47, 166
Allen, Ivan, 28
Allen, Mel, 60
Alworth, Lance, 56, 59, 259
Anderson, Bill, 49
Anderson, Dick, 118, 155, 181, 192, 218
   games played, 122, 195, 225, 244, 254-256, 259
Anderson, Donnie, 91
Anderson, Edwin, 191
Andrie, George, 262, 263
Arnsparger, Bill, 165, 178, 179, 180, 189, 194, 195, 244, 253
Atkins, George, 13
Auer, Donna, 65, 66, 95
Auer, Joe, 50, 65-67, 71, 74-75, 76, 80, 107-108, 109, 112, 120-121
   games played, 23, 69, 74, 81, 82, 92, 93, 94, 95, 104, 106, 111

Baker, Johnny, 87-88
Barber, Red, 60
Barber, Rudy, 149
Beier, Tom, 188
Bell, Johnny, 60
Bell, Upton, 6, 235, 245
Berger, Ron, 47-48
Biggs, Verlon, 107

Biletnikoff, Fred, 207
Bingaman, Betty, 200
Bingaman, Les (Bingo), 13, 38, 44-46, 48, 147, 148, 167
   illness, 156-157, 159, 165, 200-201
Bingaman, Lester III, 200
Blanda, George, 87, 152
Bradshaw, Terry, 231, 232
Bramlett, John (Bull), 109, 113, 114, 130, 142-143
Branch, Mel, 49, 75, 117, 119
Braucher, Bill, 5-6, 8, 9
Brickman, Alan, 198
Briscoe, Marlin, 128
Brittenum, Jon, 100, 103
   games played, 102
Brodie, John, 212
Brown, Aaron, 245
Brown, Bob, 48
Brown, Dean, 189
Brown, Jim, 57, 118
Brown, Paul, 12, 25, 47, 85, 100, 127, 137, 151, 152, 160, 166, 171, 179, 206, 223
Brown, Rabbit, 67
Brown, Willie, 195
   games played, 207
Bruggers, Bob, 128, 129

Index

Bryant, Paul (Bear), 4, 5, 6, 166
Buchanan, Buck, 107, 245
Budde, Ed, 245
Buford, Chris, 63, 94
Buggenhagen, Larry, 211
Bulaich, Norm, 252
Buncom, Frank, 151-152, 186
Buoniconti, Nick, 142, 143, 152-153, 155, 158-159, 162, 163, 165, 177-178, 180, 184, 192, 193-194, 200, 218, 223-224, 233, 235, 251, 260-261
  All-Star game, 162
  games played, 200, 226, 243, 245, 254, 257, 259, 260
  injuries, 156, 214, 259-260, 264
Burr, Chuck, 36-37, 38, 39, 42, 97, 135
Burroughs, Billy, 40
Burroughs, John, 39-40
Butkus, Dick, 34, 147, 178, 257
Byrd, Butch, 78

Cahill, Tom, 37
Callahan, Charlie, 31, 41, 158, 250
Callahan, Frank, 140, 141
Campbell, Woody, 195
Carlton, Wray, 66
Carpenter, Preston, 101
Casares, Rick, 38, 50, 67, 71, 76, 80, 83, 116
  games played, 69, 75
Cassidy, Butch, *see* Kiick, Jim
Caveness, Ron, 49
Chagnon, Bob, 155
Chesser, George, 67, 115-116
Clancy, Jack, 99, 113, 162, 188, 218
  games played, 112
  injury, 124, 156, 159
Clark, Mike, 259
Clark, Monte, 166, 185, 192, 193, 194, 195, 235, 262-263
Clark, Steve, 42, 155
Clifford (lion), 65
Coan, Bert, 63
Cole, Julian, 40-41, 42, 62, 63
Cole, Larry, 263
Cole, Terry, 219
Colletti, Bill, 36
Collier, Blanton, 165, 166, 171, 262
Collier, Joel, 78
Cooke, Ed, 49, 58, 75, 114

Cornish, Frank, 190, 203, 218
  games played, 244
Cosell, Howard, 202, 234
Costa, Dave, 102
Cox, Jim, 145, 159
Crusan, Doug, 118, 192, 218, 226
Csonka, Larry (Sundance Kid), 118, 119, 120, 125, 132, 134, 155, 157, 159, 163, 183, 185, 192, 208, 209, 210-213, 216, 217, 218, 224, 231, 239, 251, 258, 259, 261-262
  games played, 122, 126-127, 128, 154, 156, 197-198, 203, 204, 222, 225, 226, 232, 234, 236, 238, 241, 244, 246, 253, 256, 263
  injuries, 126-127, 130-131, 149-150, 222, 264
Culp, Curley, 245
Curry, Bill, 256
Curtis, Mike, 233-234, 256

Dammit (alligator), 66
Darragh, Dan, 126
Davidson, Jim, 49
Davis, Al, 57, 139
Davis, Bob, 225
Davis, Ernie, 118
Davis, Jim, 61-62
Davis, Ted, 190, 203
Dawson, Len, 53, 63, 87, 94, 164, 241-242, 243, 244
Del Gaizo, Jim, 218
DeLong, Steve, 81
DeMarco, Bob, 189, 192, 217-218
  games played, 234, 245, 246
  injury, 203
DeMoss, Bob, 105
Den Herder, Vern, 218
Dickinson, Bo, 112
Dooley, Jim, 190, 234
Dotson, Al, 37, 49, 58, 75, 101
Dowe, Dan, 167
Duranko, Pete, 104

Edmunds, Randall, 118, 130
Eisele, Herb, 171
Eller, Carl, 30
Ellison, Willie, 227
Emanuel, Frank, 15, 46-47, 63, 75, **79-80**, 91, 109, 125, 130, 188
Erlandson, Tom, 49, 58, 72, 75

Evans, Norm, 30, 49, 58, 73, 76, 82, 113, 117, 184, 192, 215, 218, 265
  games played, 131, 256
  injury, 149
Ewbank, Weeb, 7, 53, 67, 76, 123, 132, 160, 169, 171, 173

Faison, Earl, 11, 83-84, 92, 99, 101, 252
Farley, Dale, 218
Fernandez, Manuel José (Manny), 118-119, 133, 153, 190, 192, 200, 215, 218
  games played, 254
  injuries, 206, 215, 264
Fitzgerald, Ella, 22
Flatley, Paul, 30
Fleming, Marv, 162, 184, 188, 192, 218, 222
  games played, 194, 203, 233, 234, 241, 242, 244, 245, 246
Fleming, Sam, 101-102
Fletcher, Abe, 67, 69
Flipper (dolphin), 62-63, 74
Flood, Curt, 129
Flores, Tom, 53, 75, 82
Foley, Tim, 162, 164, 203, 214, 218, 226, 253
  games played, 255
  injury, 214
Foss, Joe, 24, 26-27, 28, 139
Foster, Gene, 81

Gabriel, Roman, 226
Gagner, Larry, 47
Gaither, Jake, 229-231, 233, 237
Gallagher, Bob, 60
Garrison, Walt, 257, 260
Gerela, Roy, 195
Gesino, Charlie, 250
Gilchrist, Carlton Chester (Cookie), 19, 71, 84, 85-87, 89-91, 92, 93, 97, 99, 116, 252
Gillett, George, 98, 135
Gillman, Sid, 11, 55-56, 59, 84, 130, 217
Gilmer, Harry, 191
Ginn, Hubert, 164, 236
Gonsoulin, Goose, 95
Goode, Tom, 49, 58, 68, 76, 89, 117, 184, 188

All-Star game, 162
  injury, 185
Gowdy, Curt, 205
Grabowski, Jim, 47, 72
Graham, Kenny, 59
Graham, Otto, 25, 114
Granger, Hoyle, 195
Gray, Jim, 68
Grayson, Dave, 152
Gree-Gree Gertie, 263
Green, Cornell, 260-261
Griese, Bill, 105, 106
Griese, Bob, 16, 32, 98, 100, 103, 104, 105-106, 113, 121, 132, 134, 142, 147, 163, 169, 177, 185, 192, 212, 216, 231, 251, 258, 261-262
  games played, 48, 103, 106, 107, 110, 111, 112, 124-125, 125-126, 127, 128, 130, 147, 152, 153, 154, 155, 156, 157, 194, 195, 197, 198, 199, 200, 203, 207, 213, 224, 226, 232-233, 234, 236, 237, 238, 241, 243, 244-245, 246, 247, 253, 254, 256, 257, 263
  injuries, 3, 107, 108, 132, 156, 164-165, 199
  personality, 105-106, 113, 197, 263-264
Griffing, Dean, 82

Hadl, John, 53, 56, 59, 80
Haggar brothers, 103
Halas, George, 4, 12-13, 22, 32, 234
Hall, Ron, 93
Hamid, George A., 31, 75
Hamid, George Jr., 31
Hammond, Kim, 121, 142, 158
Harper, Jack, 119, 120
  games played, 112
  injury, 125, 209
Hawkins, Ralph, 37
Hayes, Bob, 216
Hayes, Wendell, 245
Haynes, Abner, 99, 112
  games played, 106-107, 108
Hefferle, Ernie, 38, 148, 165, 168, 188
Heinz, Bob, 143, 190, 218, 226
  games played, 225, 243, 254, 255
Hendricks, Ted, 143, 233-234, 252
Hester, Harvey, 25-26, 195
High, Robert King, 26, 27, 28

Hill, King, 57
Hines, Jim, 118, 129-130, 188
  games played, 159
Hinton, Eddie, 254
Hirsch, Elroy, 66, 67
Holt, Jesse, 48
Hopkins, Jerry, 99
Hornung, Paul, 14, 125
Howley, Chuck, 262, 263
Hudock, Mike, 49
Hudson, Jim, 92
Huff, Sam, 69
Hunt, Lamar, 27, 29

Idzik, John, 38, 145, 148, 168

Jackson, Frank, 49, 70
  games played, 68, 81, 92-93, 102, 110
  injuries, 70-71, 80, 109
Jackson, Keith, 202
Jacobs, Ray, 109-110, 113, 119, 126
  injury, 125
Jaquess, Pete, 76, 77
Joe, Billy, 49, 56, 67, 86, 100, 116
  games played, 71, 76, 82
Johnson, Curtis, 162, 164, 180-181, 192, 218, 226
  games played, 207, 238, 242-243, 244, 254, 259
  injury, 214
Jones, Deacon, 210, 226
Jude, Saint, 25
Jurgensen, Sonny, 186

Kaine, Elinor, 9
Karras, Alex, 32, 51, 221
Keane, Tom, 38, 148, 167
Kearney, Jim, 244
Keating, Ed, 183, 211, 212
Keland, Willard H. (Bud), 98, 103, 134-137
Kelleher, Tom, 17
Kemp, Jack, 78
Keyes, Jim, 124
  games played, 122
  injury, 132
Kiick, Alice, 209
Kiick, George, 148
Kiick, Jim (Butch Cassidy), 118, 119, 132, 134, 148, 157, 162, 163, 177, 183, 184, 192, 208-213, 216, 217, 218, 253, 258, 259
  All-Star game, 162, 210
  games played, 125, 126, 131, 154, 155, 156, 197, 198, 203, 204, 222, 225, 226, 233, 236, 241, 245, 246, 256
  injuries, 209, 231, 264-265
Killy, Jean-Claude, 212
King, Larry, 20
Klosterman, Don, 6
Knight, Curt, 238
Kocourek, Dave, 49, 72, 76, 82, 103
  games played, 77, 79
Kolen, Mike, 162, 164, 179, 180, 192, 218, 226, 234
  games played, 245, 255
Kremser, Karl, 153, 191-192, 194
  games played, 154
Krug, Jack, 38, 39, 41
Kuechenberg, Bob (Cannonball), 189-190, 203, 218, 226
  games played, 234, 246

Lamonica, Daryle, 78, 207, 242
Landry, Tom, 21, 178, 263
Lane, Dick (Night Train), 81
Langer, Jim, 189
Lanier, Willie, 241, 243, 246, 261
LaRose, Dan, 99, 101
LaRue, Jim, 53
Lavelli, Dante, 25
Layne, Bobby, 33, 51
Laytner, Ron, 102
Leigh, Charlie, 219
Lilly, Bob, 263
Lincicombe, Bernie, 193
Lincoln, Keith, 59
Little, Larry, 147, 154, 185, 192, 217, 261-262
  All-Star game, 162
  games played, 225, 246, 256
  injury, 149
Logan, Jerry, 252
Lombardi, Vince, 6, 12, 14, 138, 139, 144, 170, 184, 186, 218
Lowe, Paul, 56
Lundy, Bob, 131, 149, 167
Lusteg, Booth, 79, 110, 123-124
  games played, 112, 124
Lyles, Lindy, 47

Lynch, Jim, 245, 246

McAdams, Carl, 46
McBride, Norm, 155
McCafferty, Don, 168, 237, 239-240, 249
McCauley, Don, 252, 254
McCormick, John, 82
McCrea, Sloan, 140
McCullers, Dale, 183
McDaniel, Ed (Wahoo), 37, 38, 49, 58, 69, 75, 80, 81, 86-87, 93, 94, 109, 117, 124, 125, 128-129, 133
  injuries, 91, 94
McDermott, Gary, 126
McDowell, Sam, 118
McElroy, Hercules, 102
McGeever, John, 49, 58, 76
Mackey, John, 178
Macklem, Friday, 167
McLamore, James, 140, 141
McLean, Ray (Scooter), 14, 144
McMillin, Bo, 15, 32
McNally, Dave, 212
Manders, Dave, 257, 260
Mandich, Jim, 164, 188, 218
  games played, 194
Mason, Tommy, 30
Mass, Wayne, 218
Matheson, Bob, 214, 218, 260
Mathis, Bill, 76
Matsos, Arch, 95
Matte, Tom, 252
Matthews, Wes, 80
  games played, 59, 79
Mauck, Carl, 189, 203
Mazur, John, 235
Meredith, Don, 202
Milton, Gene, 153, 154
  games played, 152
Mingo, Gene, 49, 56-57, 68, 110-111, 124
  games played, 57, 63, 75, 80, 82, 87, 93, 94, 113-114
Mira, George, 212, 213, 264
  games played, 213-214, 231-232
Mitchell, Stan (Bronko), 112, 119, 125, 265
  games played, 127, 150, 152
  injuries, 132, 156, 209, 215
Mitchell, Tom, 75, 255

Mizell, Hubert, 21
Modell, Art, 140
Moore, Maulty, 218
Moore, Wayne, 189
  injury, 215
Morcroft, Ralph (Red), 147
Moreau, Doug, 64, 103, 126, 188
  games played, 93, 126, 132
  injury, 154, 156, 159
Morrall, Earl, 234, 264
Morris, Eugene (Mercury), 143, 155, 157-158, 212, 217, 218, 258-259
  games played, 152, 153, 154-155, 203, 231, 240
  injuries, 183, 213
Morrison, Wilbur, 140, 141
Motley, Marion, 25
Mumphord, Lloyd, 143, 192, 214
  games played, 206, 238, 240, 243, 244

Nagurski, Bronko, 50
Namath, Joe, 6, 17, 37, 53, 67, 76, 77, 107, 108, 110, 132, 137, 166, 195, 196-197, 214, 215, 225, 263
Nance, Jim, 118
Neff, Bob, 76, 125, 127, 145
Neighbors, Billy (Spanky), 49, 58, 76, 89, 117, 153, 187-188
  injury, 91
Nelson, Bill, 262-263
Nicklaus, Jack, 212
Niland, John, 257, 260
Nixon, Richard, 220-221, 249, 265
Nobis, Tommy, 46
Nobles, Charlie, 20
Nolan, Dick, 189
Noll, Chuck, 231
Nomina, Tom, 49, 58, 75, 117, 119
Noonan, Karl, 58, 76, 80, 132, 215, 265
  games played, 71, 110, 203, 246-247
Norris, Bud, 145-147
Norton, Don, 56
Norton, Rick, 15, 16, 46, 52, 53-54, 67, 68, 77-78, 88, 103, 105, 121, 147, 188
  games played, 61, 75, 76, 78, 79, 87, 102, 107, 108-109, 110, 125, 126, 132, 157, 159
  injury, 87, 126
Nottingham, Don, 252, 254

Index

Nye, Blaine, 257, 260

O'Brien, Jim, 144, 149, 188
O'Hanley, Ross, 49, 100, 235, 261
Okeechobee, Joe, 224
Oliver, Jerry, 47, 48
O'Neil, John H., 31, 40-41, 42, 103, 135-136
Osborne, Dave, 30
Ostendarp, Jim, 179-180
Otis, Jim, 244

Palmer, Arnold, 212
Palmer, Dick, 189
Palmer, Potter, 135
Pardee, Jack, 213
Parilli, Babe, 53, 131
Park, Ernie, 49, 56, 58, 76, 99
Parker, Buddy, 14-15, 32
Peake, Scott, 140
Pellegrini, Bob, 38, 54, 62, 81
Perkins, Ray, 255
Peterson, Bill, 5, 157, 158
Petrella, Bob, 58, 125, 215, 265
Petrich, Bob, 101
Phipps, Mike, 161
Pinson, Vada, 129
Plunkett, Jim, 235, 236
Podolak, Ed, 241-242, 243, 244, 245
Pope, Ed, 5, 9, 21, 153-154
Powell, Jesse, 143, 218
Price, Sam, 67, 72, 73, 125
  games played, 68, 71, 106
Proper, Charlie, 36

Ratterman, George, 238
Rechichar, Bert, 167
Redman, Rick, 81
Reese, Melvin, 27
Rensch, J. Leonard, 28
Rentzel, Lance, 30
Reynolds, Dr. Frank, 164-165
Rice, Ken, 49, 76
Richardson, John, 99, 119, 190, 192, 200, 218
Richardson, Willie, 192, 215
  games played, 198, 207
Riley, Jim, 99, 153, 192, 200, 218
  games played, 238, 243, 254
Rizzo, Ben, 235
Rizzo, Salvatore (Sam), 136-137

Robbie, Elizabeth, 8
Robbie, Joe, 1-3, 4, 18, 60, 82, 86, 88, 89, 91-92, 94, 97, 100, 103, 120, 122, 129, 137, 139, 147, 151, 176, 186, 198, 213, 217, 239, 250, 257
  childhood, 29
  financial arrangements, 3, 23, 28, 31, 96-98, 134-137, 139, 140-141, 251-252
  and first training camp, 38-39, 41-42
  formation of Dolphins, 26-33, 251
  and Gaither, 229-231, 237
  hiring of Shula, 5-9, 11, 15, 172
  and Keland, 98, 103, 134-137, 140
  and Norris, 145-147
  personality, 2-3, 42-43, 70, 97
  Poly-Turf controversy, 222-223, 224
  and C. Rosenbloom, 172-173
  -D. Thomas partnership, 23, 27, 28, 29, 97, 103
  and G. Wilson, 3, 4-9, 10, 11-12, 15-16, 18, 31-32, 162-163
Robbie, Joseph (father), 251
Robbie, Tim, 60
Roberson, Bo, 49, 58, 76, 101
  games played, 68, 77, 79, 87
  injury, 80
Roberts, Archie, 108-109
Robinson, Eddie, 229
Robinson, Frank, 129
Roderick, John, 57-58, 76, 80, 83, 102
  games played, 59, 79
Rooney, Art, 140
Rosenbloom, Carroll, 6, 7, 139, 140, 172-173, 174, 184, 204
Rosenbloom, Steve, 7, 172, 173
Rote, Tobin, 51, 82
Rozelle, Pete, 7, 28, 136, 137, 173, 174, 181, 229, 230, 237
Rudolph, Jack, 49, 58, 75
Russell, Bill, 129
Rutkowski, Ed, 126

Saban, Lou, 16, 66, 86, 99, 101
Sample, Johnny, 68, 107
Saperstein, Abe, 135
Sauer, George, 76
Scarry, Mike, 167, 218
Schmidt, Joe, 51, 191
Schnellenberger, Howard, 165, 166

Schwartzwalder, Bernie, 211
Scott, Jake, 162, 164, 181-182, 192, 205-206, 214, 218, 226, 252, 261-262
  games played, 195, 199-200, 221, 243, 255
  injuries, 214-215, 264
Seiple, Larry, 99, 157, 158, 206
  games played, 106, 154, 244
  injury, 159
Sellers, Ron, 158
Shaw, Dennis, 174
Sherman, Rod, 207, 242
Shula, Dave, 248
Shula, Don, 12, 16, 118, 123, 130, 192-193, 194, 199, 200, 203, 204, 205-206, 207, 212, 213, 214, 216, 220, 222, 223, 225, 228, 233, 236, 237, 238, 239-240, 248-249, 251, 252-253, 254, 255-256, 258, 259, 265
  childhood, 170-171
  hiring of, 5-9, 10, 11, 15, 169-170, 172-174
  revamping of Dolphins, 16-17, 162, 163-167, 169-172, 173-186, 187, 188, 189, 190, 204-205
  and C. Rosenbloom, 6, 172-174, 204
  and G. Wilson, 6-7, 9, 13, 16, 17, 19, 20-21
Sibley, Harper, 140, 141
Simpson, Howard, 49
Simpson, O. J., 153
Sinatra, Frank, 137
Skinner, Sam, 196
Smalley, J. Earl, 140-141
Smith, Bubba, 184-185, 233, 252
Smith, Larry, 226
Smith, Rankin, 28
Smith, Ron, 232
Snell, Matt, 68
Snow, Jack, 30, 226
Speedie, Mac, 85
Spikes, Jack, 49
Spurrier, Steve, 98
Staley, A. E., 22
Stanfill, Bill, 143, 153, 192, 200, 218, 261-262
  All-Star game, 162
  games played, 157, 254
Starr, Bart, 238
Staubach, Roger, 259
Stead, Greg, 213

Stenerud, Jan, 240-241, 243
Stofa, John, 52, 88, 92, 100, 113, 127-128, 147, 158, 199, 212, 213
  games played, 93, 94-95, 102, 103, 104, 127, 131, 159, 198
  injuries, 104, 213
Stone, Archie, 32, 163
Storin, Ed, 9
Stowe, Otto, 213, 215, 218, 265
  games played, 220
Stram, Hank, 242
Stratton, Mike, 78
Stukes, Charlie, 256
Sullivan, Dan, 255
Sundance Kid, see Csonka, Larry
Swanson, Mrs. Robert W., 33
Swift, Doug, 179-180, 189, 192, 218, 226
  games played, 233, 255

Taliaferro, Mike, 67-68, 76
Tarkenton, Fran, 30
Taseff, Carl, 166-167, 171
  injury, 265
Taylor, Jim, 91
Taylor, Otis, 242, 244
Tensi, Steve, 80, 81, 128
Theismann, Joe, 212
Thomas, Danny, 22-25, 27, 28, 29, 31, 55-56, 59, 74, 81, 97, 103, 140, 141
Thomas, Duane, 21, 257, 258, 259, 260
Thomas, Earlie, 217
Thomas, Emmitt, 244
Thomas, Joe, 16, 29-31, 34, 35, 42, 46, 47, 48, 49, 57, 70, 86, 98, 99, 101, 118, 119, 143, 145, 146, 160-161, 163-164, 173, 181, 212, 213, 214, 228, 250
Thomson, Bobby, 21
Torczon, LaVerne, 49, 58, 75, 101
Tozer, Raleigh, 18-19
Truman, Harry, 3
Turner, Jim, 76, 123
Tutko, Dr. Thomas, 216
Twilley, Howard, 34-35, 49, 58, 76, 132, 192, 205, 213, 215, 223, 239, 265
  games played, 104, 112, 194, 196, 203, 204, 205, 220, 224, 226, 244, 245, 246
  injuries, 58, 80, 91, 154, 156, 159

274 *Index*

Tyrer, Jim, 245

Unitas, John, 96, 122, 174, 215, 233, 234, 236, 237, 252, 253-254, 255, 256, 264
Upshaw, Marv, 245

Van Brocklin, Norm, 29, 208, 209
Vataha, Randy, 235, 236
Vincent, Mike, 52
Virgin, Dr. Herb, 131, 146, 164, 231
Vogel, Bob, 255
Volk, Rick, 253, 256

Walker, Doak, 51
Walston, Bobby, 37
Wantland, Hal, 68
Warfield, Paul, 1, 159, 161-162, 183, 185, 192, 203, 204, 210, 212, 213, 215, 216, 234, 252, 258, 261-262
  games played, 195-196, 198, 206, 207, 220-221, 224, 226, 232, 241, 244, 245, 246, 253, 256, 265
  injury, 203
Warren, Dewey, 127
Warren, Jim, 49, 58, 75-76, 113, 117, 124, 181, 188
  games played, 93
Warwick, Lonnie, 30
Weaver, Rick, 237
Weir, Sammy, 67
Werblin, Sonny, 28, 196
West, Willie, 49, 73, 76, 117, 148, 181
Westmoreland, Dick, 49, 58, 75-76, 117, 126, 181, 188, 192
White, Lee, 208
Williams, Edward Bennett, 12
Williams, John, 255
Williams, Maxie, 49, 58, 76, 117, 184, 192, 203, 205-206, 265
  injuries, 189, 215
Williams, Ted, 170
Williamson, Freddie (The Hammer), 35, 91
Wilson, Claire, 18, 82
Wilson, Eddie, 49, 52, 53, 69-70
  games played, 63
  injury, 69-70

Wilson, George, 3-4, 10-21, 35, 45, 56, 77, 78, 81, 83, 86, 88, 92, 101, 102-103, 107-108, 109, 111, 113, 119, 120-121, 123, 124, 126, 132, 133, 136, 137, 138, 143-149, 151, 152, 154-158, 209
  and first training camp, 36-40, 50, 54, 64, 71
  and George Jr., 15-16, 51-52, 60, 77, 79, 92, 99-100, 102
  hiring of, 32-33
  and Norris, 145-147
  relationship with players, 67, 68, 72, 86, 115, 116-117, 138, 148, 153-154, 155, 158-159, 162-163, 171, 177
  replacement of, 9, 10, 11-12, 13-14, 157-158, 162-163, 168, 169
  and Shula, 6-7, 9, 13, 16, 17, 19, 20-21
Wilson, George Jr., 15-16, 51-52, 60-61, 77, 82-83, 88, 99-100
  games played, 63, 67, 70, 78-79, 81, 82, 87, 89, 91, 92
  injury, 80, 92
Wilson, Nemiah, 154
Wilson, Ralph, 26, 27, 139
Winston, Roy, 30
Wood, Dick, 49, 52, 79
  games played, 56, 58-59, 63, 67, 68, 71, 75, 77, 80, 87, 89, 91, 92, 93, 94
  injuries, 71, 94
Woodard, Milt, 121
Wren, Charlie, 44, 45, 201
Wright, Elmo, 243
Wright, Ernie, 151-152

Yepremian, Garabad Sarkis (Garo), 191-192
  games played, 194, 196, 197, 198, 203, 204, 221-222, 224, 226, 232, 234, 238, 240, 241, 242, 244, 246, 253, 259
Yepremian, Krikor, 191
Young, Buddy, 45

Zecher, Rich, 49, 75

A000100059311

```
GV                                    232122
956        Braucher, Bill
.M47
B72        Promises to keep.
```